Holy Spirit:
Agent of Change

Receiving the
Transforming Power
of the Holy Spirit

Dr. Lynn W. Aurich

ISBN 978-0-9838105-6-8

This book is available from Amazon.com, Barnes Noble.com, drlynnaurich.com

Author's Contact Information: www.drlynnaurich.com

Cover art by André Lefebvre/www.creativeforge.org

Inside design by Lorinda Gray/Ragamuffin Creative/www.ragamuffincreative.com

Printed in the United States of America

Holy Spirit:
Agent of Change

*Receiving the
Transforming Power
of the Holy Spirit*

Dedication

*To Alice Rao, my adopted mama, for her constant
nurturance, support, encouragement, wisdom,
and unconditional love throughout my life.
She was my island of sanity in my childhood
and is a source of joy in my adulthood.
Her influence on my life is immeasurable.*

Contents

Endorsements 8

Acknowledgements 10

Introduction 12

Chapter 1: My Story: Touched by the Agent of Change........ 19

Chapter 2: The Transforming Power of the Holy Spirit
and Apostle Peter....................................... 37

Chapter 3: The Transforming Power of the Holy Spirit
and Apostle Paul.. 55

Chapter 4: Who Is the Agent of Change and
How Does He Work?................................... 77

Chapter 5: The Holy Spirit as Teacher 125

Chapter 6: Vehicle for Change:
The Baptism in the Holy Spirit 137

Chapter 7: The Spirit Speaks:
A Historical Look at Tongues 165

Chapter 8: Psychology Speaks:
　　　　Understanding Spirit Baptism and Glossolalia... 209

Chapter 9: The People Speak................................. 229

Chapter 10: Common Questions Regarding Tongues........ 255

Chapter 11: Holy Transition: The Process of Change......... 267

Chapter 12: Moment of Truth:
　　　　Demonic, Demented, or Divine?..................... 287

Notes 316

TABLES

1. Peter's Transformation.. 53

2. Paul's Transformation 75

ILLUSTRATIONS

1. Holy Spirit Is Agent of Change, Convergent Analysis.... 252

2. Baptism in the Holy Spirit.................................. 288

Endorsements

WHY DO WE *hear so little mention of the work and ministry of the Holy Spirit today? Why is the Third person of the Godhead so often referred to as a mere influence rather than a person?*

Dr. Aurich writes clearly, insightfully, and convincingly on the Holy Spirit's power to transform and change lives. Drawing from both his personal experiences as well as the Scriptures, the writer creates a deeper hunger to understand more of the Holy Spirit's activity in the believer's life.

This book is more than a textbook, it's a workbook—read it and put into practice its truths. It will transform your life.

David Ravenhill
Author and Itinerant Teacher
Siloam Springs, Arkansas

EVERY ONCE *in a great while there is a book that qualifies as a "rare find." It takes a broad topic and covers it so well that you find yourself commenting and responding out loud as you read from page to page. "Holy Spirit: Agent of Change" is that rare find. Dr. Aurich skillfully communicates the working of the Holy Spirit from a biblical, experiential, and clinical perspective.*

I have never read such a comprehensive approach to any subject, much less the infinitely challenging topic of the Holy Spirit. I highly recommend this book to believers of every background and those who think the work of the Holy Spirit, in our time, is marginalized.

Reverend Thomas Faulk
Senior Pastor
First Assembly of God Church
Lafayette, Louisiana

Acknowledgments

The Lord dealt with me for years about writing this book. I resisted the idea because many fine books have already been published about the Holy Spirit. As usual, though, I lost the argument.

The Bible verses are quoted from the New American Standard Bible (NASB), and I am grateful for their generous policy of allowing the quotation of their Scriptures.

I have attempted to properly cite reference sources where appropriate. Unfortunately, some of my thoughts are the result of assimilating many ideas and concepts from several different authors, pastors, and friends over many years to the point that I am not entirely certain exactly who said what. My apologies in advance to those who may recognize a quote or idea for which I did not give you proper credit. Please know that I deeply appreciate all of you who have spoken God's truth into my life.

I am deeply indebted to my precious wife, Peggy, who, not only typed the original manuscript, but offered numerous suggestions for improving it. More importantly, I am grateful for her loving and staunch support over the past forty-four years. Her faith in God and in me has been consistent, especially during times when I had little of either. She is the joy of my life.

Special thanks to Reverend Thomas Faulk for his godly insights and suggestions for the first manuscript. I count it a privilege to be a co-laborer with him to prepare the way for the coming of the Lord. He is truly a pastor's pastor.

My deep gratitude to my dear friend, Rex Veron, for his obedience to the Lord that night in the swimming pool many years ago which changed my life forever. He also doggedly encouraged me to write this book, and I am grateful.

My love and appreciation to my beloved children, Susan and David, who faithfully prayed for me during the writing of this book. They are consistent blessings to their mother and me.

My deep appreciation to David Ravenhill for his wisdom, guidance, and advice in helping bring this project to fruition.

Thanks to my editor, Dave Malone, for his skill and patience in correcting my grammatical errors and to Lorinda Gray for her considerable expertise in formatting the book.

Finally, my eternal praise and thanksgiving to the Lord for saving me and baptizing me in the Holy Spirit. He is the true author of this book and deserves full credit for it.

Introduction

Many books have been written about the Holy Spirit. Some of these volumes have been very basic and are for the layperson. Other studies have been more technical and theological, penned by Greek scholars. With this book, I strive for middle ground. While it is not strictly a work on apologetics, I feel compelled to address some of the criticisms and arguments against the operation of the Holy Spirit in the contemporary church. My approach is to use a combination of logical propositions, exegetical considerations, scientific evidence, and experiential truth to bring greater clarity to the theme of this book—the transformational power of the Holy Spirit. I also attempt to integrate, where appropriate, a psychological perspective on this multifaceted aspect of the Holy Spirit.

This book is, by no means, the definitive, all-inclusive final word on the Holy Spirit. I merely want to focus on the Holy Spirit's awesome ability to produce remarkable and lasting change in individuals and to examine the methods by which He achieves it.

I believe many Christians hunger for more in their Christian walk but are unsure of what they are missing and how to get it. They desire greater intimacy with the Lord and know in their spirits that more is available to them but just do not know how to obtain it. For this audience, I write my book.

Many born-again Christians limp along in their walk with the Lord and they wonder what is missing in their spiritual life. They do not see or experience what they read about in the New Testament. They do not see or experience the power in their lives and see few answers to prayer. When the answers do come, these born-again Christians often fail to see answers due to a lack of spiritual discernment and intimacy with God. In not discerning the answers to their prayers, their faith remains weak that, in turn, hinders their walk with the Lord. It is a never-ending vicious circle. Satan glories in keeping Christians bound up in their vicious circle thus keeping them in a state of spiritual impotence. It is my contention that this is the reason why Satan has worked so hard to keep Spirit baptism out of the church today. Satan has nothing to fear if he can prevent the church from stepping into its rightful inheritance in the Holy Spirit. Christians will continue to operate at a low level of the fruit of the Spirit (Galatians 5:22) but will not function in the power of the Spirit which is what changes individuals, families, churches, communities and even nations.

We are in a war. This war is not about racism, politics, economics, religion, or national boundaries. These are merely the natural manifestations of something that is occurring in the spirit realm. The Bible is replete with descriptions of end-time scenarios that affect all of the above-mentioned areas. Nevertheless, the underlying cause of all these problems is spiritual warfare in the heavens between God and Satan. If this is true, and I believe that it is, then God's army on this earth is ill-equipped to fight in this war. Many Christians would argue that they have God's Word as their main weapon to defeat the enemy. I do not disagree with that contention. God's Word serves as bullets to wound and destroy the enemy. However, the gun that empowers, propels, aims, and directs the bullets to their intended target is the Holy Spirit.

We see in Luke 4:1-13 that Jesus used only the Word of God to defeat Satan and his powerful temptations. Why was Jesus successful? The Jews of the day certainly knew this same word and yet many struggled in sin, sickness, poverty, ignorance, and religiosity. Filled with the Holy Spirit, Jesus provided the defining difference (Luke 3:22; Luke 4:14). When Jesus used Scripture against Satan, He did not just hand throw bullets at Satan but rather fired ammunition through the most powerful armament in the universe, the Holy Spirit. They hit their target dead center and routed the enemy causing him to retreat in utter disarray. Jesus clearly manifested the power of the Holy Spirit when He commanded Satan to leave and Satan obeyed (Matthew 4:10).

God's army today is doing little more than hand throwing bullets at the enemy because their commanders (pastors, priests, theologians) have told them that the gun is no longer available to them. The baptism in the Holy Spirit (Spirit baptism) signs, wonders, and miracles were present during the first century church but do not exist today, contemporary Christians are told. Little wonder why most Christians have little motivation to face the enemy with nothing more than a handful of bullets but no gun through which to fire them. Can you blame them?

The purpose of this book is to not only define and describe the nature and function of this weapon (the Holy Spirit), but also how to receive Him and use His power in the ongoing war to defeat the enemy and advance the kingdom of God.

The issue that must be addressed by every sincere inquirer of the truth is the question of whether the baptism in the Holy Spirit, as depicted in the book of Acts, is biblical and of God or a device of Satan used to deceive Christians in the contemporary church. Or is it, as some contend, a creation of human beings that reflects hysteria, spiritual ignorance, and mental illness? The answers to these questions are at the heart of understanding God's truth regarding these issues. Clarification of these issues is vital to the health and growth of God's kingdom in these last days. In this book, we explore the overwhelming evidence that Spirit baptism is absolutely of God and is still available today for every true believer who seeks a more intimate relationship with God and has a genuine desire to be used by Him.

So many attacks have been launched on the credibility of Spirit baptism that sincere Christians simply do not know what to believe. Interestingly, most of these attacks have not come from non-Christians but rather within our own camp. It is time for Spirit-filled Christians to come out of the closet and staunchly defend what they know, by experience and God's Word, to be the truth.

In this book, we also examine exciting scientific findings that provide evidence in support of Spirit baptism by disputing some of the more common criticisms of it. Despite what secular critics believe, true science always confirms God's Word. They are not mutually exclusive.

Both old and new testaments speak of Spirit baptism. We are seeing the fulfillment of Joel's prophecy (Joel 2:28-32) in our own time. Peter also confirmed that Spirit baptism had been prophesied earlier and was being fulfilled in his time (Acts 2:14-21). God clearly says that He changes not. This spiritual phenomenon still occurs today for those who approach Him with an open heart and open mind.

The full gospel/charismatic movement has been described as the fastest growing Christian movement in the world at present. Christian leaders are both astounded and perplexed by its rapid growth. They are confused because they do not understand the driving force that is fundamental to its vitality—Spirit baptism. Many leaders cling to human tradition rather than pursue the truth of God's Word and seek this life-changing experience. One cannot fully understand Spirit baptism on a purely intellectual level. Like salvation, it must be *experienced*.

In this book, we explore the experiential aspects of this supernatural phenomenon to eliminate misconceptions about it and to show that it is intended by God to be a normal part of the Christian experience. Spirit baptism continues to thrive throughout the world, despite attempts by organized religion to prevent it, because people are spiritually starving for something that reflects the power and reality of God.

I fully expect some will read this book and be enraged by the truths in these pages and cry, "heresy." That is historically what happens any time human tradition and theology is challenged. Sir Arthur Conan Doyle once said, "There is nothing as deceptive as an obvious fact." It is curious why some Christian circles espouse such vehement opposition to such a fundamentally simple biblical truth. Hopefully, this book will shed some of God's light on this issue.

Many politicians campaign on a platform of *change*. They are often very successful with this approach because it is so appealing to the average voter. It is a powerful message because, deep within each of us, is the desire and need to be transformed—a desire which has been placed there by God.

The problem, of course, is that political candidates are often vague about exactly what kind of change they are going to produce. Change just for change's sake is not always necessary, nor is it always for the better. Even when the promised changes are good, our leaders often forget them once they are elected.

The Holy Spirit, as Agent of Change, on the other hand, always meets this driving need in us to be changed and always fulfills His promises. Powerfully illustrated in the lives of the apostles, the Agent of Change continues to transform the lives of millions of present day Christians. I pray that, as you read this book, you will open your heart and mind and allow God's Spirit to speak to you. He loves you and desires so much to have greater intimacy with you and to change you into His likeness.

CHAPTER 1

My Story: Touched by the Agent of Change

Albert Einstein once said, "The definition of crazy is doing the same thing over and over and expecting different results." It is interesting that many born-again Christians keep doing the same spiritual things over and over expecting different results. Many tell me they crave a deeper, more intimate relationship with the Lord, but they don't do anything different to achieve it. They either have not been taught about the baptism in the Holy Spirit or they have, but reject it.

The dramatic and rapid transformation in my life is ample proof for me that the Holy Spirit is the Agent of Change.

I was born in Houston, Texas. When I was eighteen-months old, my parents divorced, and my mother promptly moved my older sister and me to Detroit, Michigan. When I was eight years old, my sister got married and moved away. I was pretty much on my own because my mother worked and was gone most of the time. We moved around a lot. I went to nine different schools, but we actually moved more than that because sometimes we moved several miles away but remained in the same school district. The end result was that I was constantly either the new kid on the block or the new kid in school.

Living in the inner-city of Detroit I quickly learned that, to survive, I needed to learn how to fight. So I joined a local boxing club and learned how to defend myself. I also learned that one of the quickest ways for me to be accepted was to use my sense of humor and make people laugh. Hence, I became the class clown.

As a latch-key kid, I spent many hours alone, which was to have a lasting impact on me for many years. It instilled in me a deep sense of loneliness. I was popular and had many friends but always felt lonely regardless of what we were doing. It also instilled anger within me that eventually exploded into rage when I hit my teen years. I had a chip on my shoulder the size of a sequoia tree. The object of my rage was my mother mostly, but it really didn't matter much to me who I directed it toward. If someone looked at me wrong, I was ready for a throw-down.

My sister, who was married and had her own children by that time, thought it might be best for all parties if I relocated to Louisiana and lived with her. She concluded that it would be easier for me to live with her than for her to visit me in prison, which is where she saw me heading. I had moved so many times I really didn't care where I lived. It proved to be the right decision.

In high school I played football, which gave me a socially acceptable outlet for my rage. I also continued to make people laugh. I was voted "God of Humor" in my senior class. I had developed an attitude of never taking anything seriously. I made fun of everything and people loved it.

After high school I didn't have a clue what I wanted to do with my life. Education was never stressed in my family, so I didn't really want to go to college, which I find amusing now since I would spend half my life in college. I was in my front yard one afternoon when two friends drove up and said "Hey, Lynn, we are going down to join the Marine Corps, wanna come with us?" After contemplating it for maybe three or four seconds, I said, "Sure, why not?" I was just a tad bit impulsive in those days. I just went in whatever direction the wind blew me.

After returning home from the Marines, some friends from high school convinced me to enroll at our local university. The only reason I agreed was that I had read in *Playboy Magazine* that this particular university was rated as the number one party school in America. And partying was what I was all about. Studying was not on my agenda, but I somehow managed to not flunk out.

As I progressed through the university, I became aware of an intellectual side of myself that I never realized existed. I began wondering what life was really all about, so I started taking philosophy classes and studying the classical philosophers and the existentialists. My conclusion in the end was they didn't know anymore about life than I did. I also concluded there was no God and I became a confirmed atheist.

After completing my bachelor's degree, my wife Peggy and I were married and went off to graduate school where I could work on a master's in psychology. I still wasn't sure what I wanted to do with my life. It wasn't until I worked at a state mental hospital, after earning my master's degree, that I realized I wanted to make clinical psychology my career. I also realized I needed to know more, so I applied and was accepted into a Ph.D. program.

I returned to school with a vengeance this time. I set the curve in most of my classes and was elected president of the graduate student association. I brought in nationally recognized psychologists as speakers. I was well-known and accepted by faculty and fellow students alike. And, yet, despite these great accomplishments, I felt an emptiness inside. I now call it the "Jesus hole." Everyone has it and only Jesus can fill it.

After finishing my dissertation and completing my clinical internship, I received my Ph.D. and was immediately hired by Tulane University School of Medicine as a faculty member in the Department of Psychiatry and Neurology. I had landed a very prestigious job right out of grad school. You would think I would be elated. But, still no peace. I eventually left Tulane and accepted a faculty position at the University of Louisiana-Lafayette, which is where I had done my undergraduate work.

I enjoyed teaching, but my training was in clinical psychology, so my desire was always to be in private practice. That desire was fulfilled when a local psychiatric group invited me to join them. In a short period of time my practice boomed.

I had always been told that private practice is where the money is. I started making more money than I had dreamed possible. We bought a new home, new cars, took expensive trips, and lived the good life.

It is also true, however, that private practice is where the most stress is. I was working sixty to seventy hours a week, and it was taking its toll on me. I was physically and mentally exhausted and wasn't sleeping well. I was irritable with my wife and children. I got depressed and began asking myself "Is this it? Is this what I've worked so hard for all these years?" Still no peace. I felt myself sinking deeper and deeper into despair.

About that time I got a call from an old high school friend of mine. He told me that he was getting some of us old high school buddies together for a weekly men's Bible study and would like for me to come.

My religious training was sparse at best. My mother claimed to be a Methodist, my father a Lutheran, and my sister a Catholic. I wasn't required to attend any of those churches on a regular basis, so I had no idea what any of them believed.

After becoming an atheist in college, I often mocked religion. I developed a comedy routine I often would use at parties any time the topic of religion would come up. I would do an impression of an old-style tent evangelist where I would lead everyone in an old hymn, "Shall We Gather at the River," with my own mocking lyrics mixed in. I would then lay hands on someone's head and pray for healing but do it in a comical way where I would simulate causing him more pain than healing. Then, I would pass the plate for the offering and shout "Throw your money to the wall. All that sticks is the Lord's, all that falls is mine!"

So, I was not really interested in attending a Bible study, but I didn't want to hurt my friend's feelings. I asked, "Are we just going to sit around and discuss the meaning of life because I already did that in college?"

He answered, "Oh no, we have a Bible teacher."

"Who is that?" I asked.

"Rex," he answered.

Rex and I had been good friends in high school, but we had not seen each other in several years. We had been drinking buddies and frequented every country bar that would sell us booze.

My clearest memory of Rex was when he and I had double dated together on Mardi Gras Day our senior year in high school. We had been drinking all day. Rex got irritated with his date because she kept talking about her old boyfriend. He leaned over and said "We're taking them home."

I was having a good time with my date, but I was so impulsive, it didn't really matter to me what we did. So I said, "Let's do it."

By the time we dropped them off, it was dark and very foggy. When Rex got back in the car, he was still angry. He started the engine of his Dad's car and floored the accelerator.

We were doing about fifty miles per hour when we hit the parked car about two blocks down the street. I went through the windshield, and Rex, being the good friend that he was, reached over and pulled me back through the broken glass.

The car was totaled. Smoke was everywhere. Amazingly, we got out and stepped into someone's front yard. We didn't have a scratch on us. We looked at each other and said, "Where's our booze?"

So you can imagine my reaction when my friend told me that Rex was going to be our Bible teacher.

"You've got to be kidding," I said.

"No, really," he said. "Rex got saved a few years ago and has really become a student of the Bible."

Well, now my curiosity was stirred. I just had to see this. So I agreed to come the next Tuesday evening. I saw two things that night. First, this was definitely not the same Rex that I knew. Rex had always been a rough guy who would fight just for the fun of it. I had seen him rip the shirt off a guy's back one night just because he didn't like it. But that Rex was gone.

The guy who sat before me this night was gentle, kind, and very pleasant. He was very different from what I remembered. The second thing I observed was that Rex knew what he was talking about. He was very knowledgeable about the Bible and could apply the principles in very practical ways.

Every Tuesday night after that, I would still be at the office and think to myself, *I'm not going over there tonight*, but somehow my car would find its way to the Bible study.

I continued to attend, and an interesting thing began to happen. The evidence for the existence of God began to pile up. My academic training had been steeped in the scientific method, which states essentially that one must have evidence that supports what one believes. If the evidence contradicts what you believe, then it is incumbent upon you to alter what you believe so that it is consistent with the evidence. After several weeks, I had to admit that my atheistic beliefs might be wrong. I had always accepted the theory of evolution at face value without questioning it because it had always been taught as fact. As I actually began to review and study evolution again, it became obvious that it was only a theory and, in fact, not a very good one at that. It has lots of holes in it, and no actual evidence to support it. I realized I had believed in evolution because it was convenient and easy. If I believed in evolution, then I didn't have to believe in God. And, if I didn't believe in God, then I didn't have to be accountable to Him.

I finally acknowledged that God was real, but I hadn't settled the "Jesus issue" yet. Did I really need to accept Jesus and his death on the cross to be saved? Then one night my family had all gone to bed, and I sat alone in my den looking for something to watch on television. I came across a Billy Graham crusade, and I started watching it instead of sliding right on past it as I usually did. To this day, I can't recall the nature of his sermon, but by the end of it they flashed a phone number on the screen and said we could call if we had questions.

The next thing I knew, I was dialing that number. A very pleasant voice answered and said, "Can I help you?"

"I don't know," was my brilliant reply.

"Well, do you have some questions?" she asked.

"Oh, I have plenty of questions. I just don't have the answers."

She seemed to sense what my problem was because she asked, "Well, are you born-again?"

That term, "born-again," had always turned me off, but just then it was like hearing it for the first time. I thought, wow, born-again, wouldn't that be awesome to just start all over again.

I told her that I wasn't born-again.

She simply asked, "Would you like to be?"

I answered, "Well, yes, but what is the procedure for that?" What a nerdy question! She very patiently gave me Scripture and explained the salvation plan to me. For the first time, it made perfect sense to me.

She led me in the prayer of salvation and then asked, "How do you feel?"

I practically shouted, "Great!"

She was somewhat taken aback and said, "Well, it may take a few weeks, but you will begin to notice a difference."

I said, "No, you don't understand, I feel different right now, like a load has been lifted off of me!"

"Oh, well. Praise God," she said sweetly.

I hung up the phone, and for the first time in my life, I got on my knees and prayed. I went to bed that night and slept more peacefully than I had in years.

I would like to tell you that all of my problems went away that night but they did not. I still struggled with bad habits. I still had problems in my marriage and I was still stressed out.

Prayer helped, but I struggled with knowing whether God was really hearing me. I tried reading the Bible on my own, but I didn't always understand fully the meanings. That disturbed me because I knew I wasn't an idiot, and yet I seemed to be missing the deeper meaning of Scripture.

I continued to go to the Tuesday Bible study, which helped me get through the week. A couple of months later Rex taught on the importance and meaning of water baptism. I did not consider that to be something that I needed. It was getting late that night, and class was almost over when I got an epiphany. It suddenly dawned on me that water baptism was significant and that it wasn't optional. Jesus said to do it!

I asked Rex who could baptize me. He answered that any born-again believer can water baptize.

"Can you do it?" I asked.

He replied that he had done it many times.

I said, "Great, let's do it right now."

My friend who hosted the Bible study had a swimming pool in his backyard, so we could do it right there.

Rex said, "It's a little cool out tonight, Lynn. We can arrange to do it some other time."

"No problem," I said, "The pool is heated."

"Well, we don't have any swimsuits," Rex countered.

"No problem, we'll just strip down to our underwear," I exclaimed.

Now, Rex wasn't too keen on that idea so he said, "Well, it's getting late, and I promised my wife I would be home early tonight."

At that point I leaned toward him and stared him in the eye and said, "You don't understand, Rex. I'm getting water baptized tonight and you're going to do it!"

Rex sensed that something bigger than all of us was going on, so he agreed to do it. I went outside and started stripping off my clothes. I turned around and saw that the other ten men had followed me outside and started stripping down also. They all realized they needed water baptism too and thought it was a pretty good idea. Rex hadn't bargained on that but recognized that God was doing something.

We got into the pool, and I was the first one to be baptized. I moved off to the side while he ministered to the others. I must admit that nothing dramatic happened when I was baptized. I felt I had obeyed the Lord, but I didn't feel anything special.

Then a strange thing began happening. When every other man was baptized, they came up out of the water speaking in strange languages. The baptism in the Holy Spirit with evidence of speaking in tongues had never been discussed in the Bible study, so we knew nothing about it but there it was. It was a sovereign act of God. As I watched the other men, I could see the joy and peace they were experiencing.

I went to Rex and said, "You need to pray for me because I don't feel right."

"What's wrong?" he asked.

"I'm not sure," I said, "but I know I'm not feeling and doing what they are."

"No problem" Rex said with an authority I had not heard in him before.

The next events are forever embedded in my memory. He laid hands on me and began to rebuke the Devil. I suddenly lost all strength in my body and went down into the water. Rex and another friend grabbed me and held me up. My stomach muscles began to contract violently almost like seizures. A spasm would hit me and I would double over. This occurred repeatedly. Rex kept praying and thanking God for "dealing with Lynn."

This was completely out of my character to respond like this. I was always in control and concerned with how others perceived me. I was now under the control of something much bigger than me. These spasms went on for quite a while. When they stopped, I was suddenly filled with the most incredible peace I had ever experienced. Suddenly, I felt compelled to open my mouth and sing—which was unusual for me because I cannot sing well.

I began singing a word that I had never heard before. The more I sang it, the more I was flooded with love, peace and joy. The more of those things I felt, the more I wanted to sing in this foreign language. I lost all self-consciousness. I did not care at that moment what the others were thinking or doing. I knew I was connecting with my heavenly Father in a way I never had before. The love was overwhelming. This went on for a while, and then all of the strength returned to my body as suddenly as it had left.

I stood up and knew I had just had an encounter with the living God and that my life would never be the same. I asked Rex what had just happened to me. He told me that I had received the baptism in the Holy Spirit. I said, "Well, whatever it is, it is God, and I want more of Him!"

Things began to change rapidly for me after that night in the pool. Being born-again and knowing that my sins had been forgiven was comforting but, this—this was something else! God had actualized Himself for me in that pool. His realness was now an objective fact, not some abstract, philosophical, or religious concept. Eternal verities had been revealed in tangible, verifiable ways: God exists. He is my real Father. I am His child eternally. I have always belonged to Him and always will. He has a plan for my life. His love is unconditional. Jesus is the way, the truth, and the life.

I had a head knowledge (intellectual) of these facts after getting saved, but now they were in my spirit-man. They went from a passive, intellectual assent to an actualized confirmation in my spirit. This was a deeper level of *knowing* than I had ever experienced before. I instantly had entered into an entirely different level of intimacy with Him. He was no longer someone I just talked at when I prayed but rather my Dad who I talked with about everything in my life. He gave me the objective data in that swimming pool that, not only proved how real He is, but also that He wants to be intimately involved in my life.

I became ravenous for everything of God. I used to labor to spend five or ten minutes in prayer. Now, I spent hours with no effort at all and, in fact, would rather spend time with God than do anything else.

After being born-again, I still struggled in my understanding of the Bible. After the infilling of the Holy Spirit, revelation began exploding in my spirit and mind every time I read His Word. It felt as though I was being fed the most succulent, delicious meal I had ever had every time I studied the Bible. The author had taken up residence inside me and gave me a deeper, clearer understanding of His Word. Reading the Bible became fun. It was no longer a chore. It became my necessary food.

I started attending a full gospel church. It seemed a little strange at first because I was unaccustomed to the freedom in worship that they expressed. As I studied the Bible, though, I saw that actions like clapping of hands while singing and raising one's hands in worship of God was absolutely biblical. Moreover, I found myself automatically doing these things in my private time with God and they felt absolutely natural and easy. The Holy Spirit was teaching me how to worship God.

The thing I noticed in this church was that the people *wanted* to be there. It wasn't an obligation for them. They didn't attend services because they felt they needed to be good or religious. It was part of who they were. I also felt the love of God there, which made it easy and enjoyable to go on a regular basis. I became very active in church and, in time, began teaching the Bible in adult Sunday school classes and home Bible studies. This eventually led to teaching and preaching at Sunday morning services in my church as well as other churches.

I have gone on mission trips to Albania and India. I have taught the Bible at universities, churches, and pastor conferences in those countries. I would have never done those things before Spirit baptism.

Over the years the Holy Spirit produced many changes in me as a man. He progressively purged me of old emotional pain from my childhood and healed those wounds. He softened my heart and helped me to be more forgiving of others. I became more loving and tender with my wife and children.

I had always tied my self-esteem and self-worth to my achievements. The Holy Spirit helped me to realize that my true significance and value is in Christ and separate from my achievements in life. I have found great peace in that truth. I no longer am consumed with achievement for achievement's sake. I have learned to rest in Him and allow Him to lead me to do His will, not mine.

The way I practice clinical psychology has gone through a radical change. We had been taught that we were not to impose our values on our patients, which I later learned was virtually impossible. Every time we give an opinion, we are expressing a value. We were taught to avoid discussing anything spiritual with patients. That area was out of our purview and should be left to their pastors, priests, or rabbis. In other words, it is none of our business.

It became apparent to me that, by ignoring the spirit, I was not treating the whole person nor could I fully understand a person without knowing something about their spiritual life.

I began asking my patients a simple question. "Where are you spiritually?" The answers to that question often shape the course of therapy. The Holy Spirit taught me how to integrate clinical principles with biblical principles to more effectively resolve the presenting problems and to enhance their lives after therapy is completed.

It was amazing to me how many wanted to talk about their spiritual life. Most had questions they had been hesitant to ask their clergyman. Many had gone to church all of their lives but didn't have a clue about salvation. Those who were born-again often didn't know how to apply and integrate biblical principles and truths into their lives. As they learned how to merge their spiritual life with the psychological and emotional life, they started resolving problems and growing at a much faster pace.

Many of my patients over the years have accepted Christ as Lord and Savior, and many have also received the baptism in the Holy Spirit as a result of being introduced to those spiritual experiences in my office. Not everyone is open to spiritual exploration, so I don't press them or impose it upon them. Their spirituality is between them and God. But for those who are open to exploring their spiritual side, God has done amazing things in them and for them. The patients grew spiritually. Relationships were reconciled. Emotional wounds were healed. Lives were changed.

I have become what I once abhorred, a "Jesus freak." The job of the Holy Spirit is to magnify and exalt Jesus Christ and to draw all people to Him. After Spirit baptism, Jesus became the most important person in my life. I am not ashamed of that and make no apologies for it. I continually thank God I was touched by the Agent of Change in the swimming pool that night many years ago and that He continues to change me into His likeness.

CHAPTER 2

The Transforming Power of the Holy Spirit and Apostle Peter

Many Christians today are unhappy with themselves. They may struggle with poor self-images or low self-esteem. Often, they want to change, but they do not know how. Some try to improve themselves but find it too difficult because they lack the strength. Today, many of us can suffer from this dilemma, and we are no different than the early disciples.

For years, the full gospel/charismatic movement has placed great emphasis on Christians receiving the singular event known as the baptism in the Holy Spirit as manifested by speaking in tongues and moving in the gifts of the Spirit (Acts 2:1-4). While the latter are important, God is more interested in changing each individual's character (Romans 12:2). Nothing can produce as dramatic and permanent a change in an individual as the indwelling Spirit. This is a rather bold statement and a simple analogy may help explain it.

If a woman owns an automobile, she has several methods available to her for moving it from point A to point B. Some of these methods are much more efficient than others. For example, she could stand outside the car on the driver's side and physically push it while reaching in with her right hand to rather clumsily steer it. With great effort, she will probably be able to get it moving and be able to slowly steer it. Obviously, this method is rather laborious and inefficient. Not much ground can be covered and not much can be accomplished in a day's time. The woman also has a limited control over the vehicle using this method. On the other hand, what happens if the woman is able to get inside the car, start it up, put it in gear, press the accelerator, and safely steer it? Suddenly, the automobile becomes very responsive to the driver's commands and can be used by the owner to accomplish much in an efficient and economical manner.

This is exactly what happens when a born-again Christian receives the baptism in the Holy Spirit. A Christian instantly becomes much more sensitive and responsive to the leading of the Spirit. He now has a much greater vantage point within the person. The difference, of course, between us and an automobile is that we have a free will. Therefore, the extent to which the Holy Spirit can lead a person toward greater sanctification remains a direct function of the person's willingness to be transformed. Nevertheless, the probability that transformation will occur is significantly greater after the baptism in the Spirit than before. How do we know this? Scripture is replete with examples of this truth. A case in point is the great apostle Peter.

To illustrate, let's do a brief personality analysis of Peter before and after Pentecost.

Peter Before Pentecost

We know from Scripture and from secular records that Peter was a fisherman. His brother, Andrew, met Jesus first and led Peter to Him. Peter told Jesus, "Depart from me, for I am a sinful man, O Lord!" (Luke 5:8). Jesus reassured him by prophesying to him that he would be catching men from now on (Luke 5:10). It's possible that Peter was saved at this point because he called Jesus Lord (Romans 10:13). But even if Peter was not saved at this early point in his relationship with

Jesus, there is proof text to support the fact that Peter was saved before Pentecost. Peter clearly recognized and accepted Jesus as "the Son of the living God" (Matthew 16:13-17).

Peter had a heart toward God, but he continually *vacillated* in his faith. One stormy night he and the other disciples sailed in a boat on the sea. They saw Jesus walking on the water. Peter asked the Lord to command him to come to Him, and Jesus replied with one word, "Come!" At this moment, Peter had to put action to his faith. The only disciple in the boat daring enough to believe Jesus to participate in the supernatural, Peter boldly stepped out of the boat. Although this certainly demonstrates the potential for great faith within Peter, at that moment, he wavered. He took his eyes off of Jesus and began to look at the stormy circumstances around him and fear entered. Faith and fear are mutually exclusive. Where there is one, there cannot be the other. That is, they are opposites. You cannot do two opposite things at the same time. For example, you cannot sit down and stand up at the same time. Peter began to sink and cried out to the Lord to be saved. Peter put his eyes back on Jesus and, indeed, was spared. Jesus then gently rebuked him, "O you of little faith, why did you doubt?" (Matthew 14:22-31). This is a repetitive pattern of behavior for Peter and suggests a characteristic of *indecisiveness* in his personality fueled by personal *insecurity*.

There is no doubt that Peter loved Jesus. However, he frequently was the boldest in speech but weakest in his behavior when the real tests came. In Matthew 26:30-35, Jesus restated the prophecy by Zechariah that the sheep of the flock shall be scattered. Peter refused to believe the prophetic word and said, "Even though all may fall away because of You, I will never fall away" (Matthew 26:33). Jesus prophesied specifically that Peter would deny Him three times before the cock would crow. Peter then demonstrated his willful spirit by rejecting this prophecy as well and said, "Even if I have to die with You, I will not deny You" (Matthew 26:35). Although Peter clearly was expressing love for Jesus, he expressed *spiritual pride*. How many of us have also been guilty of thinking that we have arrived spiritually and the things that befall others will not happen to us?

In the garden of Gethsemane, Jesus experienced one of the darkest moments of His life. What agony Jesus must have been in when He said to Peter, James, and John, "My soul is deeply grieved, to the point of death; remain here and keep watch with Me" (Matthew 26:38). This must have been an all-time low point in His life for He knew that the time for the final fulfillment of God's redemption plan for the world was near. Jesus also knew the incredible suffering He was about to endure. Jesus was in desperate need of spiritual and emotional support from those He loved. Peter and the two sons of Zebedee, James and John, were unable to supply His need. They fell asleep, not once but twice, after being asked to watch with Him. After Peter's great profession of dedication to Jesus, "even unto death," he could not even stay awake and pray with Jesus for one hour. Jesus cogently defined Peter's problem when He said, "…the spirit is willing, but the flesh is weak" (Matthew 26:41). Peter often yielded to his flesh and considered his own needs first.

In Matthew 19:27, Peter brazenly asked, "Behold, we have left everything and followed You; what then will there be for us?" Peter felt that he has sacrificed everything for Jesus and demanded to know what was in it for him. This reflects a certain *self-centeredness* in Peter's character. He did not mind leaving family, home, and occupation for Jesus but was not willing to do it just for the sake of knowing Jesus. Peter wanted to be sure there was something in it for him in the end. Many of us often do the same thing. We do what we should do anyway and then expect, even demand, that God reward us for it. Peter failed to understand that God is more pleased with obedience than sacrifice (I Samuel 15:22). It's true that obedience does often entail giving up those things you hold dear if they hinder your walk with God, but it is the motive of the heart with which this is done that is the salient feature of the act. If, at any time, obedience requires sacrifice, then we need to do so with a cheerful heart.

Peter's words suggest that, while he gave up everything for Jesus, he had done so somewhat grudgingly. We are taught to give, expecting nothing in return and, in fact, to give to those who cannot give back. Peter still had his eyes on this world by demanding tangible rewards for his sacrifices. God tells us that He rewards those who diligently seek Him so we know that our obedience and sacrifice does not go unrewarded. But, notice how our Lord responded to Peter: "And everyone who has left houses or brothers or sisters or father or mother or children or farms for My name's sake, shall receive many times as much, and shall inherit eternal life" (Matthew 19:28-29). Jesus tells us that our reward will not be just material but also spiritual. Peter had difficulty comprehending this because he was *spiritually immature*.

Like many new Christians, Peter had a zeal for the Lord but lacked maturity and wisdom. In Matthew 16:21-23, Jesus explained to the disciples His suffering and death that would soon take place would fulfill God's plan. Peter's *lack of spiritual discernment* and *lack of wisdom* caused him to be an unwitting tool in the hands of Satan. Note Peter's response to the Lord: "And Peter took Him aside and began to rebuke Him saying, God forbid it, Lord! This shall never happen to You" (Matthew 16:21-23). Peter either did not understand God's redemption plan, or he refused to accept it thus allowing himself to be used as a vessel through which Satan could speak. If Peter was refusing to accept our Lord's explanation, then he was *rebelling* against God. He wasn't rebelling because he hated God but because he indeed loved Jesus. He did not want Jesus to suffer and die. Notwithstanding, the motive may be good, but the behavior is still antithetical to God's will and represents a *willfulness* in Peter's character. We still see this in ourselves today. We continue to arrogantly think that we know more than God. This is reflected in Jesus' response to Peter: "Get behind Me, Satan! You are a stumbling block to Me; for you are not setting your mind on God's interests, but man's" (Matthew 16:23). Our willfulness can delay or even prevent the fulfillment of God's plan for our lives.

Peter's spiritual immaturity and lack of wisdom is further illustrated six days later on the mount of transfiguration. Peter, along with James and John, were given the extraordinary privilege of seeing Jesus in His transfigured state: "And He was transfigured before them; and His face shown like the sun and His garments became as white as light. And behold, Moses and Elijah appeared to them, talking with Him" (Matthew 17:2-3). Again, Peter was the first to speak. He said, "Lord, it is good for us to be here; if You wish, I will make three tabernacles here, one for You, and one for Moses, and one for Elijah" (Matthew 17:4). A tabernacle is a sacred tent, and Peter was obviously attempting to bestow great honor upon the three figures he gazed upon. The problem is that, because Peter observed the three together, he thought to bestow equal honor to each. How many times do we as Christians similarly exalt the man of God equally or more than the God he serves? Peter had not yet grasped the full glory and preeminence of Jesus. The Father gently corrected this misunderstanding by interrupting Peter and saying: "This is My beloved Son, with whom I am well-pleased; listen to Him!" (Matthew 17:5). In other words, "Peter, be obedient to only My Son."

Peter had an *impetuous* nature. He often spoke and acted before the other apostles and before he had appropriately appraised the consequences of his words and deeds. On a dark night in the garden, the Roman cohort led by Judas arrived to apprehend Jesus. The Lord made no attempt to escape or to conceal His identity. He freely and openly admitted that He was the one whom they sought. However, like an impulsive and unruly child, Peter pulled his sword and angrily struck Malchus, the high priest's slave and cut off his right ear (John 18:1-11).

Instead of being sensitive and responsive to his master's lead in this tense situation, thus complying with the authorities, Peter exploded and once again yielded to his own impulses. Reliance upon his own abilities and/or fear of yielding total control to Jesus is not only reflected in this violent act but also in the very fact that he carried a sword at all. Peter had walked, talked, and lived with Jesus for approximately three and a half years and had observed firsthand countless times and in myriad ways the manifested power of God. Why the need to carry a sword? Self protection? Did he truly believe that Jesus or the Father were incapable of protecting him? This violent act also suggests Peter's less than complete understanding and compliance with God's redemption plan even though Jesus had explained it to him more than once.

Shortly after the arrest of Jesus, Jesus' prophecy concerning Peter's denial was fulfilled. On three separate occasions, Peter's vacillating faith and fear for his own safety drove him to *lie* about his association with Jesus (John 18:15-27). Peter's dedication and conviction to follow the Lord did not appear to be as titanic as he initially professed.

Some theologians argue that the dramatic change in Peter and the other apostles was caused by seeing the resurrected Christ, thus diminishing the importance of the Pentecostal experience and maintaining that it has no significance for today's church. Viewing the resurrected Christ, no doubt, was a miraculous experience, but we have no evidence that the apostles began their ministries and moved in the power of God at that point. On the contrary, Peter continued to behave in an immature and fleshly manner. The resurrected Christ described by what kind of death Peter would glorify God (John 21:18). Peter's response revealed yet another unseemly feature of his personality, *jealousy*: "Peter, turning around, saw the disciple who Jesus loved following them; the one who also had leaned back on His breast at the supper, and said, 'Lord, who is the one who betrays You?' Peter therefore seeing him said to Jesus, 'Lord, and what about this man?'" (John 21:20-21).

Peter knew that the Lord had a special relationship with John, and he wanted to know if John would experience the same death or get special treatment. Jesus rebuked Peter in saying: "If I want him to remain until I come, what is that to you? You follow Me!" (John 21:22). Again, Peter's *shallowness* and *self-centeredness* prevented him from understanding the great privilege and honor he had been given, that is, to be martyred for Christ. This childish display was in the presence of the resurrected Christ. This experience, in and of itself, must not have been powerful enough to produce the monumental personality transformation we see occurring in Peter on and subsequent to Pentecost.

It may appear from this personality sketch that Peter was a rather repugnant individual with no redeeming qualities. God, however, looks on the heart and sees, not only what he is, but what he can potentially become if he yields to the life-changing power of God through the infilling of the Holy Spirit. Peter yielded on the day of Pentecost and began the lifelong transformation process that would produce a mighty man of God.

After Pentecost

Referring to the Holy Spirit, Jesus said:

> And He, when He comes, will convict the world concerning sin, and righteousness, and judgment; concerning sin, because they do not believe in Me; and concerning righteousness, because I go to the Father, and you no longer behold Me; and concerning judgment, because the ruler of this world has been judged. I have many more things to say to you, but you cannot bear them now. But when He, the Spirit of truth, comes, He will guide you into all the truth; for He will not speak on His own initiative, but whatever He hears, He will speak; and He will disclose to you what is to come. He shall glorify Me; for He shall take of Mine, and shall disclose it to you. All things that the Father has are mine; therefore I said, That He takes of Mine, and will disclose it to you. (John 16:8-15).

Embodied in these Scriptures is the very quintessence of characterological change. If the Spirit speaks not of Himself but only what He hears from the Lord, then the more we allow Him to inhabit us, the more we begin to reflect the very likeness of the Lord. If the Spirit speaks only what He hears from our Lord, and we speak only what we hear from the Spirit, then a marvelous change begins to emanate from us. We no longer speak, feel, think, or act according to our own character but in perfect harmony with His. Jesus said, "And the glory which Thou gavest Me, I have given them; that they may be one, just as We are one; I in them, and Thou in Me, that they may be made perfected in unity" (John 17:22-23). As we are perfected in Him, and we increasingly become one with the Trinity in thought and deed, it is a spiritual impossibility to *not* change.

Before His ascension, Jesus prepared the believers for a very special experience: "But you shall receive power, after that the Holy Spirit has come upon you; and you shall be My witnesses both in Jerusalem, and in all Judea and Samaria, and even to the remotest part of the earth" (Acts 1:8). Any transition from one state or form to another cannot occur without a necessary energy source which serves as the impetus for that variation. The Holy Spirit is that impetus which provides the drive to produce change within a person.

On the day of Pentecost, after having received the baptism in the Holy Spirit with evidence of speaking in tongues, a remarkable thing began to occur within Peter. That day, some criticized and mocked the supernatural accusing that "these men are full of new wine" (Acts 2:13). At this point, Peter stood up and began, what remains to this day, one of the most anointed sermons ever preached. He eloquently explained the baptism in the Holy Spirit and defended the faith. Peter exhorted the multitude to accept the Messiah, Jesus. Although Peter was a devout Jew before the baptism and probably knew the Old Testament Scriptures, no record exists of him quoting lengthy passages of Scripture and applying them astutely to explain spiritual phenomena as we see in Acts 2:17-21, 25-

28. Jesus said the Holy Spirit would put us in remembrance of all He said (John 14:26). Following Spirit baptism, our minds become more occupied with spiritual matters and, if we *yield* to Him, He brings forth those things at the appropriate time. At Pentecost, Peter instantly became more submitted to God and, thus, was able to speak under the unction of the Spirit. We also begin to see a radical departure from Peter's fearful, vacillating nature. Whereas he lied and denied Christ to just a few people before the baptism, Peter now *boldly* declared Jesus to thousands. We are told that he testified with many words (Acts 2:40). He obviously had almost instantly become a much more *effective* and *eloquent witness* for Christ because we know that three thousand people were saved and added to the church that day. This doesn't even sound like the same man and this was just the first day.

Later, Peter and John went to the temple to pray when suddenly the Holy Spirit moved upon Peter (Acts 3:1-12). The mendicant sitting at the temple gate, who was congenitally crippled, began to beseech them for money. Unable to walk and totally dependent on others for his livelihood, this man was in a monstrous kind of bondage. We are told Peter fixed his gaze upon him. That is, his focus of attention was on this pitiful man, not himself. Instead of the self-centered Peter who was concerned with his own needs and thoughts, he had become much more *other-centered*. We see Peter giving of himself, first to God to be used by Him, then to the crippled man. He exhibited a *self-sacrificing* quality. Moreover, compassion and mercy went out of him toward the man.

There are no hindrances to the Holy Spirit moving through us when we empty ourselves of ourselves. In commanding the man to stand in the name of Jesus, Peter not only demonstrated the gift of miracles but also moved in great faith. This is diametrically opposed to the picture of the fearful man painted in earlier Scripture. Peter exhibits yet another new wrinkle in his newly developing character, *humility*. Instead of spiritual pride or arrogance, he preaches a powerful disclaimer when he mightily exalts Jesus and ultimately leads five thousand more souls unto salvation. His focus of attention was no longer on himself but rather on Jesus and on the lost lambs of Israel (Acts 3:12-26).

Peter and John were arrested the next day and brought before the Sanhedrin to defend themselves (Acts 4:5-20). Peter had little regard for himself by this time and boldly declared his association with Jesus. His degree of commitment had changed from vacillation to true dedication. He spoke with *courage, confidence,* and *selflessness,* not caring what would happen to him as long as he could testify of Jesus. The Sanhedrin commanded Peter and John to stop preaching in the name of Jesus. In the face of threats, Peter refused and declared: "... we cannot stop speaking what we have seen and heard" (Acts 4:20).

Later, Peter dealt with Ananias and Sapphira and in doing so moved in the spiritual gifts of discernment, word of knowledge, and prophecy (Acts 5:1-10). Ananias sold a piece of property, the proceeds of which would be distributed to the needy. However, with the full knowledge of his wife

Sapphira, Ananias gave only a portion to Peter. The Holy Spirit revealed the lie to Peter who confronted both of them. Upon confrontation Ananias and Sapphira both fell down and died. At this point, Peter demonstrated a quickly growing *spiritual maturity* and *sensitivity* to the Spirit.

Throughout his life, Peter continued to yield to the transforming power of God. He exhorted us to abstain from lust of the flesh and to submit ourselves to authority (I Peter 2:11-17). Peter is no longer the unruly, impulsive, and rebellious person he once was but rather a man of obedience to God and men in authority. When we submit to The Holy Spirit, He immediately begins to put our flesh and spirit under His unction and teaches us about true holiness, that is, love and obedience.

Peter spoke on the cultivation of character in (II Peter 1:3-7). He spoke of moral excellence, knowledge, self-control, perseverance, godliness, brotherly kindness, and love. By encouraging us to grow in Christ and to pursue these qualities, Peter himself exhibited these very characteristics that the transforming power of the Holy Spirit had worked in him.

Peter glorified God by being martyred and, even in his death, he displayed extraordinary humility by requesting that he be crucified upside down deeming himself unworthy to suffer the same death as our Lord. This was not the deranged act of a self-punitive psychotic, for all of the evidence indicates that Peter had become entirely *well-balanced* and psychologically and spiritually mature and healthy. No, this last act of humility was his sincere and genuine effort to exalt the God who had not only saved him from eternal hell, but had also worked a thorough metamorphosis in his character through the indwelling of His Spirit produced by the baptism in the Holy Spirit (table 1).

TABLE 1
Peter's Transformation

Before Pentecost	After Pentecost
vacillating	yielded
indecisive	effective and eloquent witness
insecure	other-centered
willful	self-sacrificing
spiritual pride	compassionate
self-centered	merciful
spiritually immature	faithful
lacked spiritual discernment	humble
lacked wisdom	dedicated
rebellious	courageous
impetuous	confident
liar	bold
jealous	selfless
shallow	spiritually mature
	sensitive to Holy Spirit
	obedient
	morally excellent
	knowledgeable
	self controlled
	persistent
	godly
	kind
	loving
	well-balanced

CHAPTER 3

The Transforming Power of the Holy Spirit and Apostle Paul

Let me tell you a true story about a man who was an accessory to murder and a chronic liar. He falsely accused many people and had them imprisoned for his own selfish ambition. He deserved death but God forgave and pardoned him. Who was this reprobate? None other than the great apostle Paul!

In examining the life of Paul (also known as Saul of Tarsus), we see the profound influence the Holy Spirit had in molding and shaping his personality and character. Numerous volumes have been written about Paul and his influence on the early church, each of which has its own emphasis and viewpoint. Some view Paul as a very controversial figure, full of contradictions and paradoxes. Some accuse him of being a misogynist for his views that women should submit to their husbands and not speak in church. It is not the intention of this analysis to debate theological points in Paul's epistles but rather to draw some reasonable inferences about his personality, based on Scripture, prior to and after his conversion to Christ and baptism in the Holy Spirit.

Before Baptism in the Holy Spirit

Some would argue that there is no specific scriptural account of when Paul received the baptism in the Holy Spirit with evidence of speaking in tongues or whether he actually received the baptism at all. In Acts 9:10-19, the Lord spoke to a man named Ananias and instructed him to locate Saul on the street called Straight, lay hands on him, and pray for him that he may regain his sight after being blinded by a vision of Jesus on his way to Damascus.

After entering the house and laying hands on Saul, Ananias said, "Brother Saul, the Lord Jesus, who appeared to you on the road by which you were coming, has sent me so that you may regain your sight, and be filled with the Holy Spirit. And immediately there fell from his eyes something like scales, and he regained his sight, and he arose and was baptized" (Acts 9:17-18).

When Saul regained his sight, God did exactly what He said He would do for him. It is not a big leap of faith, then, to believe that God also filled Saul with the Holy Spirit just as He said He would (Acts 13:9). Some argue that there is no reference to Saul speaking in tongues when he was filled with the Holy Spirit. That is true, but we see later that Paul told the church at Corinth: "I thank God, I speak in tongues more than you all" (I Corinthians 14:18) and "therefore, my brethren, desire earnestly to prophesy, and do not forbid to speak in tongues" (I Corinthians 14:39).

Therefore, it is reasonable to conclude that Paul did, indeed, speak in tongues when he was filled with the Holy Spirit just as all the others did who were recorded in the book of Acts by Luke.

The Lord made a distinction here between being filled with the Spirit and being baptized (water). He told Ananias to pray that Saul may regain his sight *and* be filled with the Holy Spirit. The Lord said nothing about Saul being water baptized, but after Ananias obeyed and fulfilled the only two instructions God gave him, then Saul was baptized.

Following this seminal event "immediately he began to proclaim Jesus in the synagogues, saying, 'He is the Son of God'"

(Acts 9:20). Something phenomenal must have happened to Saul that day. Some argue that it was the vision of Jesus on the Damascus road that changed Saul. As mentioned earlier, the appearance of Jesus in His resurrected state is a miraculous event and would have a profound impact on someone but, as with the other apostles, Paul did not begin his ministry until after being filled with the Holy Spirit (Acts 9:17).

Proclaiming Jesus as the Son of God is even more remarkable when we consider Paul's history before his encounter with Jesus and his baptism in the Holy Spirit.

Paul gave a succinct summary of his history: "…circumcised the eighth day, of the nation of Israel, of the tribe of Benjamin, a Hebrew of Hebrews; as to the Law, a Pharisee; as to zeal, a persecutor of the church; as to the righteousness which is in the Law, found blameless" (Philippians 3:5-6).

Luke corroborated this description in his account of Stephen's death and subsequent events: "And when they had driven him out of the city, they began stoning him, and the witnesses laid aside their robes at the feet of a young man named Saul" (Acts 7:58) and "Saul was in hearty agreement with putting him to death" (Acts 8:1). Following Stephen's death great persecution came against the church: "But Saul began ravaging the church, entering house after house; and dragging off men and women, he would put them in prison" (Acts 8:3).

These passages imply a great deal about Paul's personality. He began by giving his ancestry and position in the Jewish race, society, and culture. He referred to being circumcised the eighth day. This practice is traced all the way back to the covenant struck between God and Abraham. A covenant is a binding agreement between two people usually consisting of a promise with a condition. God told Abraham: "I am God Almighty; Walk before Me, and be blameless. And I will establish My covenant between Me and you, And I will multiply you exceedingly" (Genesis 17:1-2).

God's part of the bargain, His promise, was that He would multiply Abraham exceedingly. God told Abraham what He wanted in exchange for that promise: "This is my covenant, which you shall keep, between Me and you and your descendants after you; every male among you shall be circumcised, and you shall be circumcised in the flesh of your foreskin; and it shall be the sign of the covenant between Me and you. And every male who is among you who is eight days old shall be circumcised throughout your generations" (Genesis 17:10-12).

How important was this covenant? God clearly stated: "But an uncircumcised male who is not circumcised in the flesh of his foreskin, that person shall be cut off from his people, he has broken My covenant" (Genesis 17:66).

So, when Paul stated that he was circumcised on the eighth day, he wasn't just referring to some random obstetric practice of his day but rather he was establishing his bragging rights as a child of the Abrahamic covenant. For a Jewish man, being circumcised was not optional. To not be circumcised meant being cut off from his people and being out of covenant with God. The latter meant that he would not hear from God and would not receive His multiplied blessings. Nothing could be worse for a Hebrew.

Paul stated that he was "of the nation of Israel." We know that Paul was from Tarsus, the capital of Cilecia in the eastern part of southern Turkey. So why did Paul claim he is of the nation Israel? He wasn't referring to a geographic location but rather to the father of the nation, Jacob. God changed Jacob's name to Israel who then fathered twelve sons (Genesis 32:28).

Paul further stated that he was of the tribe of Benjamin. We know that Benjamin was the son of Jacob and Rachel (Genesis 35:24) and became head of one of the twelve tribes of Israel. The twelve tribes of Israel constituted the nation of Israel regardless of their geographic location at that time.

In stating that he was circumcised on the eighth day and of the nation of Israel and the tribe of Benjamin, Paul was delineating his Jewish lineage all the way back to Abraham (Romans 11:1). He obviously was very *proud* of this because he added that he was "a Hebrew of Hebrews." He was describing himself as having been *boastful* of his unimpeachable Jewishness.

Paul also stated that he was a Pharisee. *Pharisaios* is from the Aramaic word *peras* which means to separate.[1] Some Christians mistakenly believe that Pharisees were also rabbis. The Pharisees were one of two major parties or sects within Jewish society, the other being the Sadducees. The two parties had distinctly different views of religion and society. The Pharisees promoted separation of Jewish religion and society from all non-Jewish components. They placed great emphasis on the letter of the law and on the correctness of a behavior. Their emphasis was more

---

1 W.E. Vine, *An Expository Dictionary of Biblical Words*, (Nashville: Thomas Nelson Publishers, 1984).

on the external man than the internal. As a Pharisee, then, Paul was describing himself as *rigid* and *legalistic.*

He further described himself "as to the righteousness which is in the law, found blameless" (Philippians 3:6). Sounds pretty good doesn't it? But what does this really say about Paul? Notice how Jesus described these qualities: "Woe to you, scribes and Pharisees, hypocrites! For you are like whitewashed tombs which on the outside appear beautiful, but inside they are full of dead men's bones and all uncleanness. Even so you too outwardly appear righteous to men, but inwardly you are full of hypocrisy and lawlessness" (Matthew 23:27-28).

In this chapter Jesus proclaims "Woe to you" to the Pharisees and scribes a total of eight times. He describes them as hypocrites, blind guides, fools, serpents and vipers, unfair, merciless, and faithless. This would be a scourging indictment from anyone but how much more from the Son of God? Jesus was not fond of the Pharisees and scribes to put it mildly. As Paul admitted to being a Pharisee, we can infer that he exhibited these same characteristics described by our Lord.

Paul wrote "as to zeal, a persecutor of the church" (Philippians 3:6). In his case, this zeal was misguided. When religious zeal is not tempered by Godly wisdom, love and mercy, it becomes destructive. When it is not under the control and direction of the Holy Spirit, it becomes self-righteousness and can alienate people even farther from God than they might be already.

As a persecutor of the church, Paul exhibited a harsh prejudice toward a group in his society that he knew very little about. Following the letter of the law but not the Spirit of the Law, Paul only cared about complying with the directives of the Pharisees and rabbis who gave him permission to deal with the "Christian problem" in the most expedient manner possible. To fully understand the severity of Paul's treatment of Christians, let's examine the words in Acts 8:3. We are told that Paul ravaged the church. Ravaged comes from the Greek word *lumainomal*, which means to "make havoc of." Men and women were dragged off from their homes and imprisoned without trial. Their civil rights were brutally violated. And all this because they were Christians. They had broken no civil or criminal law but merely believed differently than the Pharisees who ruled the temple.

Some might say, "We can't judge Paul too harshly. Such cruelty was common during his time." That may be true, but let's put this behavior into a more modern perspective to fully capture the evil of it. We could liken it to Nazi Germany where millions of Jews were seized, imprisoned, and murdered without due process of the law simply because they were Jewish. Or more recently, during Apartheid in South Africa, blacks were arrested and imprisoned without due process of the law and many suffered "accidental" deaths while incarcerated.

These atrocities cannot be mitigated by asserting that they were the expected result of political unrest or conflict. In Paul's case, he directly attacked and persecuted Jesus Christ, the Son of God: "And he fell to the earth, and heard a voice saying unto him, 'Saul, Saul, why persecutest thou Me?' And he said, 'Who art thou Lord?' And the Lord said, 'I am Jesus whom thou persecutes'…" (Acts 9:4-5).

Now, we must recognize such behaviors for what they are, i.e., *evil*. One might argue, "But Paul didn't exterminate millions of Christians as Hitler did to the Jews." First, the exact number of Christians Paul imprisoned or had executed is unknown. The number of Paul's incarcerated must have been significant, for him to be described as "ravaging the church." For certain, Paul proved, at least, an accessory to Stephen's murder. Stephen, a deacon in the early church, was brought before the Sanhedrin, falsely accused of blasphemy, and stoned to death. Paul's complicity was obvious: "And Saul was in hearty agreement with putting him to death" (Acts 8:1). We also do not know how much worse it would have gotten had Jesus not intervened in Paul's life on the road to Damascus. Evil left unchecked usually proliferates and escalates.

Is it unfair to compare Paul with someone such as Hitler who was one of the most violent, and evil human beings to ever have lived? While that comparison may be debatable, it remains that Paul did not just treat other humans this way, as bad as that is, but rather he directly attacked and persecuted Jesus, the Son of God. I believe, and Paul would probably agree, that he was, all in all, a detestable and wicked person.

Paul labeled his evil practices "righteousness which is in the Law." What religious Jew of his day would question that description? Apparently only Jesus. Paul fell into that group that Jesus described as professing God with their lips but in their hearts are far from Him (Matthew 15:8).

Paul was, no doubt, extremely intelligent and well-educated. Paul communicated on such a high level that even Peter commented that some of the things in his epistles were "hard to be understood" (II Peter 3:16). But superior intelligence alone is not necessarily a good quality. It is how it is used that determines whether it is good or bad. There are numerous examples of brilliant individuals who misused their intellect. Albert Speer, for example, was a talented German architect. Rather than applying his intellect, skills, and training toward the accomplishment of something beneficial to mankind, he instead used them to help Adolf Hitler build the Third Reich and its concentration camps. Ted Kazinsky, the Unabomber, held a Ph.D. in mathematics and was, by all reports, a brilliant mathematician. Rather than using his considerable intellect in a positive way, he made bombs which murdered and maimed people.

Paul used his intellect arrogantly to devise schemes to persecute the early church. The Bible describes people like Paul very bluntly: "Professing themselves to be wise they become *fools*" (Romans 1:22, my emphasis). In his intellectual arrogance Paul believed he knew all there was to know about God and that he had all the answers when, actually, he didn't even have the right questions. Although in his Romans epistle many years later, Paul referred to sinners, this description accurately describes Paul during his pre-conversion years: "Because that, when they knew God, they glorified Him not as God, neither were thankful; but became *vain* in their imaginations, and their *foolish* heart was *darkened*" (Romans 1:21, my emphasis).

In accusing Christians of heresy Paul "changed the truth of God into a lie..." (Romans 1:25). One who lies is a *liar*. In persecuting, imprisoning, and executing Christians Paul exhibited a maliciousness in his character. Maliciousness comes from the Greek word *kakla* which means "wickedness, as an evil habit of the mind."[2] The ancients saw *kakla* as the wellspring of all viciousness and vices.

In Romans Paul pronounced his own sentence: "Who knowing the judgment of God, that they which commit such things are *worthy of death*, not only do the same, but have pleasure in them that do them" (Romans 1:32, my emphasis). If he had not encountered and submitted to Jesus, Paul surely would have received eternal death.

After Baptism in the Holy Spirit

As Christians we often underestimate God's ability to change someone. Many of us have been guilty of assuming that certain individuals are so bad that they will never change, and we may not even pray for them. Early Christians knew of Paul's transformation even before he preached to them: "Then I went into the regions of Syria and Cilicia. And I was still unknown by sight to the churches of Judea which were in Christ; but only, they kept hearing, 'He who once persecuted us is now preaching the faith which he once tried to destroy.' And they were glorifying God because of me" (Galatians 1:21-24).

Now why do you suppose they were glorifying God because of Paul? The church community was all a buzz about Paul. I

---

2 Spiro Zodhiates, ed., *Hebrew Greek Key Study Bible*, (Chattanooga, TN: AMG Publishers, 1984).

imagine the talk went something like this: "Can you believe it? The very guy who was evil incarnate and did everything in his power to destroy us is now a believer and on fire for God. If God can change someone like him, all things are possible with God! Hallelujah!" I can just see faith in God rising in the church because they witnessed the transforming power of the Holy Spirit manifested in Paul. This illustrates why God chooses the most unlikely people to serve him.

Jesus said, "I praise Thee, O Father, Lord of heaven and earth, that thou didst hide these things from the wise and intelligent and didst reveal them to babes" (Matthew 11:25). The word "babes" comes from the Greek work *nepios*,[3] which means infant or, figuratively, a simple-minded person or immature believer. Why would God give such revelations of Himself through His Son to unwise, immature, and unsophisticated people? I believe it shows the stark contrast between a person's former self and the transformed self. God delights in taking the most childish, foolish, selfish, arrogant, and lowliest reprobates and, by the power of His Holy Spirit, completely changing them into the total opposite of what they once were. This life-changing effect produced by the Holy Spirit separates Christianity from the other religions of the world. This is exactly what transformed Paul from an enemy of Christ into His beloved servant. This miracle of positive transformation gives glory to God because only He can completely change the heart, mind, character, and behavior of a person for purposes of good.

---

3 Ibid.

As we saw earlier, Paul boasted that he was circumcised on the eighth day thus legitimizing his identity as a Jew. Later, however, profound change occurs: "For he is not a Jew who is one outwardly; neither is circumcision that which is outward in the flesh. But he is a Jew who is one inwardly; and circumcision is that which is of the heart, by the Spirit, not by the letter, and his praise is not from men, but from God" (Romans 2:28-29). Paul's view changed entirely. He emphatically stated that our relationship with God depends not on the external man and things of the flesh, but rather, on the condition of the heart. Notice to whom he gave credit for his *changed heart*. The Holy Spirit!

Recall our earlier discussion of circumcision as an external sign of the covenant between God and His people, the Hebrews. Paul explained that the sign of the covenant was an internal circumcision made by the Holy Spirit resulting in a changed heart. What is the significance of that change? The word heart (lab) in Hebrew means "the totality of man's inner or immaterial nature."[4] In other words, when the heart changes, the whole man changes. Only the Holy Spirit can produce this change in man's entire inner being: "And I will give them one heart, and I will put a new spirit within them. And I will take the heart of stone out of their flesh, and will give them a heart of flesh, that they may walk in my statutes, and keep mine, ordinances, and do them. Then they will be my people and I shall be their God" (Ezekiel 11:10-20).

---

4 Ibid.

God is in the heart-changing business. When a person's heart is changed (circumcised), all things of God follow. When our hearts change, we not only desire to follow His laws, but also to obey them. Everything begins with and is determined by the condition of the heart: "I, the Lord, search the heart. I test the mind, even to give to each man according to his ways, according to the results of his deeds" (Jeremiah 17:10). If our hearts are right before God, then our ways will be pleasing to Him and our deeds will be fruitful. The heart controls everything. It even determines where we will spend eternity: "...that if you confess with your mouth Jesus as Lord, and believe in your *heart* that God raised Him from the dead, you shall be saved; for with the *heart* man believes, resulting in righteousness, and with the mouth he confesses, resulting in salvation" (Romans 10:9-10, my emphasis). Paul had come to understand that true righteousness is not the result of religion (law) but rather a genuine relationship with God which is determined by the condition of the heart.

Paul formerly boasted of his righteousness. He rigidly adhered to the letter of the Law. He later repudiated this doctrine when he boldly proclaimed: "...nevertheless knowing that a man is not justified by the works of the Law but through faith in Christ Jesus, even we have believed in Christ Jesus, that we may be justified by faith in Christ, and not by the works of the Law; since by the works of the Law shall no flesh be justified" (Galatians 2:16). The Holy Spirit had taken him from a state of religiosity to a pure faith in Christ Jesus.

Once the heart is changed by the Holy Spirit, the mind and body will follow suit. Paul's writings reflect a powerful paradigm shift in his own life: "I urge you therefore, brethren, by the mercies of God to present your bodies a living and holy sacrifice, acceptable to God, which is your spiritual service of worship. And do not be conformed to this world, but be transformed by the renewing of your mind, that you may prove what the will of God is, that which is good and acceptable and perfect" (Romans 12:1-2). Paul's mind had been renewed, which changed his worldview. He no longer identified with the values, attitudes, and views of the non-Christian world. A radical change occurred in his thinking. He now preached total submission to God as a way of knowing and proving God's perfect will.

Whereas Paul was formerly ambitious and boastful of his standing and achievements, a profound change in his self-image proved obvious in his letter to the Roman church: "For through the grace given to me I say to every man among you not to think more highly of himself than he ought to think; but to think so as to have sound judgment, as God has allotted to each a measure of faith" (Romans 12:3).

This reflects a Godly humility that the Holy Spirit had developed in Paul by transforming his mind. This was confirmed again when he wrote: "But may it never be that I should boast, except in the cross of our Lord Jesus Christ, through which the world has been crucified to me, and I to the world" (Galatians 6:4).

Paul's values, thoughts, and priorities had changed. He no longer adhered to the world's standards but only to God's, which produced a separation from this world. His thoughts were not his own but rather he had put on the mind of Christ (I Corinthians 2:16): "And that you be renewed in the spirit of your mind, and put on the new self, which in the likeness of God has been created in righteousness and holiness of the Truth" (Ephesians 4:23-24).

Renewing of the mind, then, produces a *new self*. What is the significance of this? Self has been the subject of many theories and discussions within psychology. Psychologist Gordon Allport defined self as "...the essence of the individual, consisting of a gradually developing body sense, identity, self-estimate, and set of personal values, attitudes, and intentions."[5] Amazing! The very essence of Paul had been changed by God. When the self changes, nothing remains the same. Some type of change in the self is often a major goal of psychotherapy. Depending on the spiritual and worldview of the therapist, changes in the self may not always be for the better and of God.

Paul urged us to put on a new self that is in the likeness of God. We are to identify totally with God. That is, we are to adopt and assimilate His attitudes, standards and personality traits. Psychologists can help people change certain aspects of the self, but only the Holy Spirit can profoundly and permanently transform the totality of a Christian's inner being.

Through the years of Paul's ministry, we see beautiful changes in his personality. A number of positive characteristics are reflected in his discussion of liberty: "If one of the unbelievers invites you and you wish to go, eat anything that is

---

5   Gary R. VandenBos, ed., *APA Dictionary of Psychology*, (Washington, D.C.: American Psychological Association, 2007).

set before you, without asking questions for conscience sake" (I Corinthians 10:27). His words instruct us to be *respectful* to all, even unbelievers: "Give no offense either to Jews or to Greeks or to the church of God" (I Corinthians 10:32). Paul exhorts us to be kind and considerate of others. This is the same man who once persecuted and imprisoned Jews. Paul goes on to write: "…just as I also please all men in all things, not seeking my own profit, but the profit of the many, that they may be saved." (I Corinthians 10:33). This demonstrates *unselfishness* in Paul. He had also developed a *transcendent view* of mankind. That is, he rejected personal profit for the greater profit of many (salvation).

Saul gave his approval and calmly stood by while Stephen was stoned to death. Paul, on the other hand, showed *empathy* for the weak (II Corinthians 11:29) and daily *concern* for all the churches (II Corinthians 11:28).

Saul previously spoke evil of all who believed in Christ. In his letter to Titus, the transformed Paul instructed Titus to teach others to malign no one and to show meekness to all people (Titus 3:2). Paul exhorted older men "to be temperate, dignified, sensible, sound in faith, in love, in perseverance" (Titus 2:2).

Saul once sowed seeds of division among the Jews by persecuting Christians. Paul, however, now promoted *unity* among Christians and within the church. The church was in danger of splitting into factions, sects, and ultimately denominations (I Corinthians 1:10-17). This is a favorite strategy of Satan. He knows that division and disunity weakens

God's church and His people. Satan knows God's Word even if man is ignorant of it: "And if a house be divided against itself, that house cannot stand" (Mark 3:25). Satan also knows that unity produces power and, therefore, has done much to bring disharmony in the contemporary church. Paul moved quickly to squelch contentions by exhorting Christians to unity: "Now I beseech you, brethren, by the name of our Lord Jesus Christ, that you all speak the same thing, and that there be no divisions among you; but that you be perfectly joined together in the same mind and in the same judgment" (I Corinthians 1:10). Paul had now become a *reconciler* and arbitrator by bringing disparate factions together and mending breeches between people in the church. Paul had become a *peacemaker* and, thus, a child of God (Matthew 5:9).

We see this theme again in Paul's letter to the church at Rome: "Now the God of patience and consolation grant you to be like minded one toward another according to Christ Jesus: that you may with one mind and one mouth glorify God, even the Father of our Lord Jesus Christ" (Romans 15:5-6). Reflected in this burning desire for unity was Paul's *humility*. He did not want to be the focus of attention in the church but consistently redirected the focus to Christ and body unity.

As Saul he, not only persecuted Christians, but wanted nothing to do with the object of their faith, Jesus Christ. We see later, however, that the transformed Paul was willing to sacrifice all for the Messiah:

> Five times I received from the Jews thirty-nine
> lashes. Three times I was beaten with rods, once

I was stoned, three times I was shipwrecked, a night and a day I have spent in the deep. I have been on frequent journeys, in danger from rivers, dangers from robbers, dangers from my countrymen, dangers from Gentiles, dangers in the city, dangers in the wilderness, dangers on the sea, dangers among false brethren: I have been in labor and hardship, through many sleepless nights, in hunger and thirst, often without food, in cold and exposure. Apart from such external things, there is the daily pressure upon me of concern for all the churches (II Corinthians 11:24-28).

Much is reflected in Paul's transformed character by these Scriptures. In willingly facing daily dangers and stresses he exhibited extraordinary *courage* and *bravery*. In enduring persecution and abuse he exhibited remarkable *determination*, *resolve*, and *strength of convictions*. These were not the result of mere intellectual beliefs but rather evolved from an intimate relationship with the person of Jesus Christ through the infilling of His Holy Spirit, which occurred after the experience on the road to Damascus.

In later being martyred, the transformed Paul made the ultimate sacrifice for the risen Savior, his life. He began as a cruel persecutor of Christians but finished his life as one of the greatest propagators and defenders of the faith to have ever lived. Paul, probably more than any other apostle, is responsible for the establishment and growth of the Christian church. This is absolutely amazing from a personality-change perspective!

The baptism in the Holy Spirit, in and of itself, did not produce all of the changes observable in Peter, Paul, and other apostles. Rather, the baptism increased their intimacy with God which, in turn, produced a malleability of character, tenderness of heart, and acceptance of the full counsel of God and godly people. Many of the transformations of the apostles took place gradually over several years with God using myriad situations and methods to transform them. But we have also demonstrated scripturally that some remarkable changes also occurred almost instantly upon receiving the baptism in the Holy Spirit. The infilling of the Spirit serves as the impetus and source of power that produces these wonderful transformations in the human character and personality (table 2).

TABLE 2

Paul's Transformation

Before Spirit baptism	After Spirit baptism
Proud	Changed heart
Boastful	Faith in Christ
Rigid	Renewed mind
Legalistic	Submissive to God
Hypocrite	New identity
Lawless	New attitude
Blind guide	New self-image
Fool	New values
Unfair	New intentions
Merciless	Unselfishness
Faithless	Transcendent view of life
Serpent	Empathy
Viper	Concerned
Destructive	Temperate
Self righteous	Dignified
Prejudiced	Sensible
Harsh	Sound in faith, love, and perseverance
Violent	Reconciler and peacemaker
Brutal	Child of God
Cruel	Humble
Evil	Determined
Arrogant	Resolute
Ambitious	Strength of convictions
Detestable	Courageous
Morally wrong	Brave
Intelligent	Self-sacrificing
Educated	
Schemer / Liar	
Malicious	
Sentenced to eternal death	

CHAPTER 4

Who Is The Agent of Change and How Does He Work?

Who is the Holy Spirit?

The most common answer to that question is, "He is the third person in the Trinity." That is correct, but that answer only describes His official title or position. It tells us nothing about who He really is. The Holy Spirit is arguably the least known and least understood person in the Trinity. In fact, many Christians refer to Him as "It." They may know a lot about God the Father and Jesus the Son but are hard-pressed to describe the Holy Spirit, our relationship with Him, and His relevance to contemporary Christian living.

As in Acts 19:2 where the disciples told Paul they had never heard of the Holy Spirit, many contemporary Christians have barely heard of Him, if at all, and if they have, certainly know little about Him. This ignorance of Him within the body of Christ is perplexing because much is written about Him in the Bible. Yet church leaders largely ignore Him. They rarely speak of the Holy Spirit and never teach how to come into a relationship with Him. In fact, many teach that He is no longer active on the earth as He was in the New Testament. If that is true, we might as well pack up our Christianity and go home. Without the operation of the Holy Spirit on the earth today in myriad ways, Christianity becomes like any other religion of the world: an intellectual belief system focused on a man (Buddha, Mohammed, Confucius, Jesus), a god, or several gods with many rules to follow.

What Kind of Impact Can the Holy Spirit Have on a Christian?

The Holy Spirit convicts of sin, reveals the truth of Jesus, and produces the spiritual, mental, and behavioral transformation from being dead in sin to alive in Christ. Born-again Christians worldwide testify being filled with the Holy Spirit is more than an intellectual belief system. People adopt belief systems all the time but may abandon them when their appeal fades due to lack of any real substance. The differentiating factor between Christianity and other world religions is obvious in the person of Jesus Christ and the continuing work of the Holy Spirit: "And I will pray the Father, and He shall give you another Comforter, that He may abide with you forever" (John 14:16).

Once we accept Jesus, the Holy Spirit stays with us forever. Intellectual belief systems rarely do that. Now, as He is with us forever, what is He doing with us? Romans 8:16 provides the answer: "The Spirit himself bears witness with our spirit that we are children of God."

The Holy Spirit continually and eternally confirms, not only in our minds but also our spirits, that Jesus is Lord and that we belong to Him. No intellectual belief system can do that because it is merely of the mind. In everyday language, Christians describe Romans 8:16 in this way: "I know that I know that I know." This all-encompassing *knowing* is evidence the supernatural has occurred in an individual and demonstrates the working of the Holy Spirit.

Non-Christians often accuse Christians of being brainwashed. If Christianity was simply an intellectual system created by human beings to control each other, that label may apply. However, Christians are not only brainwashed but spirit-washed by the shed blood of Jesus and the power of the Holy Spirit. Paul cogently explained this supernatural experience: "But when the kindness of God our Savior and His love for mankind appeared, He saved us, not on the basis of deeds which we have done in righteousness, but according to His mercy, by the washing of regeneration and renewing by the Holy Spirit, whom He poured out upon us richly through Jesus Christ our Savior" (Titus 3:4-6). It's obvious the Holy Spirit plays a key role in salvation. However, what exactly is this washing of regeneration and renewing by the Holy Spirit?

The great prophet Ezekiel helps us to understand this work of the Holy Spirit: "Then I will sprinkle clean water on you, and you will be clean; I will cleanse you from all your filthiness and from all your idols. Moreover, I will give you a new heart and put a new spirit within you; and I will remove the heart of stone from your flesh and give you a heart of flesh" (Ezekiel 36:25-26). Therefore, yes, our brains (minds) and spirits are being washed but washed from sin not reason. This is confirmed again, where the Lord refers to the church (Christians): "…that He might sanctify her, having cleansed her by the washing of water by the word…." (Ephesians 5:26). When we make the conscious decision to yield to the Word (Jesus) (John 1:1) we are cleansed of sin. Jesus said, "You are already clean because of the Word which I have spoken to you" (John 15:3).

As if that would not be enough, God then goes yet further by telling us that He will give us a new heart and put a new spirit within us. In other words, God changes the actual spiritual nature of humans. Our spiritual nature (heart) is transformed. Unless the heart changes, nothing else changes. Only the Spirit of God can permanently change a person's heart.

Ezekiel 36:27 describes what Paul means in the last part of Titus 3:5: "...and renewing by the Holy Spirit." After regenerating our spirit, an awesome thing occurs: "And I will put My Spirit within you and cause you to walk in My statutes, and you will be careful to observe My ordinances."

God puts the Holy Spirit within us to empower us to live our lives according to His will and His ways: "but you shall receive power when the Holy Spirit has come upon you..." (Acts 1:8). We absolutely need this power to obey God.

In these passages of Scripture, God reveals His immutable, interlocking sequence of life-changing events:

1. A Christian's mind is washed by the Word.
2. A Christian's heart is changed when he or she submits to the Word.
3. A Christian's behavior is changed by the infilling of the Holy Spirit.

Christians are totally transformed and renewed, which is accomplished by the awesome power of the third person in the Trinity, The Holy Spirit.

What Are the Attributes of the Holy Spirit?

As the third person in the Trinity, the Holy Spirit possesses all of the same attributes as God the Father and God the Son.

The Holy Spirit is *eternal* (Hebrews 9:14). This is a perplexing concept for humans to grasp because our worldview is finite. We think in terms of beginning and end. The clock and the calendar measure everything. Even before clocks and calendars, humans measured time by sunrises, sunsets, and seasons, which all have a beginning and an end.

To speak of the eternal means to speak of timeless or everlasting—no beginning and no end. Therefore, when the Bible describes the Holy Spirit as eternal, it means that He always was, is, and ever shall be. In other words, the spirit world is based on an entirely different dimension of time than that of the natural world. Once we grasp this, it is easier to accept even though we may not have a complete understanding of it at first. Consider trying to explain an airplane to a native deep in the Amazon who has never seen or heard of an airplane before. He may not fully understand the cognitive concept of flying in a machine because it does not fit with what he knows about his world. Nevertheless, that does not change the truth that airplanes exist. We may not fully comprehend the attribute of being eternal, but that does not vitiate the truth that the Holy Spirit is indeed eternal.

The Holy Spirit is *omnipresent* (Psalms 139:7-10). This is also a difficult concept. You have probably told someone or thought to yourself, "I can't be in two places at the same time." Presence in the natural world is what we describe as mutually exclusive. As soon as we are in one place, it excludes us from being in another. We are constrained by our own physical limitations and the dimensions of time and distance in our natural world. The Holy Spirit, fortunately, has no such constraints. He is present everywhere at once.

This attribute gives me great comfort and confidence in knowing that regardless of where I am, He is there and I can have immediate access to Him. I do not have to travel to some *holy* site to be in His presence because He is always where I am. The knowledge of this facilitates greater intimacy with Him. When someone is constantly with you, it is virtually impossible to not be more intimate.

The Holy Spirit is *omniscient*. He is all-knowing and all-wise (Isaiah 40:13-14; I Corinthians 2:10-16). This may not be as difficult to comprehend as eternal and omnipresent. The Holy Spirit was involved in all of creation: "And the earth was without form, and void; and darkness was upon the face of the deep. And the Spirit of God moved upon the face of the waters" (Genesis 1:2). The creation process may be easier to understand if we accept by faith a basic premise that God is more intelligent and more powerful than we are: "For my thoughts are not your thoughts, neither are your ways my ways, saith the Lord. For as the heavens are higher than the earth, are my ways higher than your ways, and my thoughts than your thoughts" (Isaiah 55:8-9). As space is apparently limitless, so is God's knowledge and wisdom.

Scientists and scholars have spent centuries studying man, plants, animals, and insects in an effort to understand them. In addition, we have amassed a great deal of information about many species. An arrogance pervades our world that science holds all the answers to the world's problems. Science does not have all the answers, nor does it even know all the questions. Only God knows all and He reveals it to whom He chooses (Jeremiah 33:3; Psalms 65:4).

In over thirty years as a practicing clinical neuropsychologist, I have concluded the more we learn about the human mind, the less we actually know. We have learned a great deal about the brain. For example, we can describe how some brain parts function. However, what we do not understand about this complex organ has filled volumes. Why are the effects of brain injury so variegated? Why do some individuals recover relatively well from a brain injury and others do not? The answers are complicated. As the previous passage in Isaiah asserts: God's thoughts are truly higher than our own. I personally would not want to follow God if He were not a great deal smarter than human beings.

One of my favorite characteristics of the Holy Spirit is *omnipotence*. He possesses unlimited power. This is obvious as described in the creation story in Genesis. The sheer magnitude of that power so vastly exceeds any scientific device created by man that it is immeasurable. In Micah, the Lord speaks through the prophet and asks: "Is the spirit of the Lord impatient?" (Micah 2:7).

That is, is the Holy Spirit restricted or limited? Obviously, this is a rhetorical question. This kind of power can accomplish that which is impossible to man. For example, the archangel Gabriel visited Mary, the mother of Jesus, and told her that she would conceive and give birth to a son. Can you imagine the questions that went through her mind knowing she was single and a virgin? When Mary asked Gabriel how this could be, he answered: "The Holy Spirit shall come upon thee, and the power of the Highest shall overshadow thee" (Luke 1:35). If we accept the basic premise in Genesis 1 that all living creatures were created out of nothing by the Holy Spirit, then it logically follows that He has the power to conceive Jesus in Mary's womb. Nothing in our human world has this much power. Scientists can produce in-vitro fertilization, but they still have not figured out how to do it without both ovum and sperm. However, as Gabriel told Mary: "For with God nothing shall be impossible" (Luke 1:37). The Holy Spirit is the epitome of all power in the universe. He shared His power with Mary, and He wants to share this power with you.

Jesus said "...but you shall receive *power* when the Holy Spirit has come upon you..." (Acts 1:8, my emphasis). The Greek word for power is *dunamis* from which the English word "dynamite" is derived. In other words, when we receive the infilling of the Holy Spirit we receive dynamic, explosive power. However, what is the purpose of this power? Again, we can look to Acts 1:8: "And you shall be my witnesses both in Jerusalem, and in all Judea and Samaria, and even to the remotest part of the earth" (Acts 1:8).

When Christians receive the baptism in the Holy Spirit, they not only have a greater desire to tell others about Jesus, but they instantly receive a greater ability to share the good news. Notice what happened to Peter on the day of Pentecost after he received the Holy Spirit. On that same day, he eloquently and cogently spoke to Jews about Jesus, and three thousand of them gave their heart to the Lord that day. One purpose of this power, then, is obviously for service to the Lord.

Now, you may be thinking, "But service to the Lord is for pastors and priests, not me. I'm not in the ministry." Please understand that Jesus did not speak to the rabbis or priests of the day. He preached to ordinary believers from all walks of life. Peter, e.g., was a fisherman. Matthew was a tax collector.

All born-again believers are basically in the ministry. We are all ministers in the truest sense of the word. Being a minister and serving the Lord does not necessarily mean preaching from a pulpit. Jesus said, "Love thy neighbor as thyself." This is the essence of being a minister. That is, giving to those who are needful.

The Holy Spirit also enables us to overcome weaknesses in our own lives. Most people eventually encounter a crisis or challenge that creates distress, fear, or suffering of some kind. It may be illness, broken relationships, rejection, financial loss, or death of a loved one. Life is life. No one is immune to it. When I was a young man, I thought I was invincible. Suffering could not touch me. I was naïve, of course. After the loss of two close friends due to accidental death, I realized certain things in life cannot be controlled.

No matter how talented, competent, and strong we are, likely we will run smack into something, either within ourselves, or externally, that strikes us down. This is where the power of the Holy Spirit comes in. Through His power we are able, sometimes miraculously, to get up, and rejoin life. His indwelling power enables us to confront and overcome our own limitations: "My grace is sufficient for you, for my power is perfected in weakness" (II Corinthians 12:9).

So, when Christians ask "Why do I need this kind of power?" I answer that it is essential for Christian living. We cannot afford to *not* have Holy Spirit power operating in our lives.

Let us take a closer look at the Holy Spirit's personality. "What, he has a personality?" you might ask. Of course. If He is the third person in the Trinity, then He has a "person"-ality. In addition, what a wonderful personality it is!

First, He is a person of integrity. In John, Jesus validated the Holy Spirit's integrity: "But when He, the Spirit of truth, comes, He will guide you into all the truth" (John 16:13). The Holy Spirit not only tells the truth, always, but also actually *is* truth. There is no error in Him. He bears witness to the truth and, therefore, we can be confident that He will guide us by truth.

God has deposited in our spiritual DNA a deep desire for the truth and zero tolerance for lying. Based on my clinical experience, even hardened, sociopathic criminals who make their living lying may become incensed when they discover that they have been lied to. The Holy Spirit *never* deviates from the truth. If we know people who approach this level of truthfulness, we describe them as being trustworthy and of impeccable integrity.

With regard to the Holy Spirit, Jesus extols the Holy Spirit's purpose: "...for He will not speak on His own initiative, but whatever He hears, He will speak; and He will disclose to you what is to come. He shall glorify Me; for He shall take of Mine, and shall disclose it to you" (John 16:13-14).

This reveals other personality characteristics—*humility* and *servanthood.* The Holy Spirit does not live according to his own agenda. He is constantly exalting Jesus and leading people to Him. He never brings attention to Himself but always to Jesus. This is the epitome of humility. The Holy Spirit constantly gives all credit to Jesus for all good things (John 16:14). Someone once said, "It's amazing how much you can accomplish if you don't care who gets credit for it." Solomon confirmed this by saying, "Let another praise you, and not your own mouth; A stranger, and not your own lips" (Proverbs 27:2). Perhaps we should follow this lead and model ourselves more after the Holy Spirit.

At first, it may appear rather audacious and preposterous to think we can analyze the personality of God (i.e. the Holy Spirit). As we have already said, He is infinite. How can a finite mind analyze an infinite one? No argument there. I do not presume to know all there is to know about the Holy Spirit. Scripture clearly tells us that His thoughts and ways are higher than ours. Psychologists could devote their entire careers to studying only His personality characteristics and, just when

Holy Spirit: Agent of Change

they believe they have arrived at the denouement, the Holy Spirit would reveal yet another unknown characteristic to prove that He is infinite and beyond human understanding.

However, having made that disclaimer, God *has* revealed certain aspects of His personality that, even with our limited understanding, we can grasp. He clearly desires to have an intimate relationship with us and the essence of that is self-disclosure. Through disclosing certain aspects of His personality, The Holy Spirit meets the human need to classify things to understand them. The process of classification has two primary purposes: communication and prediction.[6] These functions are essential to not only the field of science, but also to interpersonal relationships because they are the foundation of trust.

We cannot trust someone we do not know, and we cannot know them without communication and predictability. Human beings classified the environment to bring order to individual observations and promote greater understanding. In science, classification systems come and go with advances in knowledge. The system we use today to understand our world may change dramatically twenty years from now, which certainly has been the case in the fields of medicine and psychology. For many years, for example, psychology had no diagnostic classification for what is now known as Post Traumatic Stress Disorder (PTSD). In the past, some combat troops were diagnosed as having *shell shock*, a meaningless label. Since then, the

---

6 Gary R. VandenBos, ed., *APA Dictionary of Psychology*, (Washington, D.C.: American Psychological Association, 2007).

diagnostic classification system has been revised and refined several times to give a better understanding of PTSD.

So what makes us think we can analyze and classify something infinite like the personality of the Holy Spirit? The answer is in God's Word. He says "I am the Lord thy God, I change not" (Malachi 3:6). He may not reveal His entire personality to us but what He has revealed is permanent, predictable, and certainly worthy of our commitment and trust. I am not attempting to diagnose the Holy Spirit or define spiritual reality. Nevertheless, by studying His revealed characteristics, we are able to differentiate His nature and personality from ours, which is the purpose of assessment and classification.

When we say we know someone, we are referring to our knowledge of his or her personality. When we like someone, we may say, "She has personality." But, what exactly is personality? It can be defined as: "The configuration of characteristics and behavior that comprises an individual's unique adjustment to life, including major traits, interests, drives, values, self-concept, abilities, and emotional patterns."[7]

Some personality processes can change as a function of events, relationships, situations, or time. Certain characteristics, however, remain consistent and stable over time. It is the latter that we will examine in the Holy Spirit.

These enduring traits and characteristics of the Holy Spirit are outlined for us in Galatians: "But the fruit of the Spirit is love, joy, peace, patience, kindness, goodness, faithfulness,

---

7 Ibid.

gentleness, self-control: against such things there is no law" (Galatians 5:22). This is an amazing description of who The Holy Spirit is. Permit me to put my psychologist hat on for a while, and let us examine each of these personality characteristics a little closer.

1. Love

Love has been the subject of more songs, books, poems, and movies than probably any other topic. It is clearly the most powerful force in the universe. Love overpowers every evil on earth including nuclear warfare, genocide, dictatorship, economic collapse, physical violence, poverty, emotional abuse, and even plague. All human problems on earth are due to the absence of love or the presence of ungodly love. The Bible tells us that whatsoever is born of God overcomes the world (I John 5:4). Love is born of God because God *is* love (I John 4:8). Therefore, the love of God perfected in human beings overcomes all evil. Most problems I see in my psychology practice are due to rejection and/or dysfunctional (ungodly) love. If this is true, then it makes sense the solution to these problems lies in God's love. Many people have asked me "What is love?" I usually refer them to I Corinthians 13:4-7: "Love is patient, love is kind, and is not jealous; love does not brag and is not arrogant, does not act unbecomingly; it does not seek its own, is not provoked, does not take into account a wrong suffered, does not rejoice in unrighteousness, but rejoices with the truth; bears all things, hopes all things, endures all things."

After becoming a Christian, I began reading the Bible rapaciously. As I read, it dawned on me that the prevailing theme of the entire Bible is love: God's love for human beings, human beings' love for God, and human beings' love for each other. I had always viewed myself as a loving person but the more I read, the more I realized that I did not really know how to love at all, at least not how God loves. Therefore, as I was praying one night, I acknowledged that inadequacy to God and asked him to teach me how to love as He loves.

Several months later, I prayed one night—more accurately, I whined to the Lord about some difficult people in my life at the time. I did not hear an audible voice, but my inner man clearly recognized the voice of the Holy Spirit. Fed up with me, He spoke, "What's your problem, son?"

I answered "What do you mean, 'What's my problem?' They're my problem. That's obvious!"

He said, "Well, you asked for this, didn't you?"

"What are you talking about? I didn't ask to be treated like this," I answered.

"Sure you did," He said. "You asked Me to teach you to love like I love. I love the unlovable. I love those who do not love Me back. I love those who return evil for good. I am giving you an opportunity to learn how to do that by bringing those kind of people into your life."

Wow! I sat there speechless for a long time, which is what I typically do when God explodes a revelation like a nuclear blast inside of me. You see, most of us know God loves that way, but few make the connection that He wants us to love that way. At least, I didn't make the connection. God loves this way as an example of how He wants us to love. Most of us want the unlovable to straighten up and clean up their act *first*, and then we will love them. This is not how God loves. He loves us as we are, and then the overwhelming power of His love helps us to get our act cleaned up.

Immediately, I started searching the Scripture to confirm what I had just heard the Spirit speak to me. I was delighted to find one beautiful example of many on loving the unlovable: "And when He had come down from the mountain, great multitudes followed Him. And behold, a leper came to Him and bowed down to Him, saying, 'Lord, if you are willing, you can make me clean.' And He stretched out His hand and touched him saying 'I am willing; be cleansed,' and immediately his leprosy was cleansed" (Matthew 8:1-3). In biblical times a diagnosis of leprosy meant total ostracism from family and community. Lepers were pariahs—despised and rejected by others. They were unlovable. However, the man's miserable condition, as described in Matthew, did not hinder Jesus from feeling compassion and love for him and demonstrating that love by healing him.

You may think, "Yes, but that's Jesus. I'm not capable of loving like that." By yourself, you are not. Nevertheless, if you allow the Holy Spirit to manifest His personality through you, all things are possible. Mother Theresa was a perfect example of someone who operated in the love of the Holy Spirit. She ministered daily to the unlovable people of India. She reached out to the most destitute, uneducated, poverty-stricken people who had been rejected and ignored by everyone. They were part of the untouchable caste even though India had legally abolished the caste system. In Indian culture, they were considered unlovable. Mother Theresa gave full credit to the Holy Spirit for her ability to love the unlovable.

Often, we want to love only those who will return it. Jesus exposed that flaw in our nature when He said: "For if you love those who love you, what reward have you? Do not even the tax gatherers do the same? And if you greet your brother only, what do you do more than others? Do not even the Gentiles do the same?" (Matthew 5:46-47).

Jesus exemplified this characteristic while traveling to Jerusalem. He passed through a certain village when He encountered ten men with leprosy. They cried out for Him to have mercy on them, and He immediately healed them. One of the lepers fell at Jesus' feet, gave Him thanks, and worshipped Him: "And Jesus answered and said, 'Were there not ten cleansed? But the nine—where are they?'" (Luke 17:11-19).

This is a beautiful example of loving those who do not return it. Jesus pointed out that these men did not respond appropriately to His love (healed them), but He did not revoke His love (healing) for them. Can we do the same? Yes, but only by identifying with that personality characteristic of the Holy Spirit. We love because it is the right thing to do, not because we will be loved in return. We love because it is who the Holy Spirit is and who we will become if we allow Him to transform us into His likeness.

Regarding the love of the Holy Spirit, one of the most difficult characteristics to comprehend is how He loves those who return evil for good: "But I say to you, love your enemies and pray for those who persecute you in order that you may be sons of your Father who is in heaven…" (Matthew 5:44-45).

Many people I have treated in my practice have been abused in some way by the very people to whom they have shown love. This causes some of the deepest wounds of all. In these situations, the most common human reactions are emotional pain, anger, resentment, bitterness, and rage. Yet Jesus tells us to respond differently. Jesus had intimate knowledge of this type of wound due to his relationship with Judas.

Judas was one of the original twelve apostles. For over three years, he traveled with Jesus, ate with Him, and sat under His teaching. He witnessed the glory of God manifested through Jesus in signs, wonders, and miracles. Yet, still Judas betrayed Jesus for thirty pieces of silver. Nothing wounds more deeply than being betrayed by someone you love. Notice how Jesus responded to this grievous wound: "Now he who was betraying Him gave them a sign, saying, 'Whomever I shall kiss, He is the one; seize Him.' And immediately he went to Jesus and said, 'Hail Rabbi!' and kissed Him. And Jesus said to him, '*Friend*, do what you have come for.' Then they came and laid hands on Jesus and seized Him" (Matthew 26:48-50, my emphasis).

The Holy Spirit, through Jesus, still called Judas His friend. What manner of love is this? Judas was returning evil for good, and yet Jesus, through the power of the Holy Spirit, was still able to love him.

We see this extraordinary love exhibited again when Peter denied Christ three times. We know that Jesus forgave him and continued to love him because He empowered him on the day of Pentecost and afterward in order to bring thousands into the kingdom of God.

A more contemporary example of loving those who return evil for good can be seen in the life and ministry of the Vietnamese pastor and evangelist, Pastor Paul Ai. It is no secret that the communistic government in Vietnam is openly hostile and ruthless toward the Christian church. Yet, many healings, miracles, signs, and wonders accompanied Pastor Ai's ministry. Thousands of Vietnamese citizens have been blessed by Pastor Ai's love for Jesus. In return for this pastor's good deeds, the government imprisoned and mercilessly tortured him for many years. He was beaten and humiliated. All of this was designed to cause him to renounce Jesus and reveal the identities of his coworkers in the ministry.

During his years of imprisonment, Pastor Ai remained faithful to Jesus. Even more remarkable, however, was his response to his persecutors. He did not become embittered but rather consistently reached out to them with the awesome love of the Holy Spirit and continually returned love for evil. He understood the truth of God's Word that love always overcomes evil. As a result, revival broke out in every prison to which he was sent. Fellow prisoners, guards, wardens, and even political officials repented and converted to Jesus Christ as Lord and Savior. He had so thoroughly identified with this love characteristic of the Holy Spirit that the fruit of the Spirit broke out everywhere he went. [8]

The Holy Spirit loves the unlovable, those who do not return His love, and those who return evil for His love. What a remarkable person!

2. Joy

"These things I have spoken to you, that My joy may be in you, and that your joy may be made full" (John 15:11).

I love to be around joyful people. They make everyone around them feel better. They are positive thinkers, optimistic, and cheerful. They exhibit a half-glass full attitude about everything, which causes them to be perpetually happy. They light up a room when they walk into it. Quite simply, they are a delight to know and be around.

Some people ridicule joyful people and accuse them of being in massive denial of the realities of life. While it is true that some people are greatly naïve about life, that is not the case with those who are manifesting joy as a personality characteristic of the Holy Spirit. They see suffering, pain, and evil in the world, but they refuse to allow those things to rob them of the joy that God has placed within them. Joy is not dependent upon circumstances, which are subject to change, but rather on the permanence of the Holy Spirit which is never lost: "Therefore you too now have sorrow, but I will see you again, and your heart will rejoice, and no one takes

---

8 Paul Ai, personal communication, January 31, 2010.

your joy away from you" (John 16:22). When the Holy Spirit develops His joy in us, we tend to deal with the sorrow and suffering of life in an extraordinarily healthy way. It appears peculiar and incomprehensible to the nonbeliever. Joyful people are extremely strong and resilient psychologically. This is confirmed by God's Word: "...for the joy of the Lord is your strength" (Nehemiah 8:10). Inherent in joy is the component of hope. Joyful people consistently expect good things to happen. Hope is essential to good mental health. It is the loss of hope that produces depression, despair, and helplessness. The joy of the Holy Spirit enables us to rebound from trauma, loss, suffering, and pain with the hope and expectation that God will do something good with it and in us. This is indeed a strength (Romans 8:26).

A number of years ago Norman Cousins, an editor with *Time* magazine, was diagnosed with terminal cancer. His doctors told him that nothing could be done and that he should go home and get his affairs in order because he was going to die soon. He decided that, if he was going to die anyway, he wanted to enjoy his last days on earth. So, he found as many comedy movies as he could and just watched them all day long. And he laughed, and laughed, and laughed all day long every day. He did this for several weeks. When he returned to his doctor, no cancer could be found in his body. He literally had laughed himself healthy. Is that possible? Absolutely!

Scientific studies have shown amazing health benefits of laughter. Studies have shown that laughter has powerful effects on Type II diabetes, rheumatoid arthritis, coronary heart disease, and even cancer. There is a definite relationship between our mental state and our physical state. But, then this is no surprise to God: "A joyful heart is good medicine..." (Proverbs 17:22). God has amazingly designed even our bodies to respond a certain way to this wonderful characteristic of joy.

Do you want more joy in your life? I am going to tell you how to develop it. First, ask God to help you see the world through the eyes of the Holy Spirit. God Himself is the object of joy. When we see the world through the eyes of the Holy Spirit, we begin to see God everywhere—even in little things like a butterfly or a sunset. I am not being polytheistic here. There is still only one triune God, but when we take pleasure in the simple things in life, we can marvel at God's awesome creativity.

Second, as you see through His eyes, you will begin to develop an attitude of gratitude: "...in everything give thanks; for this is God's will for you in Christ Jesus" (I Thessalonians 5:18). The more you see God in everything and give thanks to Him for His creations, the more joy will well up in you. In time, you will become the joyful person I described earlier.

You will be a delight to be around and people will be blessed just by being in your presence. It is the beautiful work of the Holy Spirit that produces this precious joy in you.

3. Peace

When I ask people what they want in life, the most common answer is, "I want to be happy." When I ask them to tell me what that means for them, I usually get answers along these lines:

"I want a good marriage."

"I want a good job."

"I want a nice home."

"I want enough money to do what I want."

In other words, happiness for most people is dependent upon circumstances. And, as we know, circumstances often change in life. The philosopher Heraclitus is quoted as saying: "The only constant is change." When people tie their happiness to life circumstances, their sense of well-being is often on a roller coaster. The problem is people often confuse happiness with peace. Favorable circumstances in life can contribute to our happiness, but they will never give us peace. Happiness and peace have totally different sources. The former is the world while the latter is God. Happiness is variable and may be temporary, but peace is everlasting because the Holy Spirit is eternal.

I have counseled many multimillionaires who have everything that money can buy. While these *things* may make them temporarily happy, it is peace that they do not have and for which they are desperately searching. In addition, because they confuse happiness with peace, they keep looking for peace in the wrong places: i.e., material things, drugs, alcohol, money, sex, power, and fame. Clarity and peace originate with God: "…and God is not a God of confusion but of peace, as in all the churches of the saints" (I Corinthians 14:33). Peace is the product of harmony between human beings and God. Peter confirmed this: "The word which He sent to the sons of Israel, preaching *peace* through Jesus Christ…" (Acts 10:36, my emphasis). Peace is the resulting rest and contentment that emanates from the relationship.

For things to be in harmony they have to be in agreement or fit together. The Hebrew word for peace is *shalom* which mostly refers to wholeness. When the three parts of a human being, i.e., body, soul, and spirit, come into agreement with God through His Son Jesus, the separate parts are no longer disparate but rather are made *whole*. The end result of this wholeness is peace. The agent of this peace that passes all understanding is the Holy Spirit. He bears witness with our spirit that the barrier between us and God, i.e., sin, has been removed, and we are now in beautiful harmony with God. New converts to Christ report experiencing this wonderful sense of peace once they opened their hearts to Jesus and yielded to Him. However, how do we maintain this peace once the cares of this world come crashing back into our lives? The answer lies in this simple verse: "Thou wilt keep him in perfect peace, whose mind is stayed on thee because he trusteth in thee" (Isaiah 26:3). Maintaining perfect peace is dependent on our ability to do two things: keep our mind fixed on Him and to trust Him. The latter automatically follows if we do the former. This is not always easy but the more we have identified with the character of the Holy Spirit the more we are empowered to stay fixed on God. Peace becomes the inevitable outcome.

4. Patience

One of the more admirable traits of the Holy Spirit is patience. When I think about patience, I am reminded of the old joke about the Christian who has the revelation that, to be more like Christ, he needs more patience. Therefore, like a good believer, he decides to pray and ask God for help. "Lord, I know you want me to be more patient, so give me more patience and give it to me now!"

Some of us can be very impatient. We are often guilty of wanting what we want when we want it. In our consumerist culture, we want everything fast. We have fast-food restaurants, 30-minute film processing, drive-through and online banking, 10-minute oil changes, text messaging, email, online shopping, and overnight express mail. We can get irate if our food order is not ready by the time we drive around to the pickup window.

Impatience is fostered in the United States and in other cultures. America has a credit economy. Citizens are encouraged to put everything on credit. "Why wait, just charge it! You should have what you want now!" Instant gratification. This is contrary to the characteristic of patience exhibited by the Holy Spirit.

Patience is the ability to wait without complaint and tolerate the frustration that results from delayed gratification. Patience is so important in our relationships with other people and especially our relationship with God. Timing is everything. Fortunately, for us, God does things according to His timetable, not ours. When we refuse to wait on God and, instead, do things on our schedule, it can result in disastrous consequences.

A classic example of impatience is seen in Abraham and Sarah. In Genesis 15 and 16, God entered into an agreement with Abraham. God told Abraham that He would give Abraham an heir and that his descendants would be as the stars of heaven. Abraham believed the Lord and his faith was counted as righteousness to him.

Sounds great, doesn't it? Then impatience reared its ugly head. Sarah got tired of waiting on the Lord and took things into her own hands. She convinced Abraham to mate with her handmaid, Hagar, who promptly conceived and bore Abraham a son, Ishmael. Some may say, "So, he got a son didn't he?" Yes, but Ishmael was not the child of promise! Consequently, Ishmael and his descendants became tormenters of Isaac (child of promise) and his descendants to the present day. When we receive a promise from God, we must understand that it will always be fulfilled but only in His timing. When we get ahead of God's schedule, we can create ramifications that can reach far into the future and affect many generations beyond our own. Patience is absolutely necessary to fulfill God's will on this earth.

The Holy Spirit is a patient teacher. I cannot tell you how many times He has patiently gone over the same life lesson repeatedly with me until I finally learned it. Several years ago I became very angry with a close friend because of something he had done. The Holy Spirit patiently began speaking to me about forgiveness. He led me to passages on forgiveness every time I opened my Bible. I read them and promptly ignored them. This continued for weeks until I finally got it, obeyed, and forgave my friend. The anger instantly left me. I would have given up on me long ago, but not the Holy Spirit. He patiently hangs in there with me until I finally get it. What a beautiful trait to have! Moreover, He wants us to identify with Him and internalize this same trait into our own personalities. In fact, patience is not just an option that we can choose or not, it is a *need*: "For ye have need of patience, that after ye have done the will of God, ye might receive the promise" (Hebrews 10:36). Patience is necessary to inherit eternal life with Jesus. Our very life can be dependent upon the development of patience (Luke 21:19).

The Lord tells us several times in Scripture to wait upon Him. The reason is that it often takes time for Him to orchestrate things in the natural world in order to answer our prayers or to accomplish His will in our lives. It is like a chess match. Each piece has to be in the right place at the right time, and it may require several moves before victory is claimed. All of this requires patience but look at the benefits: "But they that wait upon the Lord shall renew their strength; they shall mount up with wings as eagles. They shall run, and not be weary; and they shall walk, and not faint" (Isaiah 40:31).

We will soar above problems and run and walk in the purposes of God with great strength. You see, patience has a great reward!

I wish I could tell you that patience comes easily but, as with all extremely valuable things in life, there is a price tag: "My brethren, count it all joy when ye fall into diverse temptations; knowing this, that the trying of your faith worketh patience" (James 1:2-3).

Paul elaborates on how this rare trait is developed: "And not only so, but we glory in tribulations also: knowing that tribulation worketh patience; and patience, experience; and experience, hope…" (Romans 5:3-4).

Therefore, tribulation and suffering are the soil in which patience develops. The trials of life force us to allow the Holy Spirit to grow something in us that enables us to cope with frustration, pain and suffering. And that beautiful fruit is *patience*. And patience leads to something even more valuable— godliness (II Peter 1:5-6). As godliness grows in us, we become useful to the Lord in producing fruit for his kingdom.

So, what's the big deal about patience? If we get impatient in waiting on God, it's not that it is going to make any difference, right? Wrong! Remember, timing is everything. God works according to His schedule, not ours. Becoming impatient and getting ahead of God implies that you know more than He does and that your timing is better than His. Fortunately, for us, the Holy Spirit is infinitely patient and, when we have an intimate relationship with Him, some of this wonderful trait begins to rub off on us.

5. Kindness

The Holy Spirit possesses extraordinary kindness. He is always interested in our welfare and consistently helps us in our time of need: "And the natives showed us extraordinary kindness, for because of the rain that had set in and because of the cold, they kindled a fire and received us all" (Acts 28:2). Paul and Luke had just been through a traumatic event. Their boat wrecked on a reef near Malta and they literally had to swim for their lives. The local natives took care of them and showed "extraordinary kindness."

Many nonbelievers and even Christians may doubt that people today are this kind—perhaps with the exception of Mother Theresa and other people viewed as holy servants. However, in 2005, we saw countless acts of "extraordinary kindness" played out before our eyes and portrayed daily on national television. The Mississippi Gulf Coast and South Louisiana were hit by two devastating hurricanes, Katrina and Rita. The levees in New Orleans were breached, causing the majority of the city to flood. Hundreds of thousands of people were suddenly homeless. They evacuated to cities in Louisiana such as Baton Rouge, Lafayette, Alexandria, and Shreveport. Social and support networks such as family, friends, church, work, and school were compromised and even shattered. A culture and way of life had been utterly destroyed.

In the events surrounding Hurricanes Katrina and Rita, unprecedented numbers of people turned to churches in unaffected regions for help. Many churches housed, clothed, and fed evacuees. Moreover, the Isaiah Project[9] was designed to prepare and train church leadership in how to:

- Organize large-scale trauma interventions for local community churches.
- Deal with the emotional impact of storm trauma experienced by survivors.
- Train coaches for small group meetings for survivors.
- Connect hurricane victims to resources provided by community churches.

---

9 Lynn W. Aurich and Mark D. Barrentine, The Isaiah Project: A Faith Based Crisis Response Ministry, (Lafayette, LA, 2005).

- Open ministry opportunities to individuals turning to the church for comfort.
- Identify those in need of professional help and provide appropriate referrals.

The Isaiah Project was initiated in the church I attend but quickly spread to other churches in other cities. In addition to the Isaiah Project, our church housed over one hundred evacuees for several months. We provided jobs, transportation, and education opportunities for many of them. More importantly, we offered emotional and spiritual support to people who had been through their own shipwreck. This is the essence of kindness that is the Holy Spirit. Kindness can produce great change in people. Paul told the Romans: "Or do you think lightly of the riches of His kindness and forbearance and patience, not knowing that the kindness of God leads you to repentance?" (Romans 2:4).

Many evacuees accepted Jesus Christ as personal Lord and Savior during this traumatic time. Many were profoundly and deeply touched in their hearts because of the Godly kindness that was shown to them. This in turn led them to repentance. None of this could have been accomplished without the Holy Spirit manifesting His kindness through His believers.

Kindness tends to be contagious. In II Samuel 2:4-6, David was anointed King over the house of Judah. He learned that the men of Jabesh-Gilead buried Saul. He was so moved by that act of kindness that he said to them: "May you be blessed of the Lord because you have shown this kindness to Saul your lord, and have buried him. And now may the Lord show loving-kindness and truth to you; and I also will show this goodness to you, because you have done this thing" (II Samuel 2:4-6). It is clear that kindness begets kindness: "thou dost show Thyself kind; With the blameless Thou dost show Thyself blameless..." (Psalms 18:25). If we are kind to others, God will be kind to us. In other words, He will help us when we need it. The Holy Spirit is the very personification of kindness. His kindness can produce profound change in an individual.

6. Goodness

Goodness is thought of as that which is morally honorable and pleasing to God. It is derived from two Greek words. The first, *chrestotes,* refers to a kind disposition as well as goodness in action. The second, *agathosone,* refers to a sterner aspect of goodness in that the means may be harsh but the result is beneficial.[10]

For example, most agree that disciplining children is a good thing: "He who spares his rod hates his son, but he who loves him disciplines him diligently" (Proverbs 13:24). Disciplining a child is, thus, an act of goodness toward him.

We see goodness reflected in Mt. 21:12-13: "And Jesus entered the temple and cast out all those who were buying and selling in the temple, and overturned the tables of the money changers and the seats of those who were selling doves. And He said to them, 'It is written, My house shall be called a house of prayer; but you are making it a robbers' den'" (Matthew 21:12-

---

10 W.E. Vine, *An Expository Dictionary of Biblical Words,* (Nashville: Thomas Nelson Publishers, 1984).

13). Some see this event as an act of violence because they do not understand what Jesus was attempting to accomplish. He restored the temple to what it was intended to be, a house of prayer. According to the definition of goodness, this was a morally honorable thing, pleasing to God and, therefore, constitutes goodness.

Many people have the basic belief that all humans are inherently good. If that premise were true, then all people would just naturally do the morally honorable thing and the world would be filled with goodness. Reality clearly tells us that is not the case. This premise also contradicts the basic premise of the gospel message. Man is not inherently good but rather is born with a sinful nature. Hence, the need for redemption through the Savior. The apostle Paul clarifies this: "For I know that nothing good dwells in me, that is, in my flesh; for the wishing is present in me, but the doing of the good is not. For the good that I wish, I do not do; but I practice the very evil that I do not wish" (Romans 7:18-19). In other words, our sin nature drives us to be and do the very opposite of goodness, i.e., evil. What, then, can change our basic nature? The author of Romans informs us: "But if the Spirit of Him who raised Jesus from the dead dwells in you, He who raised Christ Jesus from the dead will also give life to your mortal bodies through His Spirit who indwells you" (Romans 8:11). The answer is the Holy Spirit. When our mind is set on the Spirit, we can have life and peace. It is His goodness that produces this powerful change in our basic nature when He indwells us. We begin to manifest His goodness whereas we formerly manifested evil

(Romans 12:21). Goodness, in and of itself, has the manifest power of God to overcome evil. God wants us to identify with this Holy Spirit characteristic and, in so doing, we will do good rather than evil (III John 11).

7. Faithfulness

"In this case, moreover, it is required of stewards that one be found trustworthy" (I Corinthians 4:2).

Faithfulness is equated with trustworthiness. Can we be trusted to do those things that God asks of us? Do we keep our word? Trustworthiness is based on the correspondence between what we say and what we do. When that correspondence is high, we infer that someone is faithful, i.e, trustworthy. When it is low, we infer that they are unreliable, undependable, or even dishonest. A high correspondence yields *predictability*. Predictability results in trust. Trust produces security. It looks like this:

High Correspondence = Predictability = Trust = Security

Sustainable relationships cannot exist without faithfulness and trust. In fact, we can consider it to be the very linchpin of all relationships. In years of doing marital therapy with couples, I have arrived at the opinion that infidelity (unfaithfulness) is the single most damaging thing that can happen to a marriage. Couples will tolerate and even accept a whole host of dysfunctional behaviors in their spouse such as drug and alcohol abuse, physical and emotional abuse, neglect, financial irresponsibility, and sexual problems, but most couples have zero tolerance for an extramarital affair.

When the linchpin of trust is broken, the wheels come off the marriage, and it cannot move forward until the linchpin is repaired.

When we speak of correspondence, we are referring to a mutual, i.e., reciprocal relation between two things. Correspondence refers to the relative occurrence or correspondence between two separate events. In other words, it is the relative frequency at which two events occur together. In science, we speak of the correlation between two sets of data. If the two sets of data correspond with each other, say, 90% of the time, their correlation is said to be high. If a correlation is perfect, it is referred to as a correlation of +1. That is, every time one event occurs the other also occurs 100% of the time.

In nature the correspondence between events may, in some cases, be a +1, that is, perfect. Humans, on the other hand, rarely achieve that level of correspondence between what is said and what is done. Low correspondence is the source of much conflict between people.

Low correspondence between what one says and what one does leads to doubt. Scripture tells us that doubt leads to double-mindedness (James 1:8). A double-minded person is one who is doubting, hesitant, and unable to make decisions. A double-minded person is unstable in all his or her ways. Instability means that there is great variation in behavior, which makes the behavior very hard to predict with any accuracy. This, in turn, leads to mistrust which produces insecurity. It looks like this:

Low correspondence = Doubt = Double-mindedness =
Unstable = Unpredictable = Mistrust = Insecurity

Can you see how high correspondence can lead to solid, trusting, secure relationships? Similarly, notice how low correspondence can wreak havoc in relationships and eventually destroy them altogether.

Now let us examine whether the Holy Spirit meets these requirements for faithfulness/trustworthiness. Two of my favorite Scriptures are Lamentations 3:22-23, which detail unvarying faithfulness of the Holy Spirit: "The Lord's loving kindnesses indeed *never* cease, For His compassions, *never* fail. They are new *every* morning; Great is Thy faithfulness" (my emphasis). I have emphasized the words never and every in these Scriptures to point out that these are absolutes. There is no variation. His loving kindnesses and compassions *never* fail, and they are new *every* morning. These absolutistic words speak to His consistency and correspondence. This is a correspondence/correlation of +1, i.e., perfect.

This is further confirmed in Psalms: "For I have said, 'Loving kindnesses will be built up *forever*; In the heavens Thou wilt establish Thy faithfulness'" (Psalms 89:1, my emphasis). This speaks to the eternal nature of His trustworthiness. It never ends, varies or disappoints. That is, it is absolutely *predictable*: "Every good thing bestowed and every good gift is from above, coming down from the Father of lights, with whom there is no variation or shifting shadow" (James 1:17). There is absolute consistency, constancy, and predictability inherent in the Holy

Spirit and, therefore, absolute trustworthiness/faithfulness which leads to absolute security.

Having security in the Holy Spirit leads to a certainty that we are protected from all harm. He tells us that He will faithfully strengthen and protect us from the evil one (I Thessalonians 3:3). Feeling safe removes all fear, which is life changing. Fear imprisons people emotionally, physically, and even spiritually. I have seen individuals so immobilized by fear they were unable to leave their homes. There can certainly be many different causes for this problem and several different approaches to treating it. One component to a comprehensive treatment plan is to try to build the patient's trust in God, thus facilitating a feeling of security and safety. Teaching people that God is faithful and trustworthy to protect them may seem rather simplistic, but once this becomes revelation to them and part of their belief system, all other treatment components are enhanced and become more effective because hope is restored. I once treated a patient who had been in a terrible helicopter crash in the Gulf of Mexico. He was one of only two survivors. He described his panic when he managed to exit the craft in twenty-foot seas. It was February and the water was frigid. As he bobbed helplessly for several hours awaiting rescue, he was certain he was going to die. Following his rescue, he developed severe anxiety and phobias for almost anything relating to water. He could not even sit in his bathtub without having an anxiety attack. The trauma had crippled him emotionally and severely restricted his behavior.

This patient is a Christian, but his trust in the Lord had been compromised due to the accident. Fear paralyzed him. I began to show him that the Lord did not cause the accident. It was due to pilot error. The patient insisted that the Lord should have prevented the pilot from making the error. I explained that the Holy Spirit is not a dictator. He will not impose His will on someone else. Human error causes accidents, frequently. I pointed out however, that God did preserve him: "The *Lord* will protect him, and keep him alive..." (Psalms 41:2, my emphasis). The Lord kept him alive against all odds. Once the patient stopped blaming God for the accident, he was able to see it was, indeed, the Lord that brought about his rescue. At times, he even had an unusual feeling of peace while bobbing in the sea. He realized the Holy Spirit had comforted him during that ordeal. This revelation caused his faith and hopes to rise within him. He eventually recovered completely.

Hope implies a happy or favorable expectation of something good. It serves as an anchor of the soul steadying us during the trials and tribulations of life. It is the very antithesis of despair, which is produced by fear. The foundation upon which hope rests is trust in the Lord (I Corinthians 15:19), which is developed in us through the working of the beautiful Holy Spirit. Without trust and hope, people who are bound in fear will not take even the smallest step of faith to change their circumstances. Once trust and hope (belief system) begin to change, on the other hand, their value system changes which, in turn, changes their worldview, which then begins to change their behavior. It looks like this:

Belief System = Value System =
World View = Behavioral Change

In addition, it all begins by believing the Holy Spirit is worthy of your trust and that He will never disappoint or betray you. It is not difficult to see how a relationship with someone who can be trusted *absolutely* with no shred of doubt can have a powerful life-changing impact on an individual.

8. Gentleness

When we think of gentleness, we usually picture someone who is mild, tender, considerate, reasonable, and fair. Gentleness usually describes how we deal with others.

Paul emphasized this quality in dealing with difficult people: "And the Lord's bond-servant must not be quarrelsome, but be kind to all, able to teach, patient when wronged, with gentleness correcting those who are in opposition, if perhaps God may grant them repentance leading to the knowledge of the truth" (I Timothy 2:24-25).

I have been corrected many times by the Holy Spirit since being born-again and deservedly so. In these situations, I was always mystified by the Holy Spirit's ability to chastise and correct me, yet, when it was all over, I still felt his deep abiding love. I never felt rejected, humiliated, embarrassed, or condemned. That, in itself, is a miracle.

I believe His quality of gentleness assures us of His love even when being corrected (Galatians 6:1). He is never harsh, critical, discourteous or rough.

Paul paints a beautiful picture of gentleness in saying: "But we proved to be gentle among you, as a nursing mother tenderly cares for her own children" (I Thessalonians 2:7). It always touches my heart to watch a mother care for her newborn. She is so careful, tender, and soft in everything she does with her infant. If we are this gentle with our own children, how much more gentle is the Holy Spirit with us?

Today's culture often equates gentleness with weakness. A gentle person does not provoke a fight or quarrel and, therefore, is often viewed as a coward or a pushover who can easily be intimidated and bullied. Nothing could be farther from the truth. Jesus was gentle but in no way was He weak. Note what David had to say: "Thou hast given me the shield of Thy salvation, And Thy right hand upholds me; And Thy gentleness makes me great" (Psalms 18:35).

In other words, the Holy Spirit's gentleness is able to strengthen, support, and empower us. There is an element of power in Godly gentleness that can effect immediate change in a person. Has anyone ever been angry with you? Your response can often determine whether their anger escalates or dissipates: "A gentle answer turns away wrath, But a harsh word stirs up anger" (Proverbs 15:1). It is amazing how quickly an angry person will calm down if they are responded to with gentleness rather than harsh rebuke.

There is an amazing healing quality in gentleness. Physical or emotional abuse or trauma can have devastating effects on mental health. If people are to recover, they must be handled gently. Abuse and trauma victims are extremely fragile emotionally. Treating them with gentleness allows them to begin feeling safe again and to trust others. Their view of the world becomes less threatening. Gentleness facilitates the healing process.

We can see then, that gentleness has the power to correct and redirect, nurture, dissipate anger, empower, and heal. This one characteristic of the Holy Spirit can produce powerful change in a person.

9. Self-Control

God is a god of balance. We can see His absolute balance in the universe and in everything created on earth. He desires for us to achieve balance in our own lives. This is gained through self-control and temperance. It is the ability to curb our fleshly appetites and avoid excesses and extremes. No small challenge! Paul tells the Galatians: "For the flesh sets its desire against the Spirit, and the Spirit against the flesh; for these are in opposition to one another, so that you may not do the things that you please" (Galatians 5:17).

Our flesh constantly goads us to extremes and excesses, which puts us at war with the Holy Spirit. This is a war we are destined to lose one way or the other. We can submit ourselves to His restraining power, which ultimately leads to victory, or we can reject His control and pursue self indulgence to our own inevitable demise: "Like a city that is broken into and without walls is a man who has no control over his spirit" (Proverbs 25:28).

God tells us when we lack self control, we become vulnerable to every attack from our enemy—Satan from the outside and from every attack from the inside (our own impulses) as well. In today's culture, we are relentlessly bombarded with sensuality and myriad self-indulgent messages. We are constantly being told by various media sources (films, advertising, music, books, magazines, and the internet) that it is our *right* to overindulge ourselves. Moreover, if anyone tells us (like the church) to control our impulses, we have the right to be indignant and rebel. This is a "do-your-own-thing" mentality without regard to consequences to yourself or others. As a result, America cannot build enough jails and prisons fast enough to incarcerate convicted criminals. Obesity is now the number one health problem. Drug and alcohol abuse is epidemic. Abortions are the highest in the world. Unwed pregnancies are at an all-time high despite sex education in schools. STDs are rampant. Divorce rates for first marriages are well over fifty percent and even higher for second marriages. Government and the corporate world are replete with scandal and corruption. The clergy, both Protestant and Catholic, have had numerous moral failures in the past twenty-five years. Many of the clergy have faced the same temptations that daily assail other Christians: "Now the deeds of the flesh are evident, which are: immorality, impurity, sensuality, idolatry, sorcery, enmities, strife, jealousy, outbursts of anger, disputes, dissensions, factions, envying, drunkenness, carousing, and things like these, of which I forewarn you just as I have forewarned you that those who practice such things shall not inherit the kingdom of God" (Galatians 5:19-21).

Many Christians minimize these immoral behaviors by saying, "Well, nobody is perfect." While that may be true, Paul explains that practicing immoral behaviors can be a thing of the past once we submit to Christ's grace. Paul goes on to write: "Among them we too all formerly lived in the lusts of our flesh, indulging the desires of the flesh and mind, and were by nature children of wrath, even as the rest" (Ephesians 2:3). Lack of restraint and overindulgence is obviously sin and is, most likely, responsible for a large share of the world's problems today.

So, what is the big deal about enjoying ourselves, you might ask? Are we supposed to adopt a monastic existence and painfully abstain from all things that we enjoy? Many Christians legalistically define self-control in this way. This type of self-control is actually of the flesh, not the Spirit. It is just another form of extremism. God does not begrudge us pleasure. In fact, it is His good pleasure to give us good things (Luke 12:32). He wants us to enjoy life but to do so with self-control. Paul describes the outcome of self-control: "And every man that striveth for the mastery is temperate in all things. Now they do it to obtain a corruptible crown; but we are incorruptible" (I Corinthians 9:25). The reward for self-control is eternal life and an incorruptible crown in the kingdom of God. Well worth it, I would say, wouldn't you?

In II Peter, we see another benefit: "…and in your knowledge, self-control, and in your self-control, perseverance, and in your perseverance, godliness…" (II Peter 1:6). Self-control follows knowledge, which suggests that we should put into practice what we learn from the word of God. If we persevere in that, it leads to godliness. That is, we cannot achieve godliness without self-control.

Self-control is often equated with willpower. For example, a patient of mine had numerous addictive habits. He was an alcoholic, addicted to gambling, and smoked two packs of cigarettes each day. "I wish I had the willpower to break these bad habits, Doc, but I just don't seem to have it," he said one day during a therapy session. He was laboring under the premise that it takes willpower to change. However, if you do not have willpower, how do you get it to begin with? It is the old dilemma: "If it takes money to make money, then how do you get the money to begin with?"

I explained to my patient his problem arose in trying to achieve control over these habits in his own power. Therein lies the problem: "For I know that nothing good dwells in me, that is, in my flesh; for the wishing is present, but the doing of the good is not" (Romans 7:18). None of us has the willpower, ourselves, to overcome sin. If we think we can, then we are deluding ourselves and operating in pride. So, what is the solution to this willpower dilemma?

First, you must reject the false premise that your own willpower is the key to self-control and meaningful change.

Second, submit yourself and your problems to God: "Humble yourselves in the presence of the Lord, and He will exalt you" (James 4:10). The word "exalt" means to lift up and elevate in *power*. Understand that God is the source of your power, not yourself. Jesus told Paul just this: "...my grace is sufficient for you, for My power is perfected in weakness..." (II Corinthians 12:9). And Paul understood Jesus' message: "... most gladly, therefore, I will rather boast about my weaknesses, that the power of Christ may dwell in me" (II Corinthians 12:9).

Third, tap into God's power and allow Him to strengthen you, not solely for your own good, but rather for the greater good of His kingdom: "For it is God who works in you to *will* and to *act* according to His good pleasure" (Philippians 2:13, my emphasis).

When we submit our will to the Holy Spirit's will, He takes over and empowers us to *act* in accordance with His will. Our willpower is no longer the issue because now it becomes His willpower operating in and through us to accomplish that which is pleasing to Him.

God never commands us to do something without equipping and empowering us to do it. Not so with human authority figures. They may order us to do something but give us no help in getting it done: "So then, brethren, we are under obligation, not to the flesh, to live according to the flesh—for if you are living according to the flesh, you must die; but if by the Spirit you are putting to death the deeds of the body, you will live" (Romans 8:12-13).

What does living "by the Spirit" actually mean? It means that when we allow the Holy Spirit total access to us, He begins to give us *His* willpower, which then enables us to control our own impure, weak impulses. Paul explained it as a process of total surrender:

> But thanks be to God that though you were slaves of sin, you became obedient from the heart to that form of teaching to which you were

committed, and having been freed from sin, you became slaves of righteousness. I am speaking in human terms because of the weakness of your flesh. For just as you presented your members as slaves to impurity and to lawlessness, resulting in further lawlessness, so now present your members as slaves to righteousness, resulting in sanctification. (Romans 6:17-19)

Paul further exhorted us to turn our will over to God: "I urge you, therefore, brethren, by the mercies of God to present your bodies a living sacrifice, acceptable to God, which is your spiritual service of worship" (Romans 12:1).

The key to self-control is to allow the Holy Spirit to inhabit more and more of us that we might internalize more and more of His willpower: "But I say, walk by the Spirit and you will not carry out the desire of the flesh" (Galatians 5:16). There is a definite link, then, between self-control and the Holy Spirit working in and through us. I have seen many people, who had struggled for years trying to overcome weaknesses and break bad habit patterns, begin to gain victory once they received the baptism in the Holy Spirit. They began to rely on His willpower not their own. After receiving the baptism in the Holy Spirit, my patient with the addictive habits mentioned above gained greater control over his impulses, and with continued therapy completely stopped drinking, gambling, and smoking.

Therefore, in the Holy Spirit we have someone whose personality is characterized by love, joy, peace, kindness, goodness, faithfulness, gentleness, self-control, and integrity. If you were to meet another human with these same traits, you would instantly be drawn to her, and she would probably become your best friend. Why would you not want to be lasting friends with such a person? In addition, the best part is that the Holy Spirit wants to be your best friend for eternity.

CHAPTER 5

The Holy Spirit as Teacher

The School of the Holy Spirit

In the early part of the twentieth century, psychologists focused most of their research on how organisms learn. Their experiments occurred in the animal labs with rats and primates such as monkeys. Researchers I.P. Pavlov and B.F. Skinner contributed much to our understanding of how organisms learn and how we can structure the learning environment to either facilitate or inhibit the process. Many of these learning principles were later applied to humans in educational and therapeutic settings.

In exploring emotional, behavioral, and mental problems, we understand that learning results in change but that change is not always a good one. It depends upon what specifically is learned. In psychotherapy, for example, many problems such as low self-esteem, poor self-confidence, fear and anxiety, addictions, compulsive behaviors, and depression are often the product of learning the wrong things. Psychotherapy and behavior modification aims at helping people unlearn incorrect things and re-learn healthy thought and behavior patterns.

The prevailing dynamic in dysfunctional families is the operation of defense mechanisms such as denial, distortion, or outright delusion. The common element in these defense mechanisms is that they, either consciously or unconsciously, cause individuals to alter facts or refuse to acknowledge reality in spite of evidence to the contrary. These false premises create a toxic environment in which reality becomes what family members say it is rather than what it is actually. In other words, family members begin to live a lie, which eventually has devastating effects in every aspect of the troubled individual's life. These individuals may develop a poor self-image and low self-esteem due to rejection by a parent because they supposedly failed to live up to some imaginary standard created by the parent. They may learn to be fearful and anxious because a parent was unpredictable, or they were taught that people cannot be trusted and the world is a scary place. They may feel that, because parents did not love them properly, they are, therefore, unlovable. All of these reactions are based on false premises. What are false premises? To put it bluntly, they are lies.

In correcting dysfunctional thoughts and behavior, people must be exposed to the lies that they have been believing. These lies must be countered and challenged with the truth. Who can do that better than the Spirit of Truth Himself? Notice another way Jesus described the Holy Spirit: "But when He, the Spirit of Truth, comes, He will guide you into all the truth..." (John 16:13). Jesus said He would lead us into all the truth. He also said that we will know the truth and the truth will make us *free* (John 8:32). When the Holy Spirit lives inside us, that journey to total freedom becomes easier.

I believe that God has created within our spiritual DNA a desire and hunger for truth. It is so much a part of who we are as humans that we are totally intolerant to being lied to. A lie is considered an anathema even to life-long, career criminals. Politicians and celebrities can get away with practically anything if they truthfully confess it. The public will forgive them. However, if they are caught in a lie, the public will reject them and they will never be trusted again.

Why is this such a predominant characteristic of humans? Think of it like this. God's desire is for us to know Him. As we are created in His image and He is truth, then we have within our basic design an appreciation of and desire for truth. When the Spirit of truth takes up residence in us, the truth in our spiritual DNA bears witness to Him, which results in an internal integrity between our spirit and the Spirit of truth.

The Holy Spirit then begins to reveal the truth to us about ourselves, others, and the world in which we live. He consistently brings His truth into sharp contrast with the lies that have burdened and controlled us for many years. He is not only a marvelous teacher as I have already shown, but He teaches only that which is absolutely true. It is this artful teaching of the truth that produces meaningful and lasting transformation into God's divine design for each of us.

The Holy Spirit as Counselor and Teacher

Jesus predicted that the Holy Spirit would produce powerful change in His followers by the way He described Him: "And I will ask the Father, and He will give you another Helper (Counselor), that He may be with you forever" (John 14:16).

The American Psychological Association Dictionary of Psychology defines "counselor" as one who provides "… information, and suggestions designed to enhance the client's ability to solve problems, make decisions, and effect desired changes in attitude and behavior."[11]

Therefore, Jesus tells us that He is going to give us someone who will help us change our attitude and behavior in such a way that we will see solutions to our problems. We are then able to make the right choices in life resulting in greater peace and happiness.

What is the process by which the Holy Spirit achieves this powerful change? The answer is in John 14:26: "But the Helper, the Holy Spirit, whom the Father will send in My name, He will teach you all things, and bring to your remembrance, all that I said to you."

Teaching, then, is how the Holy Spirit transforms us. We are all familiar with teachers. Most of us have had a number of different teachers throughout our educational careers, whether we stopped after high school or continued on to college. We can recall those teachers who had a positive impact on us and those who were not very effective in what they did. My eighth grade teacher and my high school football coach both had a powerful impact on my life exactly when I needed it. What was it about these two individuals that made them great teachers?

We are told, "Qualities associated with teacher effectiveness include mastery of subject matter, pedagogical thinking, organizational ability, enthusiasm, warmth, calmness, and the establishment of a rapport with students."[12] These traits are

---

11 Gary R. VandenBos, ed., APA *Dictionary of Psychology*, (Washington, D.C.: American Psychological Association, 2007), 238.
12 Ibid.

the requisites for producing maximum learning by students. Learning produces change in people.

Does the Holy Spirit possess these characteristics associated with teacher effectiveness? Let us examine each of these above-mentioned qualities.

1. *Mastery of subject matter:* A characteristic of the Holy Spirit is omniscience, which means He has universal knowledge of all things. His knowledge is infinite. Is there any subject matter of which He is not master? Inconceivable. As He knows everything about everything because He, in fact, created everything, it is not a stretch to believe that He knows all there is to know about what you are trying to learn. When we attend any type of school, we want to learn from the experts in any particular subject. This increases the likelihood that we also may eventually become an expert. The Holy Spirit is the expert of all experts. There is nothing He does not know. If you need advice on how to handle your finances, ask Him. He is the master accountant. If you need answers about problems in a relationship, ask Him. He is the master therapist. If you need insight into a problem at work, ask Him. He is the master supervisor. If you are not sure how to solve a problem with your children, ask Him. He is the master parent. There is no subject matter of which He is not the master.

2. *Pedagogical thinking:* People who think pedagogically are those who constantly think about how to present their knowledge to others in ways that will facilitate the learning process. Their thoughts are geared toward how they can best teach others what they know. The Holy Spirit's thinking is structured in such a way that everything He says to us is designed to teach us something (John 16:13-14). Pedagogical thinkers use myriad ways of presenting their knowledge to others because every student is different and has a different learning style. Some students are great auditory learners. All they have to do is listen carefully to the teacher and they learn quickly. Others are great visual learners. If they read it or see it visually demonstrated, they have it. Others are better motor learners. That is, if they physically practice something, they master it easily. There are many learning styles and certainly combinations of all of them. Since the Holy Spirit knows everything about each of us, He knows what our learning styles are and exactly how to present His knowledge to us to facilitate our learning.

3. *Organizational ability:* Some teachers are masters of their subject matter, but they cannot organize their knowledge in such a way their students easily learn it. Some of my professors in college were obviously brilliant in their respective fields of learning, but they were so disorganized in their presentations that we had difficulty figuring out what in the world they were trying to teach us. We, as humans, learn best when information is represented in a structured, organized fashion. Does the Holy Spirit possess organizational ability? This is a no-brainer! Just check out the earth and the universe. Notice how perfectly everything is organized. All flora and fauna are organized according to similar characteristics into classes and species. Then God said, "Let the earth sprout vegetation, plants yielding seed, and fruit trees bearing fruit after their kind, with seed in them, on the earth, and it was so. And the earth brought forth vegetation, plants yielding seed after their kind, and trees bearing fruit, with seed in them, after their kind; and God saw that it was good (Genesis 1:11-12). The food chain is a masterpiece of organization. Remove or alter one step in it, and the entire chain is affected. The planets and stars in our galaxy are so perfectly organized that even a minute change in their orbits would have devastating effects on the rest of the galaxy. If the Holy Spirit organized all of what we see and even what we do not see, it is easy to conclude that He has the ability to organize things in our lives to facilitate the learning process.

4. *Enthusiasm:* When a teacher is enthusiastic about her subject matter, it is contagious. There is nothing so agonizing as to have to sit through a class where the teacher presents the material in a monotone, boring style. If she shows no interest or zeal for the subject, then why should we? But, if she is passionate about her subject and brings energy and fervor to the lesson, we will begin to feel the same way even if the subject is not our favorite one. Having all the knowledge in the world about something is meaningless if we cannot stimulate people to want to learn it. Our own enthusiasm is what provokes others to desire to know what we know. The Holy Spirit is the epitome of enthusiasm and hope: "But the fruit of the Spirit is love, joy, peace, patience, kindness, goodness, faithfulness, gentleness, self-control: against such things there is no law" (Galatians 5:22-23). He is enthusiastic about everything in our lives. He is especially joyful about Jesus and desires to teach us everything there is to know about Him. He even helps us to remember everything that Jesus said (John 14:26). What a teacher! He even gives us a great memory! When we are filled with the Holy Spirit, He brings this enthusiasm and joy with Him and, because it is contagious, we catch it. We instantly become more enthusiastic about the things of God and want to learn more. This is the result when the enthusiastic teacher lives inside us.

5. *Warmth:* When people are warm, we think of them as being friendly and kind. They are sympathetic, sincere, and cordial. They may be ardent about what they believe and teach, but they are very approachable. They tend to be gentle, cheerful, and loving. Warmth creates an environment that is highly conducive to learning. My first Pastor, Reverend R.S. King, exemplified warmth. I eagerly looked forward to his weekly Bible study class because he made it so enjoyable. We could ask any question or make any comment without fear of ridicule or rejection. If we were incorrect about something, he was always gentle and kind in his correction. When a teacher is cold and uncaring, the learning process is inhibited regardless of how intelligent the student. The warmth of the Holy Spirit, however, is unbounded. He creates the perfect learning environment. As we see in Galatians 5:22-23, He possesses kindness and gentleness. He always responds in a kind and friendly manner, regardless of how stupid our questions may be. This fills us with pleasant feelings (peace), which encourages us to ask more questions without fear of being criticized, mocked, or humiliated. When we feel free to ask questions and openly admit to the teacher that we do not understand something, learning is accelerated. The warmth of the Holy Spirit is the catalyst for rapid learning.

6. *Calmness:* When a teacher is calm, he is unruffled by what his students say or do. He is not reactive. Rather, he responds in a composed, peaceful manner. He may not agree with how his students are acting, but he is undisturbed by it and remains serene. This calmness is usually interpreted as patience, which is absolutely necessary in the teaching process. We, as students in the school of life, usually make many mistakes and frequently repeat the same ones. The Holy Spirit remains calm and patiently corrects us. It is His calmness in the midst of our own personal storm that generates a feeling of security and safety in us no matter what we face and try to master. You may recall when Jesus and his disciples were in the boat on the sea and a great storm arose. The disciples panicked because the boat was about to be swamped but Jesus was in the bottom of the boat asleep. They woke him begging for help: "Then He arose, and rebuked the winds and the seas; and it became perfectly *calm*" (Matthew 8:26, my emphasis). Jesus remained calm in the midst of the storm because He was filled with the Holy Spirit and then transferred this calmness to the situation and all became calm just like Him. The Holy Spirit possesses this same quality, which is why He is a great teacher.

7. *Rapport with students:* To have rapport with someone implies we are in relationship and agreement with them. There is compatibility and affinity: "Can two walk together, except they be agreed?" (Amos 3:3). When there is rapport between the Holy Spirit and us, we can walk in the same direction, which is the direction of learning, growth, mastery and maturity: "But when He, the Spirit of Truth, comes, He will guide you into all truth" (John 16:13). As a master teacher, the Holy Spirit knows us down to our core and, therefore, knows exactly how to create compatibility and agreement so necessary for learning to take place.

Therefore, we see that the Holy Spirit not only possesses all seven qualities associated with effective teaching but also possesses them infinitely, which makes Him the ultimate teacher. When we are baptized in the Holy Spirit, we become much more sensitive to all of these marvelous teaching abilities He possesses, which makes us better learners. It is this learning process that gradually transforms us.

CHAPTER 6

Vehicle for Change: The Baptism in the Holy Spirit

Spiritual DNA and Baptism
The Holy Spirit Working Through Our Spiritual DNA

God has put within the DNA and genes of humankind the hunger and ability to know Him. He has put a measure of faith in all of us. We can know Him if we desire. However, the ruler of this world, Satan, has misdirected this faith. It is misdirected toward people, drugs, alcohol, money, government, science, and false religion (John 10:10).

An eternal conflict is set up when we go against our spiritual DNA and try to be something different from what we are designed by God to be. Humankind was designed to worship and have intimate fellowship with God. When a person opposes that basic design, he or she is at conflict at the basic cellular level as well as the basic spiritual level. There will be an ongoing conflict at the deepest core, which drives a person more and more to attempt to resolve it by pursuing this eternal design in areas that are not of God. Humankind's DNA design mandates that God be found to resolve the conflict and find integrity, completeness, and rest. Only then can we function as we are designed by God to function. An automobile cannot function if you put sand, water, cement, or anything else other than gas in the tank. It will only function the way it was designed to function if you put gasoline in the tank. Humans can only function properly if they put God in their spirit. Only then, can their cellular and spiritual DNA function perfectly as it was designed.

A cat will never bark. As long as it tries to bark, it will never be the whole, complete cat it was designed to be. Human beings need to stop trying to function without the Spirit of God. We need to stop trying to be the opposite of what we are designed by God to be. Even those who know God, try to be something else based on what they have been told by others, not God. Christians have been told there is just so much they can know about God, and they cannot really get close to Him. They are told the intimacy the apostles had with Him is not available to them. This, too, goes against their spiritual DNA. Intimacy with God is programmed into our cellular and spiritual DNA. He provides that intimacy through His Spirit. Just as eye color is unchangeable, this truth is immutable.

The infilling of the Holy Spirit is the key that fits perfectly into the lock of our spiritual DNA. He completes that perfect design. Without Him we are like a gas tank with no gas, an aquarium with no water, or an oxygen tank with no air— attractive on the outside but no life inside and no function commensurate with its design.

The Church has taught for centuries that intimacy with God is unattainable by the average person. Church leaders teach that only the exceptional great men and women of God (saints) in the Bible were able to attain it. However, the church fails to point out that those great men and women were just average and some even below average before they sought and found God. He is the one who made them exceptional and great after they found intimacy with Him. *The baptism in the Holy Spirit is the vehicle by which this intimacy is attained and by which powerful change is produced.*

The Gifts of the Holy Spirit Extend to Us— Not Just to the Apostles

Some argue that the baptism in the Holy Spirit, as well as the gifts of the Holy Spirit, ended with the apostles. They contend that by the end of the Book of Acts signs and wonders were diminishing and, therefore, ended with the apostolic age. There is no scriptural support of this.

In fact, we see the gifts still being reported in the later chapters of Acts. In Acts 27:9-34 we see prophesy; Acts 28:3-6, healing; Acts 28:8-9, signs and wonders; Acts 23:11, visitation by Jesus.

If the gifts of the Holy Spirit were for only the apostles, why would Paul teach the church so extensively on the gifts in I Corinthians 12? He specifically urged believers to pursue the gifts, especially that of prophecy. If Paul believed, as contemporary critics say, that only the apostles operated in the gifts, then he was wasting a lot of time and energy teaching other believers how to properly operate in them.

No Scripture supports the contention that the gifts and baptism in the Holy Spirit were only for the Apostles and that they ceased. Jesus clearly gave these gifts and signs to all who believe in Him: "And these signs will accompany those who have believed: in my name they will cast out demons, they will speak with new tongues; they will pick up serpents, and if they drink any deadly poison, it shall not hurt them; they will lay hands on the sick and they will recover" (Mark 16:17-18). If salvation through Christ, water baptism, communion, the great commission, and everything else in the New Testament did not pass away with the apostles, why would the gifts of the Spirit and the baptism in the Holy Spirit pass away?

The critics argue that Spirit baptism and the gifts of the Holy Spirit were given to only the apostles specifically to empower them to fulfill the great commission (Mark 16:15). Did the Lord's commandment to go to the uttermost parts of the earth with the gospel apply only to the Apostles? Does it not also apply to all who believe in the Lord Jesus? If so, wouldn't Jesus empower and equip us in like manner, as He empowered the Apostles? Did He love them more than He loves us? What kind of father would tell his children to do something that they were not equipped to do? No, the truth is that Jesus still empowers His people to accomplish His work and that empowerment is the baptism in the Holy Spirit! Peter offered proof: "Repent, and be baptized every one of you in the name of Jesus Christ for the remission of sins, and ye shall receive the gift of the Holy Spirit. For the promise is unto you, and to your children, and to all that are afar off, even as many as the Lord our God shall call" (Acts 2:38-39). On logical and scriptural grounds, we can conclude that the baptism in the Holy Spirit was not an experience exclusive to the Apostles.

The writer of Hebrews made a powerful statement: "Jesus Christ the same yesterday, and today, and forever" (Hebrews 13:8). In other words, what Jesus did in the apostolic age, He continues to do today. Jesus is the baptizer in the Holy Spirit. He baptized the apostles and He continues to baptize those today who choose to believe and receive. One cannot separate the person of Jesus Christ from his actions. They are one and the same.

Salvation and Spirit Baptism: Separate Events

Many are taught they received the Holy Spirit when they were saved and water baptized. "Isn't this the same baptism you are talking about?" they ask. They equate their salvation and water baptism with the baptism of the Holy Spirit.

It is very difficult to convince someone they need something if they believe they already have it. So, let's see if we can clear up this confusion by looking into the Word of God. Several Scriptures speak to this issue of salvation, water baptism, and Spirit baptism being separate events. For example, in the Gospel of Luke, "John answered, and said to them all, 'As for me, I baptize you with water; but One is coming who is mightier than I, and I am not fit to untie the thong of His sandals; *He will baptize you with the Holy Spirit and fire*'" (Luke 3:16, my emphasis).

John was differentiating between what he had been doing and what Jesus was about to do. John baptized unto repentance and told the people to believe on Him that was coming (Jesus). Repentance and water baptism are elements of salvation. Essentially, then, John was leading many unto salvation. But he also taught that the Savior was coming who would baptize them in yet another way "with the Holy Spirit and with fire."

If the Holy Spirit baptism and John's water baptism were identical events, why would John make it a point to discuss them as being separate? Jesus Himself made the same differentiation: "And gathering them together, He commanded them not to leave Jerusalem, but to wait for what the Father promised, 'Which,' He said, 'you have heard of from Me; for John baptized with water, but you shall be baptized with the Holy Spirit not many days from now'" (Acts 1:4-5). Jesus continued, "But ye shall receive power, after that the Holy Spirit is come upon you: and ye shall be witnesses unto me both in Jerusalem, and in all Judea, and in Samaria and unto the uttermost part of the earth" (Acts 1:8).

Notice that Jesus said His followers would receive power *after* the Holy Spirit had come upon them. In other words, those who believed in Him had yet to receive the Holy Spirit. Jesus added that this separate event would occur in a few days further verifying that this baptism was different from the one they had already received (water baptism).

To whom was Jesus speaking? It was not to non-believers but rather to those who believed in Him. That is, they were already saved: "Now you are clean through the word which I have spoken to you" (John 15:3). The word "clean" is from the Hebrew word *katharos*, which means literally or figuratively clean, clear, and pure. Jesus was telling them their sins had been forgiven and, because they believed in Him, they were saved (John 3:16). That is one spiritual event, but He prophesied that they would have another one, Spirit baptism.

Jesus explained the difference between the two events: "... that is the Spirit of Truth, whom the world cannot receive, because it does not behold or know Him, but you know Him; He abides *with* you, and will be *in* you" (John 14:7, my emphasis). The words *with* and *in* are prepositions that describe two different relationships or proximate positions.

Jesus was telling saved believers they already knew the Holy Spirit because He was *with* them, that is, alongside them, a position which was established when they repented of their sins, were water baptized, and believed in Jesus as Messiah. He went on to tell them yet another positional relationship with the Holy Spirit was about to be established. He was going from being *with* them to being *in* them. Clearly, these are two different experiences. *In* means inside or within.

When we are saved and water baptized, the Holy Spirit comes alongside us to comfort, guide, and direct us. When we are baptized in the Spirit, He moves from alongside to inside us. Think of it like this: When we get saved, it is like being doused with a bucket of soothing water (Holy Spirit). But, with the baptism in the Holy Spirit, we jump into the whole swimming pool and the water (Holy Spirit) gets all of us. The word "baptism" comes from the Greek word *baptizo* which means, to immerse. Jesus was, thus, explaining that the relationship with the Holy Spirit was about to change from a close friendship to one of being totally immersed in Him and engulfed by Him.

We see in John that Jesus again differentiated between salvation and Spirit baptism: "He that believeth on me, as the Scripture hath said, out of his belly shall flow rivers of living water. But this spake he of the Spirit, which they that believe on him should receive: for the Holy Spirit was not yet given; because that Jesus was not yet glorified" (John 7:38-39).

Holy Spirit: Agent of Change

He was saying that *believers* had not yet received the Holy Spirit (i.e. immersed in Him) because He was not yet given. They were already *believers* but had not received the baptism in the Holy Spirit. His use of the word *should* in verse 39 is equivalent to *ought to*, both of which express obligation and necessity.

The Lord was instructing believers that it was an obligation to receive the baptism in the Holy Spirit, but implied in the definition of "should" is the reality that not all would choose to receive. It was clearly a choice just as salvation is appropriated by an individual's free will choice.

The eighth chapter of Acts gives another example of the distinction between water and Spirit baptism. Phillip preached Christ with great anointing and performed miracles, which had great impact in the city: "But when they believed Phillip preaching the things concerning the kingdom of God, and the Name of Jesus Christ, they were baptized, both men and women" (Acts 8:12).

The word believed is from the Greek word *pisteuo*, which means: "to have faith (in, upon or with respect to, a person or thing), i.e. credit; by implication to entrust (especially one's spiritual well being to Christ): believe, commit (to trust), put in trust with."[13]

This verse clearly indicates these Samaritans were born-again at this point. Most contemporary pastors and evangelists would be totally thrilled and satisfied with the majority of a city's population accepting the Lord and being born-again.

13 Spiro Zodhiates, ed., *Hebrew Greek Key Study Bible*, (Chattanooga, TN: AMG Publishers, 1984).

They would call it a revival and consider it a mighty victory for the kingdom of God. However, we see in verse 14 that the apostles in Jerusalem apparently were not content with people just being born-again, so they dispatched Peter and John to Samaria to complete God's work. Moreover, just how might they bring completion to this work? The author of Acts explained: "Who, when they were come down, prayed for them, that they might receive the Holy Spirit: (For as yet he was fallen upon none of them: only they were baptized in the name of the Lord Jesus.) Then laid their hands on them, and they received the Holy Spirit" (Acts 8:15-17).

Clearly, another distinction is being made between salvation and Spirit baptism. If the Samaritans had received the infilling of the Holy Spirit at the time of their salvation as a result of Phillip's work, then there would have been no need for Peter and John to travel to Samaria and pray specifically for them to "receive the Holy Spirit." What would be the point?

Later in chapter 19, Paul arrived in Ephesus and encountered about twelve disciples. Paul got right to the point with these believers by asking a probing question: "He said unto them, 'Did you receive the Holy Spirit when you believed?' And they said unto him, 'We have not so much as heard whether there is a Holy Spirit'" (Acts 19:2). Paul clearly delineated that believing in Jesus Christ and receiving the Holy Spirit were two separate spiritual events and experiences. If salvation and Spirit baptism were one and the same thing or always occurred simultaneously, then why would he ask the question? Again, what would be the point? Paul's response to their answer was to lay hands on them and then "the Holy Spirit came on them; and they began speaking with tongues and prophesying" (Acts 19:6).

In chapter 18 of Acts, we are introduced to a mighty man of God, Apollos. He is described in glowing terms: "And a certain Jew named Apollos born at Alexandria, an eloquent man, and mighty in the Scriptures, came to Ephesus. This man was instructed in the way of the Lord; and being fervent in spirit, he spake and taught diligently the things of the Lord…He began to speak boldly in the synagogue" (Acts 18:24-26).

This brief description illuminates the kind of man Apollos had become. He was fluent, vivid, forceful, and persuasive in speech. He was knowledgeable in Scriptures, could wisely apply them, and was skilled in apologetics. He understood the mode and means of how Jesus operates and in what He does for us. He was an impassioned and zealous preacher. He was persevering, attentive, careful, untiring, and industrious. That is, he was no quitter. Moreover, Apollos was fearless and courageous in the face of rejection and persecution. What more could you want in a man of God? And yet something was missing. In verse 25 we are told that he knew "only the baptism of John." This suggests he lacked something. Apparently, Aquila and Priscilla felt his spiritual knowledge was incomplete. They took him aside and "expounded unto him the way of God more perfectly" (v. 26). Notice that they were not refuting Apollos' teaching and interpretation of Scripture but rather were laying open, i.e., giving a more complete and full explanation of the *way* of God. The *way* meaning the mode in which Jesus operates in us.

Now, it does not specifically say that Aquila and Priscilla instructed him in Spirit baptism, but it is easy to deduce from what was discussed above in chapters 8 and 19. In both of these instances, the disciples had only received the baptism of John just as Apollos had, but they had not received the Holy Spirit yet. When Peter, John, and Paul expounded unto them Spirit baptism, they all received. As Apollos was clearly not lacking in anything else in his spiritual walk with the Lord, it is logical to conclude that Aquilla and Priscilla explained to him the one thing of which he had no knowledge—the baptism in the Holy Spirit.

It is clear from the above three examples from Acts that Salvation and Spirit baptism were considered to be separate spiritual experiences. Additionally, the early church did not believe that Spirit baptism was rare, weird, or bizarre. Rather, they saw it as *normal* Christianity and an absolute prerequisite to true intimacy with God and unequivocally necessary to move in the power of God.

Spirit Baptism: Demonic or Divine?

A tendency exists in the body of Christ to explain things one does not understand or disagree with as being *not of God* or, even more condemning, *demonic* or *of the Devil*. Some say that Spirit baptism with evidence of speaking in tongues is demonic. If this is true, then it would follow that all those who have received this spiritual experience are indeed demon-possessed. Following this logic, then, those who receive it would begin to follow the Devil and increase in sinful behaviors.

Satan's ultimate goal is to lead people away from Christ and deeper and deeper into sin. This would become blatantly obvious to even the casual observer. This can readily be seen in those who join cults. They begin to engage in all manner of ungodly behaviors and even lose their relationship with God.

Jesus gave us the method of identifying whether an individual is of God or not of God. In describing false prophets, He declared: "Ye shall know them by their fruits. Do men gather grapes of thorns, or figs of thistles?" (Matthew 7:15-20). He continued to say that, "every good tree bears good fruit but a bad tree bears bad fruit" (v. 17). To stress His point, Jesus emphatically repeats that a good tree *cannot* bring forth bad fruit and neither can a bad tree produce good fruit (v. 18). In fact, these are impossibilities! The simplest way, then to discern whether something is or is not of God is to judge the fruit.

As mentioned above, if Spirit baptism is of the Devil, then all Spirit-filled people would reject Christ and embrace sin. In reality, however, the opposite occurs for those who come into the fullness of the Spirit. They report a more profound closeness to God through Jesus and greater desire to know more of Him. Their time spent in prayer increases. Their time spent studying the Scriptures increases. Their time spent in church increases. Their service to the Lord and others through various ministries increases. In short, all things of God in their life increase. Spirit-filled Christians tend to move from a life of passive assent to one of active faith and service to the Lord. Their understanding of the Scriptures and the things of the Spirit tends to accelerate at light speed. A greater sensitivity to and revilement of sin grows in the Spirit-filled believer. There is a greater tendency to reject the unfruitful works of darkness and have no fellowship with them (Ephesians 5:11). I believe it is safe to say that all of these things can be interpreted as good fruit! How can a good tree bear bad fruit? Jesus said it is impossible.

We see in I John 22-23 more characteristics of good fruit: "Who is a liar but he that denieth that Jesus is Christ? He is antichrist, that denieth the Father and the Son...Whosoever denieth the Son, the same hath not the Father; but he that acknowledgeth the Son hath the Father also" (I John 22-23).

I contend that the Spirit-filled believer not only acknowledges Jesus is the Christ but actively worships and serves Him. My experience is that demon-possessed people do not witness to others about Jesus and lead them into a saving knowledge of Christ. They do not eagerly study and teach others the Word of God. They do not express their love in service to God and His people. Rather, they engage in works of the flesh such as adultery, fornication, uncleanness, lasciviousness, idolatry, witchcraft, hatred, various emulations, wrath, strife, seditions, heresies, envying, murders, drunkenness, and revelings (Galatians 5:19-20).

No, Spirit baptism with evidence of speaking in tongues is not of the Devil. It is but one of the good and perfect gifts sent down to us from our Holy Father and it is tangible, concrete proof of His reality (James 1:17). I believe that the contention that Spirit baptism is of the Devil is, in itself, a deception by Satan (John 8:44). It is used by him to deceive God's children and prevent them from receiving the power from on high. In so doing, he renders them spiritually impotent if they believe the lie. Jesus said, "I am the way, the truth and the life." Believe Jesus and receive His power through the Holy Spirit.

Unity: A Fruit of Change

It is this baptism in the Holy Spirit that produces greater unity among believers. It eradicates the denominational barriers that have separated believers and made the body of Christ powerless. If you gather together a group of non-Spirit-filled believers in the same room and ask them to share their spiritual beliefs, you will soon be able to identify the denomination to which they belong. Why? Because they will begin discussing religion and what their denomination believes.

However, if you gather a group of Spirit-filled believers together, you will be hard-pressed to identify their denominations because they usually do not talk about church or religion. They talk about God, Jesus, or the Holy Spirit and what He is doing in their lives. There is unity in their main belief system. This is a primary result of Spirit baptism.

Jesus said that He is coming back for a body without spot or blemish. Most interpret that to mean a body without sin, but it also means *one* body, i.e., a body that is in unity and not fractionated into denominations (Romans 12:4-5). Spirit baptism is the vehicle by which He will accomplish this.

There is much said in American society about the benefits of diversity. America is a nation of diverse people from different races, ethnic backgrounds, religions, educational levels, languages, socio-economic levels, and cultures. We are told that these differences are good and that we should accept those varieties without question. Otherwise, you will be labeled as intolerant. Unlikeness is a good thing. I do not necessarily disagree with that concept. However, what the proponents of diversity fail to tell you is that without some central unifying force, diversity, if left to its natural progression, is divisive, fractionating, and ultimately destructive. Without a central unifying force, diversity eventually ceases to be beneficial to a society and instead breeds ongoing disagreement, intolerance, prejudice, bigotry, and hatred.

The unifying force, a belief in God, is powerful. The Holy Spirit is part of this. When people are in agreement spiritually, God begins to assemble them together like very different pieces fit together in a jigsaw puzzle. Their differences make a beautiful whole because they have a vision of the final picture, not just their one small piece. They are in agreement with the final beautiful product because they are all in agreement with God regardless of the diversity of their separate puzzle pieces. God loves variety and diversity but only if He is the unifying force. Paul spoke to this issue in his epistle to the Corinthians: "Now there are a variety of gifts, but the same Spirit. And there are varieties of ministries, but the same Lord. And there are varieties of effects, but the same God who works all things in all persons. But to each one is given the manifestation of the Spirit for the common good" (I Corinthians 12:4-7). Clearly, then, the Holy Spirit is the unifying force that transforms diversity into a beautiful strength.

In the first century, striking differences thrived between the Jews and Gentiles (heathens). These two cultures could not have been more disparate. Jews and Gentiles disagreed on everything. They differed in culture, language, spiritual beliefs, behavior, customs, and worldviews. Jews wanted nothing to do with Gentiles. Diversity separated them.

But then a marvelous, supernatural thing began to happen. This is illustrated when Peter defended his ministry to the Gentiles. He explained that the Holy Spirit sent him to a household of Gentiles in Caesarea to explain salvation to them. As Peter began speaking, the Holy Spirit fell on them: "And I remembered the word of the Lord, how He used to say, 'John baptized with water, but you shall be baptized with the Holy Spirit.' If God therefore gave to them the same gift as He gave to us also after believing in the Lord Jesus Christ, who was I that I could stand in God's way?" (Acts 11:16-17). The separating barrier of diversity between these groups came crashing down in one fell swoop. The differences that once separated them remained but no longer mattered because they had been joined together at their cores (spirits) by the one unifying force of the universe, the Holy Spirit.

Paul spoke to this reconciliation of Jews and Gentiles: "For He Himself is our peace, who made both groups into one, and broke down the barrier of the dividing wall, by abolishing in His flesh the enmity which is the Law of commandments contained in ordinance, that in Himself He might make the two into one new man, thus establishing peace..." (Ephesians 2:14-15). The cross was the event that put to death the enmity but the Holy Spirit was the facilitator of unity: "... for through Him we both have our access in one Spirit to the Father" (Ephesians 2:18). It is this common access to the Father by way of the Holy Spirit that produces unity.

This unifying power of the Holy Spirit was seen even among the Jews on the day of Pentecost. After explaining to them exactly what it was that they were observing (i.e. tongues), Peter told them: "Repent and let each of you be baptized in the name of Jesus Christ for the forgiveness of your sins; and you shall receive the gift of the Holy Spirit" (Acts 2:38). Three thousand souls were saved that day and baptized in the Holy Spirit. Notice what began happening then: "And all those who had believed were together, and had all things in common. And day by day continuing with one mind in the temple, and breaking bread from house to house, they were taking their meals together with gladness and sincerity of heart..." (Acts 2:44-46). These were Jews from at least fifteen different countries and regions who spoke many different languages, but the Holy Spirit rapidly brought them into unity. Although these people were from diverse backgrounds, they now had one mind and one heart. Similarly, the Holy Spirit unifies Christians from different denominational backgrounds into one body of believers. He shifts their focus from religious traditions, doctrines, and practices to that of Christ and His preeminence in all things.

What happens to diversity without the unifying power of the Holy Spirit? Jesus gave us the answer: "...Any kingdom divided against itself is laid waste; and a house divided against itself falls" (Luke 11:17). American culture and society promotes diversity, but it has taken God out of the equation. Prayer has been removed from schools. The name of Jesus can no longer be used in prayers by military chaplains. There have been attempts to remove *under God* from the pledge of allegiance and *in God we trust* from our currency. Students cannot read their Bibles in school. Diversity without God is ultimately destructive. The United States is no longer united. Many feel that the causes of disunity are due to racism, sexism, political ideologies, socioeconomic, and educational differences. These are mere symptoms and reflections of disunity. The underlying cause is that the unifying core, the Holy Spirit, is no longer welcome in America. The Christian church carries much of the responsibility for this tragedy because Christians have been taught that He is no longer relevant and active in our modern society. Satan has used this error to his advantage by taking diversity to its natural outcome—division, disagreement, and fractionation among God's people. Satan knows that unity brings power. If he can keep God's people divided, they will pose no threat to him and his kingdom.

The good news is that God has had enough. He is about to pour out His Holy Spirit in unprecedented ways. Thousands are going to receive the baptism in the Holy Spirit in the next move of God because the Lord desires to unify His people. As barriers come crashing down, the Spirit of Unity will draw all His people together regardless of race, ethnic background, sex, age, or culture. He will create a holy paradox, and diversity will become a strength through unity, i.e., unity in the Spirit.

Intimacy: Pathway to Transformation

Many in full gospel/charismatic circles teach that the main reason for receiving the baptism in the Holy Spirit is to receive power, i.e., the gifts of the Holy Spirit (I Corinthians 12:8-10). This is certainly a good reason for receiving, but I believe there is a more important reason: intimacy.

Most people have intimate relationships in their lives, but it is rarely with God. Even born-again Christians often complain that God seems to be someone who is far off in the heavenlies and difficult to reach. I have spoken with many people who believe in God and believe that He created us but that He is not really involved very much in our lives. He is merely a distant observer. How sad that would be if that were actually true. We are told that it is possible to grieve the Holy Spirit (Isaiah 63:10). If He was aloof and distant from us, then how would our actions grieve Him? Grief can only occur in close, intimate relationships.

Psychology has an interesting definition of intimacy: "an interpersonal state of extreme emotional closeness such that each party's personal space can be entered by any of the other parties without causing discomfort to that person. Intimacy characterizes close, familiar, and usually affectionate or loving personal relationships and requires the parties to have a detailed knowledge or deep understanding of each other."[14]

When the Holy Spirit engulfs you, He has entered the deepest part of your personal space (Ephesians 3:16). There is no discomfort with that but, rather, a feeling of extreme

---

14 Gary R. VandenBos, ed., *APA Dictionary of Psychology*, (Washington, D.C.: American Psychological Association, 2007), 238.

emotional closeness and all that that entails such as trust, commitment, self-disclosure, and unconditional love. All of these are produced by a detailed knowledge or deep understanding of each other. In addition, who could know us better than God? He told Jeremiah that He knew him before he was even in his mother's womb (Jeremiah 1:5). How is that for detailed knowledge of someone? God knows everything there is to know about you and still loves you unconditionally. And we can know Him as well: "...but let him who boasts boast of this, that he understands and knows Me, that I am the Lord who exercises loving kindness, justice, and righteousness on earth; for I delight in these things" (Jeremiah 9:24). It is this mutual knowledge and understanding of each other that produces the emotional closeness characterized by His love we call intimacy. Faith in Christ regenerates our spirit, which was dead in sin. It is the infilling of the Holy Spirit, however, that softens the heart by giving a deeper revelation of who He is. Our love for Him is instantly magnified which automatically increases our intimacy with Him.

It is not that we do not come into a knowledge of Him when we are born-again, we do. When I came into a saving knowledge of Jesus Christ, I quite rapidly began to see Him differently. I had a relationship with Him and could talk to Him daily. But our God is a *god of more*. Just when we think we know Him well, He shows us another aspect of Himself and His aspects are infinite. Deeper layers always exist. God is sort of like an onion. When you peel one layer off, there is yet another one except that his layers never end.

I have spoken with many born-again Christians who love the Lord and manifest the fruit of the Spirit (Galatians 5:22). However, when I share with them about the baptism in the Holy Spirit, some get a bit defensive. "I already know the Lord and talk to Him everyday," they say.

"That's great," I reply, "but there are levels of knowing just like there are levels of education."

Having a high school diploma is a good thing and documents that you have a certain amount of knowledge. A bachelor's degree from a university documents that you have gained more knowledge over and above high school. A graduate degree documents yet more knowledge. Just as there are deeper levels of education and knowledge, deeper levels of intimacy with God are possible.

Think of it in this way. I have watched Billy Graham on television over the years and feel that I have come to know Him somewhat. But what if I went to his house in North Carolina and spent every day in person with him for a month? I suspect that I would have a deeper understanding of who he is. There is nothing wrong with my current knowledge and understanding of him, but I am certain there is probably a lot more about him that I do not know. So it is with the Holy Spirit.

When we come into the fullness of the Spirit through Spirit baptism, all of the fruit of the Spirit (Galatians 5:22) are intensified within us which creates greater intimacy with the Lord. It is not that you do not already experience the fruit if you are born-again, but when baptized in the Spirit, intimacy is magnified. It is like turning the volume up on your television.

You may have struggled to hear it at a lower volume, but now you hear it loud and clear.

It is this greater intimacy with God that creates the pathway for ongoing change in us. When we feel this extreme emotional closeness with God, who is full of love and acceptance, we become more teachable. The defenses come down, our hearts open up, and we become more willing to be transformed because our level of trust has deepened. As I have already shown, the Holy Spirit is the ultimate teacher. As our intimacy with Him grows, our willingness and ability to learn grows. As we learn, we change. How quickly we change is a direct function of the level of intimacy we have with Him. Spirit baptism produces a continual level of intimacy that is quantitatively and qualitatively deeper than what we experience when we are born-again.

Some Christians feel they already have enough intimacy with the Lord. They do not need anymore. I am always a bit nonplussed by that attitude. It is like saying, "I don't need any more air to breathe." Why would you not want to be closer to God? These are the same people who want to go to heaven for eternity. Guess who permeates all of Heaven? God!

Intimacy with the Lord is the very essence and purpose of life. It empowers you to die to the flesh and to live and walk by the Spirit (Galatians 5:25). When the Holy Spirit lives in the core of your personal space, the intimacy is a continual experience. It does not just come and go or occur only in heightened spiritual moments in church or prayer. It becomes the best part of who you are. There is an old saying, "You become who you associate with." Bad company corrupts good morals. The more intimate we become with the Holy Spirit, the more we are transformed into His likeness. It is inevitable.

Spirit baptism not only allows Him entrance into the deepest part of our personal space, but it also gives us access to the deeper parts of His as well. Is this really possible? Let us look at a few things and see.

The Lord gave Ezekiel some remarkable visions concerning the temple of God. He gave him specific measurements for the outer court and the inner court. The inner court was separated from the outer court by a barrier "to divide between the holy and profane" (Ezekiel 42:20). The average person was not permitted access to the inner court. Only the Levitical priests were allowed in to minister to the Lord, and they were permitted to wear only linen garments. They were not to wear anything that made them sweat (Ezekiel 44:18). When they were finished ministering and exited the inner court, they had to change clothes again and put their linen garments in holy chambers: "Then they shall put on other garments that they may not transmit holiness to the people with their garments" (Ezekiel 44:19). Not only could the average person not enter the inner court, but was also not allowed to experience the holiness of God either.

Ezekiel described a remarkable experience: "And the Spirit lifted me up and brought me into the inner court; and behold, the glory of the Lord filled the house" (Ezekiel 43:5). Notice who brought him into the inner court to experience the glory of God: the Holy Spirit. Ezekiel had access to the Holy of Holies and the glory of God by way of the Holy Spirit. This is an old-testament typology of the Holy Spirit leading us into greater intimacy with God. It was a prophetic symbol of what was to occur some six hundred years later at Pentecost and continues to occur down to the present day.

Jesus' death on the cross is the singular event that now makes it possible to enter the Holy of Holies. At the moment of His death several miraculous things occurred: "And behold the veil of the temple was torn in two from top to bottom, and the earth shook; and the rocks were split, and the tombs were opened; and many bodies of the saints who had fallen asleep were raised..." (Matthew 27:51-52). The separating barrier between the holy and the profane had been split wide open, thus giving the common person access to the Holy of Holies. The shed blood of Jesus opened the door to the deeper recesses of His personal space. But how do we actually enter in?

Stephen showed us the way. He was described as "a man full of faith and of the Holy Spirit" (Acts 6:5). Like Ezekiel, he had a stunning vision: "But being full of the Holy Spirit, he gazed intently into heaven and saw the glory of God, and Jesus standing at the right hand of God; and he said, 'Behold, I see the heavens opened up and the Son of Man standing at the right hand of God'" (Acts 7:55-56). The Scripture does not say, "But being *born-again*, he gazed intently into heaven." Stephen certainly was born-again, but the emphasis here is that he was *full of the Holy Spirit*. Obviously, it is being filled with the Holy Spirit that transports us into the deeper, more intimate places of His personal space. The blood of Jesus gives us confidence that we can approach the throne boldly in time of need, but it is the Holy Spirit who serves as the vehicle for getting us there. He desires to carry us as deep into the personal space of God as we wish to go. There are no limitations because God has no limits. He is open twenty-four hours a day, seven days a week. We have complete access to Him for as long and as often as we wish. This is the epitome of intimacy, and it is this continual intimacy that transforms us into a new creature.

How close can we get to God? We are told that we are the apple of His eye (Psalms 17:8). Apple is translated literally as pupil. The pupil of the eye is the opening in the very center of the iris. It contracts and dilates to allow light rays to enter the eye. No light enters the eye and, thus, the brain without a fully functioning pupil. If we are the pupil of God's eye, then His light can illuminate us through revelation (self-disclosure) in an ongoing manner: "It is He who reveals the profound and hidden things, He knows what is in the darkness, and the light dwells with Him" (Daniel 2:22).

There is a dynamic interaction between the pupil of the eye and light. The pupil (i.e. the believer) needs the light (revelation, i.e., God's self-disclosure) to function as it was designed and the light needs the pupil to give purpose to that which it stimulates and illuminates. There can be no more intimate relationship than that which exists between the pupil and the light. The pupil of the eye contracts and dilates to control the amount of light entering the eye. It contracts to protect the eye from being damaged by too much of the wrong kind of light (e.g. ultraviolet). It dilates to allow more light into the eye under low light condition, so we can see where we are going. And just how is His light transmitted to the apple of His eye? A passage from Ephesians explains: ". . . that by revelation there was made known to me the mystery, as I wrote before in brief. And by referring to this, when you read you can understand my insight into the mystery of Christ, which in other generations was not made known to the sons of men, as it has now been revealed to His holy apostles and prophets *in the Spirit...*" (Ephesians 3:3-5, my emphasis).

The Holy Spirit controls how much and what kind of light (revelation) we receive. He protects us from false teaching and error (contracts us) and leads us into all truth. During dark times, He is a light unto our feet to provide greater illumination (dilates us) to lead us into greater light. The intimate relationship between God's light and us is mediated and facilitated by the dynamic power of the Holy Spirit. When He gives us deeper insight and understanding, we have awesome "Eureka!" experiences or what psychologists call "Aha" moments. "I've got it, I see!" As that happens, we begin to change in some way. Intimacy with God, as created by the Holy Spirit, then, is indeed the pathway to total transformation in every aspect of our life.

CHAPTER 7

The Spirit Speaks: A Historical Look at Tongues

Speaking in tongues remains the most controversial aspect of Spirit baptism. Tongues first appeared on the day of Pentecost: "And they were all filled with the Holy Spirit and began to speak with other tongues, as the Spirit was giving them utterance" (Acts 2:4). Much confusion, misunderstanding, and error surround this supernatural experience. Praying in tongues is in perfect harmony with the Holy Spirit's role as Agent of Change.

It is through language that God has initiated every monumental change on the earth. Initially, the whole earth used the same language, which produced great understanding, achievement, and unity: "Now the whole earth used the same language and the same words" (Genesis 11:1). However, humankind's vanity and pride caused people to misuse it:

> And they said, 'Come, let us build for ourselves a city, and a tower whose top will reach into heaven, and let us make for ourselves a name; lest we be scattered abroad over the face of the whole earth.' And the Lord came down to see the city and the tower which the sons of men had built. And the Lord said, 'Behold, they are one people, and they all have the same language. And this is what they began to do, and now nothing which they purpose to do will be impossible for them. Come, let us go down and there confuse their language, that they may not understand one another's speech.'"
> (Genesis 11:4-7)

Holy Spirit: Agent of Change

When God changed the languages at Babel, He literally changed the entire course and direction of humanity. The people of the earth were not only scattered but also splintered into thousands of different groups, tribes, and nations. This event created the ultimate disunity and fractionation. Why would God do such a thing? I believe it was to protect human beings from themselves. When left to his own pride, arrogance and vanity, man is self-destructive.

After Babel, God dramatically changed the earth again with Moses, and He used language again to do it. In Exodus 4, we see Moses arguing with God about journeying to Egypt to lead the Hebrews out of bondage. One of Moses' arguments focused on his inability to use language well. He said he was ineloquent and slow of speech and tongue. God responded, "Who has made man's mouth? Or who makes him dumb or deaf, or seeing or blind? Is it not I, the Lord?" (Exodus 4:11-13).

The Lord was telling Moses to let Him control his mouth and tongue since He created it in the first place. Yet, Moses persisted and begged God to send the message by someone else (Exodus 4:11-13). The Lord had enough and said, "Is there not your brother Aaron the Levite? I know that he speaks fluently" (Exodus 4:14).

Moses was looking for a way out. He felt his language skills were not commensurate with the monumental task God called him to do. How often do we react the same way when the Lord asks us to do something that is even a lot easier than that of which He asked of Moses? We come up with all kinds of excuses why we cannot do what God asks of us. I recall an occasion when God gave me a strong prophetic word of correction for another believer and I refused to give it. I offered the same excuse that Moses did in Exodus 4:1. When God told Moses to go to Egypt, he said, "…What if they will not believe me, or listen to what I say?" (Exodus 4:1).

God does not take excuses very well, and in my case I simply refused to deliver it. "I'm not doing that, Father, he won't receive it!" Every morning for three weeks on my way to work, the Holy Spirit said, "When are you going over there and deliver the word?" And every morning I replied, "I'm not going!" Finally, as with Moses, He had enough of my excuses and disobedience.

He said, "If you don't do what I am telling you to do, I will turn and deal with you!"

That shook me right down to my core.

"Okay, Lord, I'm going today," I said.

After delivering the word from the Lord, I said to Him on my way home, "See, I told you he wouldn't believe me."

The Holy Spirit said, "That's not your problem. Now it is between him and Me. You were simply the messenger. Your job is done."

God has a way of exploding excuses. God solved Moses' problem by telling him to use Aaron to convey His message to the people: "And you are to speak to him and put the words in his mouth; and I, even I, will be with your mouth and his mouth and I will teach you what you are to do. Moreover, he shall speak for you to the people; and it shall come about that he shall be as a mouth for you, and you shall be as God to him"

Holy Spirit: Agent of Change

(Exodus 4:15-16). God spoke the Ten Commandments, among other things, to Moses who spoke them to Aaron who then spoke them to the people. This unique use of language once again changed the direction and course of humankind.

Moreover, it established a pattern and served as a typology of things to come. Most theologians agree that many events and phenomena observed in the Old Testament are foreshadowings and typologies of things we read in the New Testament. For example, it is generally agreed in Christian circles that the Passover described in Exodus 12 is a typology of the crucifixion of Christ and redemption through His shed blood as is described in the New Testament (Exodus 12). We see the same typology in Genesis 22 where God told Abraham to offer his only son, Isaac, as a sacrifice unto Him. This, clearly, is a foreshadowing of God, the Father, offering Jesus, the Son, as a sacrifice for our sins (Genesis 22).

The unique and unusual way in which God used language through Moses and Aaron literally changed the world and foreshadowed the gift of tongues and the gift of interpretation of tongues as seen in I Corinthians 14. God gave His message to Moses, who then gave it to Aaron, who then gave it to the people. This is exactly how God uses the gift of tongues and the gift of interpretation of tongues. He gives a message in tongues to the body of believers and someone with the gift of interpretation then gives its meaning to the people.

As in the days of Moses and Aaron, many Christians today are distant from God and have not developed the level of intimacy necessary to discern the voice of God when He speaks. It is God's desire to have intimate conversation with us. He has many ways of achieving this. He frequently uses others to speak to us in a variety of ways. He may speak to us through His word, a minister, a family member, friend, book, song, or movie. Why is tongues any different? When God speaks, regardless of the method or vehicle He chooses, it is supernatural and reveals His glory.

At Babel, God confused language to bring disunity among His people to protect them from themselves. At Pentecost, God initiated another great change in the direction and course of humanity using language, but this time it was to reunite His people.

Unity in Tongues

Tongues produce God's unity among His people not because everyone understands the prayer languages, but precisely because they do not. The languages are different but the experience is the same. Just as in childbirth, each woman gives birth to a uniquely different child, but each share the same experience, that is, childbirth. Put a group of mothers in the same room and see what happens. They can be from different races, socio-economic, education, ethnic, and cultural backgrounds. Nevertheless, as soon as the conversation turns to childbirth, an instant bond of understanding unites them.

Recipients of Spirit baptism know they have been touched by the living God because tongues are supernatural (not created by humans), and, therefore, they share a common life-changing experience. It is this shared experience that promotes unity whether the language is understood or not.

Language is what separates the people of the earth. It is fitting that God would use language to reunite and bind people to each other and to Him. Tongues are manifested instantly upon receiving the infilling of the Holy Spirit. Only God can cause us to be instantly bilingual. It is beyond man's ability. Hence the supernatural nature of tongues.

Some would argue that Jesus' life, death, and resurrection is what changed humankind. I would, in no way, disagree with that contention. However, there was no Christian church until Pentecost. The disciples had done very little on their own to spread the gospel until Pentecost. It was only after they received the baptism in the Holy Spirit that they went to the utter most parts of the earth and planted churches. Granted, it was not tongues per se that changed the world, but it was one sign that God had done something supernatural in these believers. It was the power resulting from this supernatural experience accompanied by this unique use of language that changed things through the establishment of the Christian church.

Opponents of Spirit baptism with initial evidence of speaking in tongues offer several arguments against this experience. I would be remiss if I did not respond to some of these because it is important to consider both sides of this issue.

Spirit Baptism without Tongues

Some believe it is possible to receive the baptism in the Holy Spirit without the initial evidence of tongues. I suppose anything is possible given God is sovereign and can do anything

He desires. It appears highly unlikely, however, as there is no scriptural support for that contention. On the contrary, there is a clear pattern established in the book of Acts that shows a consistent linkage between Spirit baptism and tongues. In every instance in Acts where people received Spirit baptism, they spoke in tongues (Acts 2:4; 10:44-47; 11:15-17; 19:6). In two other instances, it does not say specifically that they spoke in tongues, but it is strongly implied. The first was when Peter and John traveled to Samaria and began laying hands on people and praying they would receive the infilling of the Spirit.

Acts does not say specifically that when these believers received the Holy Spirit they prayed in tongues, but notice what happened. Simon, a new convert to Christ, observed Peter and John praying for people: "And when Simon saw that through the laying on of hands the Holy Spirit was given, he offered them money, saying, 'Give me also this power, that on whomsoever I lay my hands, he may receive the Holy Spirit'" (Acts 8:18-19). Simon *saw* something happening that impressed him enough to pay money for the same power. What did he see? Can you see the Spirit? No, but you can see an external manifestation of Him. Since the nexus of Spirit baptism and tongues was clearly established by that time, it is reasonable to infer that Simon *saw* people speaking in tongues. He knew something supernatural was occurring, which is exactly the purpose of tongues.

The second instance of tongues being implied is when Paul received the infilling of the Spirit. It does not say that he spoke in tongues at that moment but Paul later wrote, "I thank God, I speak with tongues more than you all" (I Corinthians 14:18).

Holy Spirit: Agent of Change

It is not unreasonable to conclude that he spoke in tongues when he received Spirit baptism since everyone else did, and he certainly taught on it extensively.

In the early part of the last century, the school of thought that not everyone speaks in tongues when they are filled with the Holy Spirit emanates from the early work of R.A. Torrey.[15] Torrey used the twelfth chapter of First Corinthians to support his argument: "Are all apostles? Are all prophets? Are all teachers? Are all workers of miracles? Have all the gifts of healing? Do all speak with tongues? Do all interpret?" (I Corinthians 12:29-30).

Torrey stated that while all in the Corinthian church were baptized in the Holy Spirit, at least some did not speak in tongues. He concluded: "So I saw that the teaching that speaking with tongues was the inevitable and invariable result of being baptized with the Holy Spirit, and that anyone who had not spoken with tongues had not been baptized with the Holy Spirit, was utterly unscriptural and anti-scriptural."[16]

Torrey admitted that he had never seen anyone speak with tongues and wrote, "I wondered if this gift was not confined to the apostolic age."[17] Although Torrey had many wonderful things to say about the baptism in the Holy Spirit, I believe he was wrong in his understanding and interpretation of this particular aspect of Spirit baptism.

Torrey reasoned syllogistically in this way: Major premise: All tongues observed in the Bible have the same purpose and

---

15 R.A. Torrey, *The Holy Spirit: Who He is and What He Does* (1927, Reprint, Shreveport, LA: Glimpses of Glory, 1997).
16 Ibid.
17 Ibid.

function. Minor premise: Not all have the gift of tongues or gift of interpretation. Conclusion: Therefore, not all have to speak in tongues to be baptized in the Holy Spirit. This sounds logical but, if even one of the premises is not factually true, then it follows that the conclusion will be false also. For example:

Major premise: God is love.

Minor premise: Love is blind.

Conclusion: God is blind.

Well-meaning Christians have cloaked scriptural truth in error, which leads to distorted conclusions, which, then, deprives believers of their rightful inheritance in the Spirit. Torrey's major premise is a universal affirmative. That is, all tongues are the same as that discussed in I Corinthians 12 and 14. Herein exists the error. He assumed that the tongues discussed by Paul in I Corinthians 12 and 14 are exactly the same in purpose and function as those observed in Acts 2:4, 10:44-47, 11:15-17, and 19:6. The whole context of Paul's discussion in I Corinthians 12 and 14 is about the gifts of the Holy Spirit, which are for the edification of the Church. As with all universal generalizations, all I have to do is find one exception to disprove it. Tongues seen in the book of Acts are devotional tongues and have a different purpose upon which I will elaborate later in this chapter. Torrey missed the distinction between the gift of tongues and devotional tongues.

Why Tongues?

Many people have asked me "When I receive the baptism in the Holy Spirit, do I have to speak in tongues?" This question reflects an underlying prejudice and ignorance of what tongues are all about. My answer is usually, "No, you don't have to speak in tongues. God will not force you to do anything, but when you are baptized in the Spirit, He will give you a prayer language (tongues). What you do with it is up to you. You are in control of it. But I can assure you that when you receive it, you will want to exercise it because it feels so good when you do."

As cited above in Acts, every time someone was baptized in the Holy Spirit, they spoke in tongues. This was consistent. Why do Christians have such a problem with it? People ask "Why tongues?" That is like asking "Why miracles?" God does things in certain ways to reveal His glory and validate His existence. Jesus gave tangible proof of His resurrection by actually appearing to His disciples: "And He said to them, 'Why are you troubled, and why do doubts arise in your hearts? See My hands and My feet, that it is I Myself; touch Me and see, for a spirit does not have flesh and bones as you see that I have'" (Luke 24:38-39). Merely hearing that Jesus was raised from the dead did not constitute proof of that supernatural act. Jesus gave them tangible, observable evidence of the miracle of resurrection by physically appearing to them. The purpose of signs, wonders, and miracles is to give tangible, observable proof of His existence and deity. Merely saying that you have been filled with the Holy Spirit does not constitute proof. God gave us the sign of tongues to prove that something supernatural has occurred.

In order to understand the experience of tongues, let's look at a testing process. Josh McDowell, author and apologist, points out that there should be an objective reality that supports a subjective experience. He notes that two tests that can be applied to subjective experience to determine its validity and truth: "First, what is the objective reality for the subjective experience and second, how many other people have had the same subjective experience from being related to the objective reality?"[18] The objective reality of a salvation experience is the person of Jesus Christ and his resurrection. The answer to the second question is that millions of people have had their lives transformed by salvation.

Let us apply these same tests to Spirit baptism. First, the objective reality for the subjective experience of Spirit baptism is the person of the Holy Spirit who made Himself physically known in history by manifesting Himself in an observable way at Pentecost and subsequently several times, which is historically recorded in Scripture. The subjective experience (Spirit baptism) resulting from this objective reality is tongues and accelerated transformation. The Spirit gives utterance (tongues) to our spirit, which validates His existence and our subjective experience.

If the Holy Spirit cannot be seen, then how do we know for certain that we have been filled by Him or that anyone else has been filled? Some may say that it is determined by how we feel at that moment. However, feelings alone are temporal and can be misleading based on circumstances. The Holy Spirit can come upon us and we will feel something unique but "upon"

---

18 Josh McDowell, *Evidence That Demands a Verdict*, vol. 1, (San Bernardino, CA: Here's Life Publishers, 1986).

is not the same as "within." "Upon" is temporary; "within" is permanent. I have spoken to many believers who received prayer for the baptism in the Holy Spirit but did not speak in tongues and felt no differently afterward. They were told that they had received the infilling of the Spirit simply because they had been prayed for although there was no observable evidence for it.

The purpose of prayer is to get a tangible, observable answer as Jesus said: "If you ask Me anything in My name, I will do it" (John 14:14). If we ask for something (prayer), we can know that it has been done because He gives us tangible proof in the answer. For example, let us say you have a dire need for $87.37 to pay your utility bill and, so, you decide to pray and ask the Lord for it. Then, one hour later, someone shows up at your door with a check for the exact amount, $87.37. You would probably rejoice and thank God for answering your prayer. Why? Because you have tangible, observable proof ($87.37) that your prayer was answered. If, on the other hand, you never received the money and your lights were cut off, then you might conclude that your prayer had not been answered. When prayers for specific things are answered we, or others, can see tangible, observable change occur. Otherwise, how would we know that God had done something supernatural? If I pray for someone to be healed, but he remains gravely ill and, perhaps, even dies, should I adamantly maintain that he was healed because I prayed for him even though there was no objective evidence for this healing? If not, then why would we expect the same thing with Spirit baptism? Tongues are the initial evidence of the Holy Spirit's objective reality. It is the tangible, observable answer to prayer for the baptism in the Holy Spirit.

The answer to the second test of subjective experience is that millions of Christians across denominations from all walks of life have received the baptism in the Holy Spirit with evidence of speaking in tongues and a transformed Christian life. Multitudes of Spirit-filled Christians report remarkably similar experiences after receiving Spirit baptism, as we will see later in this book. No longer can opponents chalk it up to mindless babbling of uneducated, ignorant, emotionally disturbed holy-rollers. God is continually restoring His fundamental truths to his body of believers.

Interpretation of Scripture

Some argue that the Scriptures regarding Spirit baptism have been misinterpreted. Many want to theologically debate the *true* meaning of each and every Greek word. There is an old saying: "Theology is at the mercy of personal experience." Personal experience is what validates the truth of Scripture. If, after reading the Scriptures pertaining to salvation, we do exactly what they instruct, we will receive salvation, which, consequently, begins to change us. Without acting on the Scriptures, we will have no personal experience with Christ, which results in no change in us. Moreover, the Scriptures will have no tangency and relevance to us. It is the subjective experience, which results from believing and acting on the Scriptures that, in turn, validate the truth of them.

Therefore, if millions have read the verses relative to Spirit baptism and then received it with observable evidence, (tongues) then that, in and of itself, validates that specific interpretation of those Scriptures: "Wisdom is vindicated by her results" (Matthew 11:19). When truth is conjoined with experience, all doubt is erased.

The problem with contemporary Christianity is that it uses propositional logic and exegetical considerations alone to persuade people that Jesus is the Messiah. They present only half of the equation. In fact, they often denigrate the other half, subjective experience. However, this other half validates the first half. The modern church operates on the premise that people should believe what the Bible says simply because the church says it is true. The current generation, on the other hand, replies, "That's not enough. Prove it!" Hundreds of viewpoints in the world bombard potential believers, which results in mass confusion, doubt, and cynicism. They simply do not know what to believe. One belief system sounds as good as the next. The potential believers hunger for some certainty in life. When they have a truth-validating subjective spiritual experience such as provided by Spirit baptism, all arguments about what is correct or incorrect are over. They now know. Doctrinal debate and exegetical nitpicking are vaporized. They now have tangible, observable, experiential evidence of the reality of God. Once that happens, no theologian, pastor, priest, or professor can convince them that what they experienced and continue to experience is false or just a figment of their imagination.

Controversy over Tongues: Known Languages

Some critics maintain that the tongues observed at Pentecost were simply known, understandable languages that people understood and that they had a specific, limited purpose. This does not account for the need for someone with the gift of interpretation as expounded by Paul in I Corinthians 13-14. The Corinthians spoke in tongues in church, but no one understood, thus, the need for interpretation. If the only purpose of tongues was to speak in known languages, why did no one in the Corinthian church understand any of the languages? God is not the author of confusion. If tongues had a limited purpose (i.e., day of Pentecost), why do they appear again several times in different places much later after Pentecost? Why would Paul discuss tongues at such great length if they were just a passing phase that God used just once at Pentecost as an attention getter and He never intended to use them again? To say that tongues was just for Pentecost, or even just for the apostolic age, and that tongues has a limited purpose is to stretch dispensationalism to an illogical extreme. Just as the Ten Commandments were not just relevant for Moses' generation alone, the baptism in the Holy Spirit with evidence of speaking in tongues is just as relevant today as it was in the first century church.

Ecstatic Utterance

It is maintained by some that the tongues operating in the Corinthian church (I Corinthians 12-14), as well as those observed today, are not the same as those observed on

Pentecost. These tongues are merely "ecstatic utterance," which was a common practice in the pagan religions of the day. That is, the Corinthians were engaging in pagan worship practices (i.e. demonic). As Paul clearly had the gift of discerning of spirits, he most certainly would have rebuked the demon behind this practice and commanded it to leave. We see that he did this very thing in Acts 16:16. A slave girl with a spirit of divination kept following Paul and Luke around harassing them by crying out that they were God's servants. Finally, Paul got enough of it, turned to the girl, rebuked the demon, and commanded it to come out of her. The demon left her immediately, much to the dismay of her masters who were making a profit from her fortune telling. No, Paul did not perceive the tongues in the Corinthian church to be demonic. His comments were directed at the proper order and usage of this particular gift in the church.

To be sure, there have always been pagan counterfeits of biblical phenomena. However, equating biblical tongues with pagan ecstatic utterances is simply not supported by biblical facts or personal experience. A classic example is blood sacrifice. God commanded the Hebrews through Moses to offer up blood sacrifices for atonement for sin. This biblical practice is not disputed by any of the critics of biblical glossolalia (tongues). Yet, it is a widely established archaeological and historical fact that many pagan cultures also engaged in blood sacrifices. Does this, then, mean that the Hebraic blood sacrifice unto God was really a pagan practice and not a commandment from the one, true, living God? Similarity and simultaneity of conduct does not mean identical motive and purpose. Or, in the words of scientists, "Correlation does not equal causation."

According to the critics, then, the Corinthians were all out of control of their emotions, if not their minds too, and were, in essence, babbling incoherently in meaningless gibberish. The alternative explanations of what was going on at Corinth is that it was either

1. Demonic or
2. Mental illness (madness)

Paul did not address the root and nature of the tongues at Corinth. Therefore, it can be readily concluded that he considered it to be of God, the more reasonable explanation. He did not accuse them of being demon-possessed, nor did he impute mental illness to them because they were out of control and behaving irrationally. Rather, Paul's comments were directed at the manner in which this gift was being exercised in the church.

"Ecstatic utterance" implies that tongues are a human creation and merely a manifestation of people who have lost control of their minds, emotions, and senses. That is, these people are engaging in neolalia. The APA Dictionary of Psychology defines neologism as "a word made up by an individual. Neologisms, whose origins and meanings are usually nonsensical and unrecognizable (e.g., 'klipno' for watch), are typically associated with Aphasia or Schizophrenia."[19] From the same source, "eulogistic jargon" is defined as "unintelligible

---

19 Gary R. VandenBos, ed., *APA Dictionary of Psychology*, (Washington, D.C.: American Psychological Association, 2007), 616.

speech containing a mixture of inappropriately combined words and bizarre expressions coined by the speaker."[20]

In the medical and psychology professions, neologistic jargon is considered a sign of severe mental illness in an individual. If the tongues that Paul observed at Corinth was nothing but neologistic jargon, then the entire Corinthian church was, no doubt, psychotic. If so, Paul would surely have addressed this issue. Instead, Paul referred to them quite differently: "...To the church of God which is at Corinth, to those who have been sanctified in Christ Jesus, saints by calling, with all who in every place call upon the name of our Lord Jesus Christ, their Lord and ours...Grace to you and peace from God our Father and the Lord Jesus Christ...I thank my God always concerning you, for the grace of God which was given to you in Christ Jesus that in everything you were enriched in Him, in *all speech* and all knowledge" (I Corinthians 1:2-5, my emphasis).

This does not sound like Paul is addressing a group of mentally deranged people, does it? In fact, notably, he refers to their speech and describes it as being enriched in Christ Jesus. "All speech" obviously would include tongues. Apparently, Paul did not see a problem with tongues in general but only the manner in which the specific gift of tongues was operating in the Corinthian church. Some argue that, as mentioned above, Corinthian tongues were not the gift of tongues as seen on Pentecost but merely ecstatic utterances.

However, note in verse 7 Paul said: "...so that you are not lacking in any gift, awaiting eagerly the revelation of our Lord

---

20 Ibid., 616.

Jesus Christ" (I Corinthians 1). It is easy to conclude that all the gifts of the Spirit, as outlined in I Corinthians 12, were extant at Corinth, including the gift of tongues.

The Gift of Tongues and Devotional Tongues

When reading chapter 14 of I Corinthians in its entirety, we see that Paul was not admonishing the Corinthians for speaking in tongues, accusing them of being mentally disturbed or of being demon-possessed. Instead, the main theme in this chapter is the proper, orderly use of this gift as well as the gift of prophecy. Paul clearly instructed the Corinthians that, for the gift of tongues to achieve its purpose in the church, i.e., edification, it must be used in combination with the gift of interpretation of tongues. In the church these gifts are not to operate separately and, when operating in concert with each other, are equal to prophecy (I Corinthians 14:5).

In elucidating the proper usage of this gift, Paul also made a clear distinction between the gift of tongues and devotional tongues that are evidence of the infilling of the Spirit (I Corinthians 14:7-19).

Paul explained that when we pray or sing in tongues our spirits pray, but our minds are unfruitful (meaning we do not understand). Note that tongues come from our spirit as the Holy Spirit gives utterance. It does not come from or through our minds as would be the case if it were ecstatic utterance. Paul explained in verse 15 that we can pray with our spirit (i.e., tongues) and with the mind (i.e., our native language). He was referring to devotional tongues in that he referred to the act of praying not the act of giving a message in tongues in the church. Praying in the spirit is obviously quite possible and to be desired because it is one way of "giving of thanks" (v. 16). Paul condoned this form of tongues (i.e., devotional tongues) in verse 17 because he said that in doing so we *give thanks well enough*. But if done in the church it should be accompanied by interpretation so that all can be blessed, not just the individual praying in tongues.

Paul further distinguished the two forms of tongues by explaining the difference in their purposes. He stated in verse 4 that when one speaks in a tongue one is edified.

The purpose, then, of devotional tongues is to build up, strengthen, establish, and bring spiritual enlightenment to the individual. The purpose of the gift of tongues is to edify the body of Christ in the church.

Another distinction between devotional tongues and the gift of tongues is the direction in which it is flowing. Paul indicated the direction for devotional tongues: "For one who speaks in a tongue does not speak to men, but to God; for no one understands, but in his Spirit he speaks mysteries" (I Corinthians 14:4).

Paul gave equal importance to prophecy and tongues and interpretation (v. 5). The direction of prophecy was from God to humankind (v. 3). Therefore, it is reasonable to conclude that the direction of flow is also the same in the gift of tongues, i.e., from God to Christians for the edification of the church. In other words, in devotional tongues, a Christian speaks to God but in the gift of tongues, God speaks to a Christian.

Further support for this distinction between the two forms of tongues is made in verses 18-19 of I Corinthians 14: "I thank God, I speak in tongues more than you all. *However, in the church* I desire to speak five words with my mind, that I may instruct others also, rather than ten thousand words in a tongue" (my emphasis).

Paul clearly indicated that tongues can occur both outside of the church (devotional tongues) and inside the church (gift of tongues). He acknowledged that he loved speaking in tongues, but the point is in verse 19 when he wrote, "*However, in the church...*" He exhorted us to only speak in tongues in the church if someone has the gift of interpretation. Paul obviously did both—outside and inside the church.

If there was no difference between devotional tongues and the gift of tongues—i.e., there was only one purpose and function of all tongues, i.e., the gift—then why would Paul pray in the spirit (tongues) outside of church? Certainly, the church would not be edified. What would be the point if there was only one purpose of tongues?

In verse 4, Paul stated that "one who speaks in a tongue edifies himself." To be edified is a good thing as explained above. Paul clearly was speaking about the act of praying in tongues as a solitary act because no one was being edified but the person praying. If devotional tongues were, as some critics assert, merely "ecstatic utterances," or gibberish, it is doubtful that Paul would consider it edifying, and thank God that he prayed in tongues more than everyone else did.

Paul differentiated between the two forms by stating that one could exercise tongues in prayer as a solitary experience for one's own edification (v. 4) without an interpreter. For others to benefit, however, one should have the gift of interpretation. Moreover, the gift of interpretation is not merely having a prior knowledge and familiarity with a recognized tongue so that one can translate it. If so, it would not qualify as a supernatural gift of the Holy Spirit. It would simply fall in the category of knowledge. It is not just the ability to understand a known language as on the day of Pentecost. It is also the ability to understand the meaning of a message in an unknown tongue. Hence, the supernatural quality of it. It is of God, not of humans.

Some critics conclude that when Paul wished that all spoke in tongues in verse 5, he surely meant languages rather than "ecstatic utterances." We would agree, as we have already stated, that the tongues Paul referred to were not "ecstatic utterances." However, the tongues in verse 5 does refer to a different form of tongues, i.e., devotional tongues, because he is differentiating between tongues used for personal edification and tongues used for corporate edification. It may be the same language in both instances but for different purposes. Just as our native language is used for different purposes in different situations but is the same language, so it is with spiritual tongues.

This is further supported by what is described in Acts 10:44-47 and 19:6. Believers received Spirit baptism and began praying in tongues. Neither Peter nor Paul attempted to dissuade or stop them from speaking in tongues simply because no interpretation was given. This would seem inconsistent with Paul's lengthy instruction to the Corinthian church on the proper usage of the gift of tongues. As there are no inconsistencies in Holy Scripture, there must be another reason why Peter and Paul made no objections to what they observed. The explanation is simple. They knew the difference between "devotional" tongues and the "gift" of tongues.

Some contend that in verse 4 Paul is again referring to "ecstatic utterances." Based on the definitions offered above, it is incomprehensible that gibberish would be edifying to an individual. If, indeed, this form of self-edification was a manifestation of pride, as some suggest, then why did Paul not correct them for it? Why, in verse 5, would he say: "Now I wish that you all spoke in tongues." If it were nothing more than the senseless babblings of mentally disturbed people, why would he encourage people to speak in tongues?

Order of Importance

R.A. Torrey, among others, assumed that the gifts of the Holy Spirit were always listed in the order of their relative importance. In referring to I Corinthians 12:8-10, Torrey wrote, "...and I also discovered that speaking with tongues was way down at the bottom of the list."[21] The implication here is that tongues are the least of the gifts of the Holy Spirit because it was mentioned last. Therefore, tongues were unimportant. As mentioned earlier, if any of the premises can be proven wrong, then the conclusions are also wrong.

---

21 Torrey, *The Holy Spirit*, 98.

The basic premise that last equates with least is disputed by I Corinthians 13: 1-2 where tongues are listed first and I Corinthians 13:8 where it is listed second. The rule that last equals least only holds up if there is consistency in the order of listing of the various charismas. Moreover, the premise that, because it is least, it is unimportant is contrary to Scripture and logical reasoning: "Every good thing bestowed and every gift is from above, coming down from the Father of lights, with whom there is no variation or shifting shadow" (James 1:17).

I Corinthians 12:14-18 further elucidates the equal importance of the members of the body. The gifts are equal in importance but different in function and specific purpose. The general purpose of all the gifts is edification of the body of Christ.

To imply that tongues are unimportant is to say that something that God is doing is unimportant. This defies rational thought and everything that we know about God. To attribute greater superiority to one gift of the spirit vis-à-vis another is a theological splitting of hairs. It would be like saying that the miraculous healing of a blind man is greater than the healing of a deaf-mute. Tell that to the deal-mute who, because of the gift of miracles, can suddenly clearly hear the voice of his child for the first time.

Ervin cogently points out that the subordination of one gift to another does not imply inferiority.[22] Even if the theological premise is true (which it is not) that tongues are the least of

---

22 Howard M. Ervin, *Spirit Baptism: A Biblical Investigation*, (Peabody, Mass.: Hendrickson Publishers, 1987).

the gifts, so what? Being valued as least of the gifts does not imply that it is nonexistent today or unimportant. The least of something from God is still infinitely greater than anything of this world. If the choice is between the least of God or the best of this world, then give me all of the least of God that I can get!

Paul stated in I Corinthians 15:9 that he is the *least* of the apostles. Are we to conclude, then, that Paul was an unimportant apostle, if there even could be such a thing?

In his own words, Paul said: "But by the grace of God I am what I am, and His grace toward me did not prove vain; but I labored even more than all of them, yet not I, but the grace of God with me" (I Corinthians 15:10).

Tongues as Judgment

Opponents of tongues offer Isaiah 28:11-12 as an explanation for what occurred at Pentecost in Acts 2: "Indeed, He will speak to this people through stammering lips and a foreign tongue, He who said to them, 'Here is rest, give rest to the weary,' and, 'Here is repose,' but they would not listen." The argument is that tongues were a sign of judgment upon God's people, which was to come specifically from Assyria. The foreign language would be Assyrian, which would be spoken on the streets of Jerusalem. A correlation is drawn between this passage and Paul citing it in his discourse on tongues in I Corinthians 14. The tongues observed at Pentecost were supposedly a sign of the judgment that was to come, that is, that Jerusalem would be occupied by Romans whose language would not be understood without an interpreter. It is argued that the Jews at Pentecost (Acts 2) were familiar with the Law and the Prophets and, therefore, would understand immediately what they were seeing (tongues) in light of Isaiah 28:11-12. They would know that the judgment of God was upon them.

Several problems exist with these interpretations. First, Isaiah prophesied about a future foreign occupation of Jerusalem. At the time of Pentecost, Jerusalem had already been occupied by Romans for some time. Roman soldiers crucified Jesus. If the tongues observed in Acts 2 were a sign of coming judgment (i.e., foreign occupation) as seen in Isaiah 28:11-12, then they appeared a bit late.

Second, the tongues spoken on the day of Pentecost were not just of the foreign occupiers: "And how is it that we each hear them in our own language to which we were born? Parthians and Medes and Elamites, and residents of Mesopotamia, Judea and Cappodocia, Poutus and Asia Phrygia and Pamphylia, Egypt and the districts of Libya around Cyrene, and visitors from Rome, both Jews and proselytes, Cretans and Arabs—we hear them in our own tongues speaking of the mighty deeds of God" (Acts 2:8-11).

If the judgment was foreign occupation by Romans, then why all the other languages from regions that did not and never have occupied Jerusalem? It is also clear from the above passage that people in the Middle East were multilingual then, as they are now, and certainly would have already understood Latin, the language of their occupiers.

Third, the similarity between Isaiah 28 and Acts 2 is not so much in the signs but rather in the response of the people to both. The unbelievers during Isaiah's time rejected him as well as the prophesied tongues sign because their hearts were hardened. Similarly, at Pentecost many hardened their hearts: "But others were mocking and saying, 'They are full of sweet wine'" (Acts 2:13).

Fourth, the contention that the Jews at Pentecost would have discerned immediately that the observed tongues meant judgment breaks down when we note their reaction in Acts 2:12: "And they all continued in amazement and great perplexity, saying to one another, 'What does this mean?'" It sounds like they did not have a clue what was happening. Hence, the need for Peter to get up and quote the prophet Joel in order to explain this supernatural phenomenon. Notice that Peter did not quote Isaiah 28. Paul's citation of Isaiah was in the context of teaching the Corinthians the proper usage of the gift of tongues. He was pointing out that tongues without interpretation would be perceived by unbelievers as crazy and thus harden their hearts just as in Isaiah's time (Isaiah 28:11-12).

Fifth, nowhere in the New Testament do we see Peter, Paul, or anyone else for that matter, refer to tongues as judgment. If it was a sign of judgment, then surely those manifesting tongues would have given messages of God's judgment and wrath, such as in Revelation 14:10, 19; Revelation 15:1, 7; and Revelation 16:19. When God pronounces judgment and wrath upon a people, He is very explicit, clear, and definite, as we see throughout the Bible. God leaves nothing to guesswork or subjective interpretation.

Paul referred to tongues as a sign for unbelievers. However, what kind of sign? A sign that the kingdom of God is here—that God is real and present! It is also a sign that the third person in the Trinity is manifesting His presence and operation on the earth just as Jesus prophesied. This verified and established Jesus' credibility in all things and as Messiah.

A sign is often used to bring people to repentance, to verify God's instructions, and to bring deliverance, refreshing, and rest. The sign itself is not necessarily the judgment. Throughout the Bible before God brought judgment upon the earth, He always poured out His grace first and gave people an opportunity to repent and escape His wrath, usually by providing a sign to draw them into His kingdom. The people of Nineveh received and accepted the sign of Jonah. They repented and God withheld His judgment. In the New Testament, the sign was John the Baptist, Jesus, and Spirit baptism with evidence of speaking in tongues.

In Isaiah 28:11-12 we see that tongues itself is not described as judgment or even as a sign of pending judgment but, rather, is described as a *rest* to the weary and as the *refreshing*. The last part of verse 12 says: "...but they would not listen." It is not the sign that brings judgment but rather the rejection of the sign. That is, humans rejected the goodness of God (sign) and, in doing so, they rejected God Himself. Then God pronounced judgment upon them (Isaiah 28:15-17).

In every instance where tongues are mentioned in the Bible, it is associated with something positive, good and beneficial: refreshing and rest (Isaiah 28:11-12), edification of the individual (I Corinthians 14:4), edification of the church (I Corinthians 14:12), and giving of thanks (I Corinthians 14:16-17). In Mark 16:17-18 we see it juxtaposed with several benefits of being a believer: "And these signs will accompany those who have believed: in My name they will cast out demons, they will speak with new tongues; they will pick up serpents, and if they drink any deadly poison, it shall not hurt them; they will lay hands on the sick, and they will recover."

Speaking in tongues is mentioned in the same breath as deliverance, divine protection, and healing the sick. If it was meant for judgment or a sign of coming judgment, why is it associated with these wonderful signs of God's mercy, love, and protection? And why would this sign accompany *all* those who believe in Jesus Christ? Typically, judgment was pronounced and declared through a prophet. Not all believers are prophets.

Signs often signify the goodness of God and further argue against the idea of tongues as judgment. For example: "And this will be a sign for you: you will find a baby wrapped in cloths, and lying in a manger" (Luke 2:12). Jesus, himself, was and is a sign of mercy and salvation to a sinful world. The purpose of signs is shown again in Hebrews 2:4: "God also bearing witness with them, both in signs and wonders and by various miracles and by gifts of the Holy Spirit according to His own will." Signs and wonders are used to confirm the deity of Jesus Christ and salvation through Him and Him alone.

We know that the day of Pentecost occurred fifty days after Easter (Christ's resurrection). Certain numbers have special significance in God's kingdom. The number fifty is the number of jubilee or deliverance. E.W. Bullinger, expert on biblical numerics, states that it points to deliverance and rest as "…the result of the perfect consummation of time."[23] Spirit baptism with tongues represented a new move of God. What is this "perfect consummation of time"? It is officially the end of the old order and the beginning of the new order (the Church). This new order brought deliverance from sin, rejoicing, and rest in God. This is precisely what the number fifty signifies. It is no accident that Jesus baptized His believers in the Holy Spirit on this particular day. The day itself was a sign to the people.

Tongues were the initial evidence and external manifestation of this new order under God. It was not, itself, intended to be a sign of judgment and wrath. Instead, it clearly was and is a sign of God's goodness, mercy, love, and intimacy. Judgment only comes when people reject the goodness of God. The church did not officially begin until Pentecost. It was only then that the apostles began to evangelize the entirely known world and bring large numbers into the Church. As with all major moves of God, He started this one with a supernatural sign— tongues. As a sign to unbelievers, it brought three thousand people into God's kingdom that day. The people heard the disciples glorifying God in tongues (Acts 2:11). They did not hear decrees of judgment or wrath. Moreover, I Corinthians 14:15 refers to one singing in tongues. There is no mention anywhere in Scripture that God pronounced judgment in the form of singing. Singing is always associated with praise and worship of God, not judgment.

---

23 E.W. Bullinger, *Number in Scripture*, (Grand Rapids, MI.: Kregel Publications, 1984).

In Acts 2 and Acts 10:44-46, those speaking in tongues were magnifying and glorifying God and giving thanks well to Him. We do not see any pronouncement of judgment against the Jews of that time. Rather, God attempted to draw them unto Himself by providing that *rest* and *refreshing* to them in a supernatural way that could not be mistaken for the creation of man.

If tongues are indeed a sign of judgment upon a perverse generation, then those who reject this supernatural phenomenon today would do well to heed their own words. For, out of their own mouths, they bring judgment upon themselves for rejecting the goodness of God.

Tongues No Longer Exist

Some critics argue that all of the sign gifts, including tongues, were limited to the apostles and ceased with the apostolic age. They use as proof text I Corinthians 13:8: "Love never fails; but if there are gifts of prophecy, they will be done away; if there are tongues, they will cease; if there is knowledge, it will be done away." Clearly, the text states that these three gifts will cease to exist but no specific deadline is indicated, only that they will end sometime in the future. To solve this obvious problem with their logic, the opponents offer I Corinthians 13:9-10 in an attempt to prove their basic premise: "For we know in part, and we prophesy in part; but when the perfect comes, the partial will be done away." Verse 10 gives us a clue as to when exactly the gifts listed in verse 8 will end. They will cease when "the perfect comes." The problem is in how the critics define "the perfect." In an effort to support their exegetical bias against "tongues," they define it as the completed canon of Scripture. This would be amusing if it were not so erroneous, misleading and, therefore, dangerous to the corporate body of Christ. Let us look at the full context of these Scriptures. In verse 12 Paul wrote: "For now we see in a mirror dimly, but then face to face; now I know in part, but then I shall know fully just as I also have been fully known" (I Corinthians 13:1-12).

To illustrate the convoluted logic that "the perfect" is the completed canon, Ervin paraphrases verse 12 thusly: "...Now, wrote Paul, I know in part; but then (when the canon of the New Testament is completed) shall I know fully even as also I was fully known."[24] Ervin points out that Paul was martyred long before the New Testament and, therefore, never saw the completed canon.

A more logical and reasonable definition of "that which is perfect" is the second coming of the Lord Jesus Christ. "Perfect" refers to the Lord Himself. When Paul said he sees in a mirror dimly, he was referring to his incomplete understanding, knowledge, and intimacy with Jesus. The term "face to face" obviously refers to a person-to-person relationship, not "person to canon." In the last part of this verse: "...then I shall know fully just as I also have been fully known" (I Corinthians 13:1-12). Paul was again referring to the intimacy that results from two people fully knowing one another. He intimated the person of Jesus Christ, not the canon of Scripture. As stated above, Paul

---

24 Ervin, *Spirit Baptism*, 176.

was dead before the canon was completed and, therefore, could not possibly know it fully. Moreover, how could Paul be fully known by the canon? A thing does not "know" a person.

As I have shown, the church age began with signs and wonders. There is no compelling, scriptural, logical, or experiential evidence that they ended with the apostolic age. For example, Peter declared: "And Peter said to them, 'Repent, and let each of you be baptized in the name of Jesus Christ for the forgiveness of your sins; and you shall receive the Gift of the Holy Spirit" (Acts 2:38).

I have already shown that the baptism in the Holy Spirit was accompanied by the sign of tongues. Peter goes on to inform us of exactly who can receive this sign: "For the promise is for you and your children, and for all who are far off, as many as the Lord our God shall call to Himself" (Acts 2:39). Does this sound as if it was restricted to only the apostles or just the apostolic age? "Children" and "as many as the Lord shall call" clearly indicates future generations. The Lord Himself said, as we have already seen, that tongues would accompany all those who believe (Mark 16:17-18). God made no limiting comments restricting these signs to the apostles or the apostolic age. Why would Paul teach extensively on the gifts of the Holy Spirit to the Church if they were restricted to the apostles? He was not teaching the apostles but rather the average believer.

Recall our earlier discussion in the previous chapter regarding syllogistic reasoning. If either the primary or the secondary premises are erroneous, then the conclusion is false. Their reasoning goes something like this:

Primary Premise:

Signs (tongues) ceased when "the perfect is come."

Secondary Premise:

"The perfect" is the completed canon of Scripture.

Conclusion:

Therefore, present-day tongues are *not* of God.

Both of these premises have been shown to be incorrect. Therefore, the likelihood that the conclusion is also incorrect is extremely high.

Some authors contend that Hebrews 2:3-4 proves that signs (tongues) are outdated: "...how shall we escape if we neglect so great a salvation? After it was at first spoken through the Lord, it was confirmed to us by those who heard, God also bearing witness with them, both by signs and wonders and by various miracles and by gifts of the Holy Spirit according to His own will." This passage references that God confirmed His word by signs and wonders, first through Jesus, and then through the apostles. It does not say that signs ceased. The Scriptures refer to what Jesus did in the past, but they do not imply that what He did then no longer exists currently. If that were true, there would be no salvation for any of us today. It is faulty logic to conclude that when the Bible describes events of the past, they no longer apply to us now. For example, the eleventh chapter of Hebrews describes the honor roll of faith. Just because all of these heroes of faith were from ancient times does not mean that faith has ceased to exist.

Tongues as a definitive sign of the infilling of the Holy Spirit continues to exist today and, as has been shown scripturally and logically, is extremely beneficial to those who receive.

Biblical Tongues Were Always Known Languages

Some critics maintain that biblical tongues observed at Pentecost in Acts 2 were known languages and were used to declare the gospel and bring people to salvation. I have no problem agreeing with that as far as it goes. However, the critics then stretch the text to fit their doctrinal belief system. They then say that this gift does not operate this way today and, therefore, present-day tongues are counterfeits. Their reasoning goes like this:

Primary Premise:
All biblical tongues were known languages.

Secondary Premise:
No one today claiming to speak in
tongues speaks in a known language.

Conclusion:
Therefore, present-day tongues are just
gibberish, i.e., an "ecstatic utterance."

This reasoning reflects a narrow understanding of tongues such as the difference between devotional tongues and the gift of tongues as has been clearly shown earlier in this chapter. It also reflects an inadequate, biased investigation of the phenomenon.

Like all universal affirmatives, all that needs to be done to disprove it is to find one exception to it. For example, if I say all dogs are black, all you need do is find one white one somewhere in the world to disprove my statement. Similarly, the above premises are rather easy to disprove.

As we know, the tongues observed on the day of Pentecost certainly were known languages. However, was this the only way that God used tongues in the New Testament? Let us see what Paul had to say about this aspect of this charisma: "For one who speaks in a tongue does not speak to men, but to God; for *no one* understands, but in his spirit he speaks mysteries" (I Corinthians 14, my emphasis). Paul described the act of praying in tongues (devotional). It appears self-evident that Paul was indicating that not all tongues are known, recognizable languages. Moreover, Paul clearly accepts this fact and does not make a big deal of it as modern-day critics attempt to do.

In describing the signs that will accompany all believers, Jesus said, "they will speak with new tongues..." (Mark 16:17-18). The word new comes from the Greek word *kainos* meaning new (especially in freshness).[25] The word tongues is from the Greek *glossa* meaning "the tongue;" by implication a language (specifically one naturally unacquired).[26] An easy inference to draw is that the tongues spoken by believers are, not only brand new to them, but also can be new to the listener as well. Thus, all tongues are not always recognizable languages known to all who are present. An unknown language always sounds

---

25 Spiro Zodhiates, ed., *Hebrew Greek Key Study Bible*, (Chattanooga, TN: AMG Publishers, 1984), 58.

26 Randy Hurst. "Christianity in China," *Today's Pentecostal Evangel*, April 5, 2009, 13.

foreign and, perhaps, even strange or bizarre to our ear, but our perception of it does not determine the factual truth that it is a language. Imagine that you are attending a prayer meeting where there are several individuals from different countries in attendance. Several may be moved by the Holy Spirit to pray aloud in their native tongues. One may speak the language of the state of Andre Pradesh in Southern India. One may speak Albanian; another may speak the clicking dialect of the Zulu tribe in Africa. I promise you that all of these languages will sound bizarre to you and, perhaps, even like gibberish. It makes no sense to you. Nevertheless, does that invalidate them as languages just because they are unknown to you?

Now, let us examine the secondary premise. Documented examples, all of which are too numerous to mention, of believers show them speaking in languages unknown to them but recognizable and known to others present at the time. An interesting account of an incident occurring in the early twentieth century in Northwest China was reported by W.W. Simpson who worked as a missionary in the area for many years. During a Bible study a Chinese cook, who was well known by Simpson, was suddenly filled with the Holy Spirit: "The man lay on the floor, speaking in tongues—first in an unknown language, then in a high form of classical Chinese understood by the Confucian scholars at the gathering. Finally, the man spoke clearly in English, though he had never spoken a word of it before."[27] Later, after returning to America, Simpson was

---

27 Ibid. Hurst
28 Ibid. Hurst

at a camp meeting where a woman received the baptism in the Holy Spirit and spoke in tongues. She did not understand what she was saying but Simpson recognized the language as that of Northwest China where he had ministered for many years. Moreover, the Spirit, through the woman, instructed Simpson to return to China to minister in the same region as he had before.[28]

John Sherrill, staff writer for *Guideposts* magazine, recounted an event reported by the Church Missionary Society of Great Britain.[29] A teenage girl in India began speaking in tongues. No one understood the language so they invited several friends to the prayer meetings in an attempt to identify it. Finally, someone recognized it as Arabic and was able to translate her prayers, which were for Christians in Libya, "…a country of which, as far as anyone knew, she had never heard."[30]

Reverend Kenneth E. Hagin reports several experiences where the gift of tongues was manifested in a known language.[31] For example, a pastor friend traveled to Mexico to bring supplies to a mission. While there, he witnessed an old Mexican woman receive the baptism in the Holy Spirit and speak in tongues. Interestingly, she spoke in fluent English! The pastor said, "At first when I heard the old woman speak in fluent English, I thought she knew the language. But then I learned that she had never been to school a day in her life! It was such a thrill to listen to her magnify, worship, and praise God in a language known to me but completely unknown to her."[32]

29 John L. Sherrill, *They Speak with Other Tongues*, (Reading, UK: Spire Books, 1965).
29 John L. Sherrill, *They Speak with Other Tongues*, (Reading, UK: Spire Books, 1965).
30 Ibid.
31 Hagin, Kenneth E., *Tongues: Beyond the Upper Room*, (Tulsa, OK: Kenneth Hagin Ministries, 2007).
32 Ibid., 247.

Reverend Hagin related a personal testimony in which he was preaching in a church in New Jersey. The pastor and his wife were former missionaries in China. During a service Hagin gave a message in tongues in a language unknown to him. The pastor and his wife recognized it as a dialect of Chinese from a region near where they had ministered.[33]

Several years ago, a gentleman acquaintance of mine began attending a full gospel church that believed in the baptism in the Holy Spirit with evidence of speaking in tongues. The subject of tongues came up in conversation, and he expressed his skepticism about the authenticity of what he observed at church. I outlined the scriptural foundation for Spirit baptism but he was not convinced. So, I simply asked him if he would be willing to ask the Lord to show him, one way or the other, if it was of Him. He agreed that he could do that. I saw him about a week later and could see that something was different about him. I greeted him and asked how he was doing.

He said, "You're never going to believe what happened. I asked the Lord, as you suggested, to show me if this tongues thing was the real deal or not."

"So did He?" I asked. My friend was about to burst at the seams.

"Big time!" he almost shouted.

"What happened?" I asked.

"I went to church that Sunday after I prayed that way. I was standing there during the worship service and there was an older lady standing next to me. She started praying softly aloud. It caught my attention. When she stopped, I leaned over and asked

---

33 Ibid., 248.

her where she had learned Latin. She said that she did not know Latin. I told her that she had just prayed in Latin but again she denied knowing it. I got more forceful with her and told her that I had been an alter boy in the Catholic Church for many years and that she had just prayed the Lord's Prayer in perfect Latin."

"What did she say?" I asked.

"She said that she had been asking God if her prayer language (tongues) was a known language. I asked her if that was her tongues language, and she said that she received it when she was baptized in the Holy Spirit but never knew what it was and God just showed her. Then, she started hugging and thanking me for identifying it for her."

"What did you do then?" I asked.

"Well, I was convinced by that time, so I went up to the altar when the pastor invited people up for prayer. I told him I wanted to receive the baptism in the Holy Spirit, so he laid hands on me and prayed and I received. Now I have my own prayer language. I do not know what language it is, but it is not Latin. Maybe He'll show me someday what it is like He did that lady at church."

"Do you still have any doubts about the authenticity of Spirit baptism with tongues?" I asked.

"Are you kidding?" he exclaimed. "This is the most real thing I have ever experienced in my life!"

Another life changed by the Holy Spirit.

Mark Rutland, President of Southwestern College of the Assemblies of God, shared a miraculous experience he had on a missionary trip to rural Mexico. He and his father-in-law, who was an unbeliever, traveled to a remote village deep in the mountains for Mark to preach the gospel. Unfortunately, their interpreter never showed up. Mark's Spanish was limited to three phonetic phrases: "God is love", "Jesus loves you," and "So do I." Mark's plan was to simply say his three phrases and then the Mexican pastor would preach. God had another plan. As Mark completed his three phrases, he began to think whole Spanish sentences, and he preached in Spanish for thirty minutes. The Mexican pastor explained to the villagers that they were witnessing a miracle because Mark did not speak Spanish. Mark then translated the pastor's words for the Americans who were with him and went on preaching in Spanish. Mark's father-in-law was so overwhelmed by the experience that he accepted Christ as Savior. Many of the Mexicans were saved that night as well.[34]

You see, the Holy Spirit will sometimes speak directly to someone in a language known to the listener but unknown to the speaker. When He uses it this way, it is serving as a *sign* to get the hearer's attention.

In his signal book on tongues, John Sherrill tape-recorded over forty people praying in tongues. He then assembled an impressive panel of university linguists who specialized in modern and ancient languages and language structure. He asked them to listen to the recordings and comment on them. Sherrill hoped they would be able to identify some of the languages. Although the panel was unable to identify any particular language, they all agreed that the tongues recordings

---

34 Mark Rutland, "Ordered Steps," in *Life in the Spirit: Devotions from the Pentecostal/Charismatic Revival*, ed. Robert White, (Minsk, Belarus: Spirit Life Books, 2000), 261.

had identifiable language patterns: "The 'shape' of real language, the variety of sound combinations, infrequency of repetition and so forth, is virtually impossible, so they said, to reproduce by deliberate effort."[35]

Sherrill also included two recordings of made-up gibberish to see if the linguists could differentiate them from the tongues recordings. The linguists were not fooled. They identified the gibberish immediately and noted that it was not language but rather "just noise." The consensus by the experts was that, while they did not recognize any of the specific languages, they were, nonetheless, languages. They pointed out that there were approximately 2800 known languages and dialects spoken in the world, not counting the number of languages that once existed but are now extinct. Therefore, the odds against recognizing a tongues language are huge. A failure to identify a language, however, does not invalidate the fact that it is, indeed, a language. It is interesting that most Spirit-filled Christians are only mildly curious about whether their prayer language is a known language on the earth today. It is just not that big of an issue to most. They are content that it is a language that the Holy Spirit gives them from which they reap great benefits in their spiritual lives.

It has been shown that not all Biblical tongues were necessarily always recognizable languages (primary premise) and that some present-day tongues languages are known languages (secondary premise). It has also been shown, as concluded by expert linguists, that there is a recognizable difference between tongues and gibberish.

---

35 Sherill, *They Speak*, 101.

CHAPTER 8

Psychology Speaks: Understanding Spirit Baptism and Glossolalia

In studying Spirit baptism psychologists have concentrated mainly on the one aspect of it that gets the most attention—glossolalia (tongues). In an effort to understand this phenomenon, most studies either ignore or implicitly refute the basic premise that glossolalia has a purely spiritual etiology and is rooted in a more all-encompassing spiritual experience, that is, Spirit baptism. Instead, researchers and theorists attempt to explain this phenomenon in purely psychological terms by using various psychological theories of personality and psychopathology. In refusing to consider its spiritual origins, many of the researchers reflect in their writing their own hostility toward a belief in God and the supernatural world. Many of the earlier studies during the 1920s and later in the 1960s and 70s describe Spirit-filled Christians (glossolalic) in very denigrating ways with very little, if any, empirical evidence to support their views. If one starts with the basic premise that glossolalia is a symptom of severe psychopathology, then everything related to it is seen through that distorted prism. The error of this approach is that it violates the scientific method, which, essentially, teaches us to let the empirical data determine our conclusions about a phenomenon rather than starting with a preconceived conclusion and then attempting to fit the observations to support the conclusions.

In the case of Spirit baptism, it is intellectual folly to attempt to explain a supernatural spiritual experience exclusively with psychology, the study of mind and behavior. This is analogous to building a house with only one tool. If all you have is a hammer, then everything will look like a nail to you. Simply put, you just do not have enough tools to finish the job. To deny Spirit baptism's supernatural origin is to take it completely out of its true context. This will do violence to the search for truth, which is what science should be all about.

We can certainly study the psychological aspects of Spirit baptism and glossolalia but not separate from acknowledging the fact that its origin is of God, not human beings. For example, in understanding the various roles food plays in the lives of humans, it is prudent to first accept the fact that hunger is a basic human drive and that humans need food for physical survival. Without accepting that fundamental truth, all studies of eating habits will probably be distorted and arrive at erroneous conclusions and theories about why we eat. An important piece of data would be omitted from the research. So it is with Spirit baptism. If its origin is viewed as human, then all explanations of it will be strictly mental and behavioral in nature. For example, early studies described Spirit-filled Christians as "childish or infantile, egocentric, mentally-ill (paranoid schizophrenic type reaction), anxious, unstable, suspicious, grandiose, guilt-repressing, illiterate and ignorant, projecting, having few formalized thought processes, punitive, uncertain in their relations with other people, and having threatened, inadequately organized personalities."[36] These studies attempted to explain glossolalia in terms of a social

---

36 Jesse Coulson and Ray W. Johnson, "Glossolalia and Internal-External Locus of Control, *Journal of Psychology and Theology*, no. 4, (1977): 312-317. These studies included: G.B. Cutten, *Speaking with tongues: Historically and psychologically considered*. (New Haven, CT: Yale University Press, 1927); J.B. Oman, "On Speaking in tongues: A Psychological Analysis," *Pastoral Psychology* (1964): 14, 48-51; F. Stagg, E.G. Hinson, and W.E. Oates, *Glossolalia: Tongue Speaking in Biblical, Historical,and Psychological Perspective*, (New York: Abingdon, 1967); W.W. Wood, *Culture and Personality Aspects of the Pentecostal Holiness Religion*. (Paris: Mouton, 1965).

pathology or defective individual model.[37] Other studies, however, clearly ruled out psychopathology as an explanation for the phenomena.[38] An impasse had been reached.

Rather than accept the Spirit etiology as an explanation, psychology desperately turned to unproven theories such as psychodynamic theories of Freud, Jung, Hartman, and psychology of the self and narcissism to explain the reason for glossolalia. While acknowledging that glossolalia can no longer be associated with psychopathology, these authors clung to psychological explanations. One study suggested that, since most practitioners of glossolalia are from fundamentalist backgrounds, they suffer "narcissistic injury" when they enter the secular, scientific world because their sense of reality, value, and selfhood are challenged.[39] A study explains:

> The person inquiring about glossolalia brings to the group a battered, enfeebled, dependent self. Because it has come to feel itself severed from the supernatural setting of its earliest nurture, it is depleted in vitality, certitude, ambition, self-esteem, stability, and creativity. Unless sufficiently re-educated to reinterpret the presence of the supernatural in non-literal ways as in the liberal religious traditions, the conservative Christian who accepts in a non-

---

37 I. Zeretsky, and M. Leone, eds., *Religious Movements in Contemporary America.* (Princeton, NJ: Princeton University Press, 1974).

38 V.H. Hine, "Pentecostal Glossolalia: Toward a Functional Interpretation," *Journal of Scientific Study of Religion*, no. 8 (1969), 211-226.

39 John Donald Castelein, "Glossolalia and the Psychology of the Self and Narcissism," *Journal of Religion and Health*, vol. 23(1984), 47-62.

symbolic, literalistic fashion the supernatural world of the Bible simply knows of no other source of meaning, value, purpose and guidance for his life.[40]

It is in this context that the conservative Christian is said to turn to glossolalia in an effort to seek reassurance and healing of his or her "narcissistic shame."

While disavowing the "defective individual" model, this view, nonetheless, describes glossolalics in very negative terms. They are broken individuals who turn to glossolalia in an effort to reintegrate the self and adjust to a godless society. This explanation is mere speculation even when applied to American culture but completely falls apart when applied to foreign cultures where Spirit baptism is even more prevalent. Many of those cultures do not have strong influences of Protestant fundamentalism and, in fact, many are atheistic in their cultural belief systems. Many individuals in these cultures have never heard of Spirit baptism but, after accepting Christ, may quickly receive the infilling of the Spirit and begin speaking in tongues.

The problem with these theoretical explanations is that they all view glossolalia as a human ability rather than a spiritual one. These explanations are in terms of the human mind instead of the human spirit and the Holy Spirit. Therefore, their understanding, interpretation, and conclusions are inherently flawed.

40 Ibid.

Problem with Psychology: Cognitive Dissonance

These descriptions of glossolalics do not sound very appealing, do they? Why would anyone want to receive Spirit baptism if it is associated with these pejorative characteristics? I found it a bit perplexing that these earlier authors discuss glossolalics in such negative terms in spite of Spirit-filled believers uniformly reporting such marvelous benefits from the experience. What is going on here?

I believe psychology may offer us an explanation. We have a term, "cognitive dissonance," which may explain the critics' attitudes. This refers to an unpleasant psychological state resulting from inconsistency between two or more elements in a cognitive system.[41] This creates a motivational drive to reduce the dissonance. How does this apply to these early researchers? It goes something like this. For most of them, one of their primary cognitive beliefs is:

1. There is no God or supernatural world. This works fine for them until another cognitive element challenges it such as:

2. Thousands of Christians are reporting beneficial effects of Spirit baptism with an accompanying supernatural sign (tongues).

Contradiction creates a lack of harmony (dissonance) in the researchers' cognitive belief system, which results in a very unpleasant psychological state. Humans will typically do anything to reduce or eliminate unpleasant feelings. Some turn to alcohol, drugs, or gambling. Some turn to obsessive-

---

41 Gary R. VandenBos, ed., *APA Dictionary of Psychology*, (Washington, D.C.: American Psychological Association, 2007).

compulsive rituals. In this case, researchers turned to the psychological, social, or behavioral to explain what was being observed. Hence, Spirit baptism with glossolalia had to be shown to be pathological and purely of a psychological nature rather than of supernatural origins. To do otherwise would require the refutation of their primary cognitive element, i.e., "There is no God or supernatural world." This, then, would lead to a new cognitive element, i.e., "God exists and I, therefore, am accountable to Him." As this cognitive belief is totally repugnant to atheists, they would rather do anything than to give it honest consideration. As a result, they offer theoretical speculations to resolve their cognitive dissonance. The absence of empirical data to support their psychobabble ramblings does not seem to bother them as long as it reduces their own unpleasant psychological state.

One method of reducing the dissonance is by discounting the importance of an inconsistent element or by discrediting it altogether. In Spirit baptism, the critics simply reject it as being a genuine spiritual experience because it is inconsistent with their atheistic cognitive system. The critics then discredit all people claiming to receive Spirit baptism by attributing this spiritual event to psychological disturbance and abnormality.

We can apply this same reasoning to contemporary theologians and pastors. Their main cognitive element is:

1. Spirit baptism with evidence of speaking in tongues ended with the apostolic age. The conflicting cognitive element is:

2. Spirit baptism with *tongues* is occurring among thousands of born-again Christians today.

To resolve their dissonance, theologians conclude that it is either of the Devil or human (i.e., mental illness). Again, this conclusion cannot be supported scripturally or empirically, but, it doesn't seem to matter to them as long as it makes these critics feel better. Their mindset appears to be "Don't confuse me with facts, my mind is made up."

By discrediting those Christians who receive Spirit baptism, theologians, and pastors who oppose Spirit baptism reduce their own cognitive dissonance by attributing the phenomenon to either demonic activity or mental illness. Ostensibly, this may sound reasonable, but there is no sound evidence to support either conclusion. The opponents may be entitled to their own beliefs, but as Daniel Patrick Moynihan, author and U.S. Senator, once said, people are not entitled to their own facts.

Internal Orientation Studies, Locus of Control

So, let us dispense with speculative theorizing and review a few studies that report some objective, empirical facts. There has been considerable research concerning the concept of locus of control. This concept has been dichotomized into internal and external constructs. By way of definition: "Internal control refers to the perception of positive and/or negative events as being a consequence of one's own actions and thereby under personal control; external control refers to the perception of positive and/or negative events as being unrelated to one's own behaviors in certain situations and therefore beyond personal control."[42]

Several researchers have investigated the relationship between locus of control and personality characteristics. In one study, tests measuring locus of control, anxiety, and neuroticism were administered to males and females. Results indicated a positive relationship between external control and high anxiety rather than the reverse.[43]

An interesting study correlated measures of locus of control with two measures of personality.[44] The findings indicated that internal individuals were higher than externally oriented people regarding dominance tolerance, good impression, sociability, intellectual efficiency, and well-being. Moreover, internally-oriented people were likely to describe themselves as active, striving, achieving, powerful, independent, and effective. Externals were more likely to describe themselves in opposite terms. The authors concluded that an internal locus of control is "...consistently associated with indexes of social adjustment and personal achievement."[45]

One researcher summarized the personality characteristics of internally and externally oriented individuals by describing the following personality picture: "The findings depict externals, in contrast to internals as being relatively anxious, aggressive, dogmatic, and less trustful and more suspicious of others, lacking in self-confidence and insight, having low

42 H.M. Lefcourt, "Internal Versus External Control of Reinforcements: A review," *Psychological Bulletin*, vol. 65 (1966), 207.
43 N.T. Feather. "Some Personality Correlates of External Control, *Australian Journal of Psychology*, 1967, 19, 253-260.
44 P.D. Hersch and K.E. Scheibe, "On the Reliability and Validity of Internal-External Control as a Personality Dimension," *Journal of Consulting and Clinical Psychology*, vol. 31 (1967),609-614.
45 Ibid., 613.

needs for social approval, and having a greater tendency to use sensitizing modes of defense."[46]

These studies regarding locus of control are highly relevant when we consider an insightful and cogent study that compared glossolalics with nonglossolalics on a measure of locus of control.[47] These researchers hypothesized that because of the suggestion of psychopathology in glossolalics and the relationship between external locus of control and psychopathology, glossolalics would probably be more externally-oriented than nonglossolalics.

The results of this study were exactly opposite than predicted. Glossolalics were significantly more internal, as measured on a locus of control scale, than nonglossolalics. As it is generally agreed, that internal locus of control is analogous to psychologically healthy, and competent functioning,[48] these results contradict the belief held by some psychologists and theologians that glossolalia (tongues) is an indication of psychopathology. These findings also suggest that glossolalics are not only well adjusted but, in fact, may be better adjusted than those who do not speak in tongues.

This study raises yet another interesting question. Were the glossolalics more internal in locus of control already prior to receiving Spirit baptism, or did they develop a greater internal orientation after receiving Spirit baptism. If the former is true,

46 V.C. Joe, "Review of the Internal-External Control Construct as a Personality Variable," *Psychological Reports*, vol. 28, (1971), 623.

47 Jesse Coulson and Ray W. Johnson, "Glossolalia," 314.

48 Lynn W. Aurich, "Risk Taking Behavior as a Function of Sex, Age and Locus of Control," (PhD diss., University of Southern Mississippi, 1975).

then we cannot necessarily attribute an internal locus of control to the empowerment of the Holy Spirit through Spirit baptism with glossolalia. If the latter is true, then perhaps Spirit baptism helps individuals develop a more internal locus of control and, hence, healthier personality characteristics.

One study appears to support this hypothesis. Researchers found that individuals who had been members of Pentecostal-type churches less than six months had substantially higher scores on external locus of control than members who had been in those churches six to ten years.[49] While a number of variables may contribute to the difference in locus of control orientation between those two groups, it seems reasonable to infer that Spirit baptism is associated with internal locus of control, which may increase as a function of time. That is, the longer one has been Spirit-filled, the greater internal locus of control and, therefore, the greater degree of mental health. This would confirm the Holy Spirit's role as Agent of Change.

A thought-provoking series of studies conducted in Wales examined the relationship of charismatic experience with certain personality characteristics.[50] These studies administered

---

49 G. Javillonor, "Toward a Social Psychological Model of Sectarianism," (PhD diss., University of Nebraska, 1971), cited in Coulson and Johnson , "Glossalalia."

50 L.J. Francis and Mandy Robbins, "Personality and Glossolalia: A Study Among Male Evangelical clergy," *Pastoral Psychology,* vol. 51, (2003), 391-396. These studies included: L.J. Francis and S.H. Jones, "Personality and Charismatic Experience Among Adult Christians," *Pastoral Psychology,* vol. 45,(1997): 421-428; L.J. Francis and W.K. Kay, "The Personality Characteristics of Pentecostal Ministry Candidates," *Personality and Individual Differences,* vol. 18, (1995), 581-594; L.J. Francis and T.H. Thomas, "Are Charismatic Ministers Less Stable? A Study among Male Anglican Clergy. *Review of Religious Research,* vol. 39,(1997), 61-69; S.H. Louden and L.J. Francis, "Are Catholic Priests in England and Wales Attracted to the Charismatic Movement Emotionally Less Stable?" *British Journal of Theological Education,* vol. 11, (2001), 65-76; M. Robbins, J. Hair, and L.J. Francis, "Personality and Attraction to the Charismatic Movement: A Study among Anglican Clergy," *Journal of Beliefs and Values,* vol. 20, (1999), 239-246.

a standardized personality test[51] to clergy and committed Christian lay adults. The findings of all of these studies agreed that charismatic experience was positively correlated with stable extroversion, negatively correlated with neuroticism, and unrelated to psychoticism.

In a related study examining glossolalia, the results indicated no empirical evidence to support a relationship between glossolalia and neuroticism, and "...indeed, some evidence to suggest that glossolalia is in fact associated with greater psychological stability."[52]

Another groundbreaking study examined the neuropsychological correlates of glossolalia.[53] Researchers at the University of Pennsylvania Medical Center utilized a neuroimaging technique known as single photon emission computed topography (SPECT) to measure cerebral activity during glossolalia. A radiopharmaceutical substance is injected intravenously, and the uptake of this compound in the brain reflects the amount of regional blood flow under normal and pathological conditions. Reduced cerebral blood flow (CBF) in various regions of the brain suggests that those areas are less active than expected when the patient performs an activity that is associated with those areas. Increased CBF suggests increased cerebral activity in the corresponding region. SPECT has been shown to provide accurate information about a variety of abnormalities.[54]

---

51 S.B.G. Eyesnck and H.J. Eyesnck and P. Barrett, "A Revised Version of the Psychotism Scale," *Personality and Individual Differences*, vol. 6, (1985), 21-29, cited in L.J. Francis and Mandy Robbins, "Personality and Glossolalia."

52 L.J. Francis and Mandy Robbins, "Personality and Glossolalia," 395.

53 Andrew B. Newberg and others, "The Measurement of Regional Cerebral Blood Flow During Glossolalia: A Preliminary SPECT Study," *Psychiatry Research:Neuroimaging*, vol. 148, (2006), 67-71.

This study used Spirit-filled volunteers and viewed their CBF under two separate conditions: glossolalia (tongues) and singing in English. Several predictions were made:

- Glossolalia, associated with the perceived loss of intentional control, would be associated with decreased activity in the frontal lobes as compared with singing.
- There will be no decreased activity in the superior parietal lobe as compared with practices such as meditation which report an altered sense of self. Glossolalics report no such altered state of consciousness.
- There will be increased CBF in the thalamus because glossolalia is a very active state.
- Because glossolalia is a highly emotional state, there should be increased CBF in the limbic system, specifically the amygdala.

The results indicated there were significant decreases in CBF in the prefrontal lobes, left caudate nucleus, and left temporal lobe. There were increases in the left superior parietal lobe (SPL) and a slight increase in the right amygdala.

The researchers concluded that the decreased activity of the frontal lobes corresponded with loss of intentional control over speaking in tongues reported by glossolalics.

---

54 J.T.L. Wilson and D. Wyper, "Neuroimaging and Neuropsychological Functioning Following Closed Head Injury: ET, MRI and SPECT, *Journal of Head Trauma Rehabilitation*, vol. 7, (1992), 29-39; Thomas James Callender, Lisa Morrow, and K. Subramania, "Evaluation of Chronic Neurological Sequlae after Acute Pesticide Exposure Using SPECT Brain Scans," *Journal of Toxicology and Environmental Health*, vol. 41, (1994), 275-284.

The expressive language parts of the brain were not directly involved in speaking in tongues.

Given no significant decreases in the SPL, it was concluded no loss of the sense of self existed in these glossolalics (unlike a trend with practitioners of meditation). There was no increased activity in the thalamus as hypothesized. The researchers were uncertain what this finding might represent from a neuropsychological perspective. The marginally increased activity in the amygdala and the significant decrease in the left caudate are of uncertain significance, the researchers concluded. The authors found that glossolalia is associated with complex brain activity due to changes in several brain structures.

Understanding the Study Findings

The authors did not attempt to correlate these findings with what Scripture says about glossolalia. So let us take these findings one step further and see if they make any sense from a scriptural and experiential perspective.

First, the decreased activity in the prefrontal lobes and language centers and no increase in the thalamus make perfect sense scripturally.

The prefrontal lobes of the brain are associated with a number of skills such as new problem solving, planning, organizing, judgment, abstract reasoning, concept formation, mental flexibility, mental efficiency, and decision making. The thalamus is also known to participate in higher cognitive processes such as memory and learning. We may describe these parts of the brain as mind. Activity in these brain structures either decreases or remains the same during glossolalia, and thus the mind is inactive during this type of praying. Practitioners of glossolalia contend that this form of praying does not go through the mind but rather goes directly from the spirit to God. That is, it bypasses human reason: "For if I pray in a tongue, my spirit prays, but my mind is unfruitful. What is the outcome then? I shall pray with the spirit and I shall pray with the mind also; I shall sing with the spirit and shall sing with the mind also" (I Corinthians 13:14-15).

In this passage, Paul elucidates that there are two types of prayer—one with the mind and one with the spirit. These two different types of prayer, then, should be correlated with two different types of brain activity. This is exactly what was shown in this study. These findings support the Scripture cited above.

The authors stated that the decreased activity in the prefrontal lobes is consistent with the perceived lack of intentional control during glossolalia. Just to clarify, there is intentional control over starting and stopping glossolalia but no intentional control over the specific words spoken. What would account for this finding? Acts provides an answer: "And they were all filled with the Holy Spirit and began to speak with other tongues, *as the Spirit was giving them utterance*" (Acts 2:4, my emphasis).

Glossolalia does not originate in the human mind or human spirit but rather with the Holy Spirit. The specific words come from Him and are under His control. They merely are passed through the human spirit directly up to God and thus bypass the mind. The neurophysiological findings appear to support this Scripture.

This study also found that the expressive language parts of the brain are not directly involved in glossolalia. What is the significance of this finding? It would seem that, if glossolalics just make up their language (gibberish) themselves, as some critics have contended, then we would expect to see increased perfusion (blood flow) in the expressive language centers of the brain. This was not the case in this study. Even though glossolalics vocalize the words, the expressive language center is silent. This strongly suggests that something or someone else is in control. This is an amazing finding and confirms Scripture and experiential reports. The prayer language (tongues) being vocalized emanates directly from the Holy Spirit and is merely being repeated by the glossolalic. This then would be consistent with the lack of brain activity in the frontal lobes, expressive language centers, and thalamus observed in this study.

There were no significant decreases in CBF in the Superior Parietal Lobe (SPL) as has been observed in practitioners of meditation in which there is a perceived sense of loss of self. Glossolalics report no similar experience. This rules out the explanation offered by some critics that glossolalics exhibit a dissociative trance disorder. Dissociative trance is characterized by disturbances in consciousness, identity, memory, and restricted awareness of surroundings or behaviors that are beyond one's control.[55] It is viewed as an involuntary state that

---

55 *Diagnostic and Statistical Manual of Mental Disorders*, 4th ed. (Washington, D.C.: American Psychiatric Association, 1984).

Holy Spirit: Agent of Change

causes clinically significant distress or functional impairment. Glossolalics do not report any disturbances in their sense of self or identity or functional impairment. These neuroimaging findings appear to confirm these reports.

In this study, there was a trend towards increased activity in the right amygdala. The amygdala is a very complex brain structure. Early studies showed that the removal of the amygdaloid complex produced a striking increase in emotional reactivity.[56] It is believed that one function of the amygdala is to exert a restraining influence on emotional reactivity emanating from sub-cortical structures. Therefore, with increased amygdaloid activity during glossolalia, as observed in this study, one conclusion is that an increased restraint of emotional reactivity exists rather than a loss of emotional control (as suggested by critics of glossolalia). The finding supports that there was no observed increase in activity in the thalamus, which has links with areas involved with emotional behavior.

The caudate nucleus of the brain is part of the basal ganglia and plays an important role in motor inhibition. Lesions in the caudate can cause conditions such as obstinate progression, and insufficient dopamine at the caudate synapse can lead to Parkinson's disease.[57] This study demonstrated a decrease in caudate activity during glossolalia, which may be responsible for the involuntary hand tremors that are occasionally observed

---

56 P. Bard, "Central Nervous Mechanisms for the Expression of Anger in Animals," in *The Second International Symposium on Feelings and Emotions*, M.L. Raymert, ed. (New York: McGraw-Hill, 1950); P. Bard and V.B. Mountcastle, "Some Forebrain Mechanisms Involved in Expression of Rage with Special Reference to Suppression of Angry Behavior," (Res. Publ., Ass. Res. nerv.ment.Dis.), vol. 27, (1948), 362-404, cited in S.P. Grossman, *A Textbook of Physiological Psychology*, (New York: John Wiley and Sons, 1967), 533.

57 Diana M. Goodwin, *A Dictionary of Neuropsychology*, (New York: Springer-Verlag, 1989), 48.

in individuals engaged in prolonged periods of glossolalia. This would suggest that these behaviors are neurophysiological in etiology rather than due to hysteria or emotionality as has been suggested by critics.

Let us summarize these complex findings. The supposed loss of emotional control that is typically associated with glossolalia by its critics does not have the neurophysiological correlates one would expect if, indeed, this loss of control had a purely emotional or psychological etiology. If so, we would expect to see increased activity in the thalamus and frontal lobes and decreases in the superior parietal lobe and amygdala. The results, in fact, revealed the opposite.

These findings also support Scripture relevant to two different types of prayer, that is, one with the mind and one with the spirit—two different types of prayer and, therefore, two different types of brain activity. Glossolalia passes from the Holy Spirit through the human spirit and bypasses the mind. Hence, those brain structures associated with the mind are relatively silent neurophysiologically during this activity. Similarly, the expressive language structures are inactive during glossolalia, which suggests that glossolalics do not create the language themselves but are merely repeating what they are hearing in their spirit.

We may never fully understand the complex relationship between glossolalia and brain activity. However, the results of this preliminary study lend strong support to the conclusion that glossolalia is of the Holy Spirit, not the human mind.

It appears from even this brief review of the literature that Spirit baptism with initial evidence of glossolalia (tongues) is unrelated to psychopathology (mental disturbance) and is associated with psychological stability.

CHAPTER 9

The People Speak

Psychologists are often asked to evaluate a patient for diagnostic purposes. We are trained to collect as much information from as many different sources as are available. This includes interviewing the patient and assessing presenting symptoms, social history, educational history, employment history, military history, and medical history. We may also interview other individuals who know the patient well. Additionally, we may administer a comprehensive battery of psychological tests that assess the level of cognitive and emotional functioning of the patient. The information from these different sources typically converge leading to reasonable inferences regarding the patient's functioning, which ultimately leads to a clinical diagnosis. A diagnostic conclusion is never based on only one stream of information but rather on how all of the streams converge and what logical inferences can be drawn from that convergence. We can also utilize convergent analysis to assess the validity of Spirit baptism.

Thus far, we have examined several sources of evidence for the Holy Spirit's role as Agent of Change through Spirit baptism. We have examined scriptural, scientific, and logical streams of evidence.

Another important source is that of personal testimony (experiential). Scientists often discount personal testimony by positing it is merely anecdotal and does not necessarily prove anything. This may be true if we consider this stream in isolation of all other streams of evidence. In utilizing convergent analysis, however, the combination of multiple streams of evidence increase the probability that one's inferences and conclusions will be accurate and valid.

Can we consider personal testimony to be a valid and powerful source of information? Certainly. It is used daily in several professions such as law, medicine, and business. In law, many legal verdicts are based on the testimony of witnesses. In medicine, the effectiveness of a treatment is often based on the report (testimony) of the patient. In business, advertising agencies often use personal testimonies of customers to sell their products. The more customer testimonies advertisers have, the more powerful their ads. Advertising firms may also enlist a famous individual who has some credibility to endorse a product, which gives personal testimony even more power to influence people. If personal testimony were not valid as a source of evidence, it simply would never be used by any of these professions.

Personal testimony obviously has validity and great power. With regard to Scripture, this is reflected in John's revelation: "And they overcame him because of the blood of the Lamb and because of the word of their testimony, and they did not love their life even to death" (Revelation 12:11). Testimony is so spiritually powerful it can subdue and overcome even Satan himself. It is so powerful it defuses the fear of death in people willing to die for what they believe (testimony) and in whom they believe (Christ).

Personal testimony can also destroy meaningless theology. When Jesus healed the blind man, the Pharisees discounted it because He did not keep the Sabbath (John 9:16). When they examined the man, they accused Jesus of being a sinner because he worked on the Sabbath and, therefore, was incapable of performing miracles. This is a good example of legalistic theology flying in the face of actual spiritual reality and truth. Notice how the formerly blind man responded: "He therefore answered, 'Whether He is a sinner, I do not know; one thing I do know, that whereas I was blind, now I see'" (John 9:25). This man could care less what the Pharisees said and what could or could not happen based on their rules and theology. He had a personal experience with the living Christ that totally transformed his life. Thus is the power of personal testimony.

The following testimonies are a small but representative sample of individuals who have experienced the transformational power of Spirit baptism. They are from different backgrounds, cultures, professions, and races.

LESLIE B.
Occupation: Operations Director, Therapeutic Boarding School
Education: B.A. Degree

"I was raised in a mainline denomination church and had been born-again since I was fifteen. After graduating from college and beginning my career, I began attending a full-gospel church. At a special church service I responded to an altar call for those who wanted to receive the baptism in the Holy Spirit.

"I was nervous that nothing would happen because I had waited for over a year and prayed many times that it would happen. Two people prayed with me and encouraged me. It took several minutes to stop thinking and relax. When I did, I was overcome with a peaceful feeling but at the same time was filled with intensity to connect with the Holy Spirit. Eventually, I found the courage to have faith and spoke out loud what I heard in my head—silly sounds that meant nothing. But when I spoke them out loud, I was consumed with what God was feeling which, at that moment, was love for me. It was overwhelming and wonderful. I sat for a while and just kept speaking in tongues. It was like finding something that you desperately need and have been searching for—like finding your parent after being lost as a child and hugging them with intense peace.

"Since then I feel a greater intimacy with God when I pray and a greater sense of what God feels when I pray for others. When I pray in tongues, I feel more closely connected to God. It makes the Holy Spirit more alive to me. It makes Him a real person. It magnifies whatever He is doing at the moment for me or someone else. It gives me peace and empowerment.

"The biggest change I have noticed in myself is that the baptism in the Holy Spirit improved my self-confidence and self-image. He reminds me that He came to *me* and filled *me* with power to overcome anything if I choose to let Him handle it."

JEAN B.
Occupation: Nurse
Education: B.S. Degree

"I received the baptism in the Holy Spirit in a Pentecostal church in Orange, New Jersey. I had been prayed for several times to receive the baptism but nothing happened. It wasn't until 1992 after a Sunday church service that I went home and decided to pray some more on my own. While I was praying, I realized that I was speaking a language different from my native tongue, which is French, and what was coming out of my mouth was not English.

"Initially, it felt strange speaking a language I did not understand. However, the personal experience of speaking it was very uplifting. One thing I noticed right away was an increase in boldness in spiritual warfare and boldness in evangelism. I felt like Peter in the book of Acts on the day of Pentecost with the courage to speak the Word of Truth.

"The baptism gave me a better outlook in overcoming problems and facing new challenges. It gave me a stronger identity in Christ. I have a deeper knowledge of who I am in Christ and that is not determined by how I feel or by daily circumstances.

"I pray in tongues daily and I feel that it gives me power—power to do what I cannot do on my own, the power to pray, to evangelize, power to carry out what God has for me."

MARGARET B.
Occupation: Massage Therapist
Education: B.S. Degree

"About a year after I was saved, I was given some tapes on the baptism in the Holy Spirit. I prayed and asked God for it and started speaking in tongues. The enemy told me it was not real, so I stopped doing it for a few months. One Sunday night at church there was an altar call for various things. I went forward and stood next to one of the elderly women, 'Grandma.' She asked me if I had received the baptism in the Holy Spirit, and I told her that I was there to pray about something else. The next thing I knew, I felt something burning through my midsection, and I was speaking in tongues again. I don't know if she touched my stomach or my back, or if she touched me at all, but Jesus certainly did.

"The fire burned within me. A number of things changed. I went on a mission trip to Kenya, East Africa. I taught Sunday School, became a youth group leader, and joined the choir. I began attending the six a.m. prayer meeting faithfully at my church. I had done none of these things before receiving the infilling of the Holy Spirit. I began spending more time alone with God, which greatly increased my intimacy with Him. His voice became unmistakable.

"My relationships with others have improved because He taught me to use discretion and think before I speak. My self-confidence improved because I learned to put my confidence first in Him.

"When I pray in tongues, I sense the power of God in me, and I know that I'm praying God's perfect will. I also have an amazing peace about things. The most significant change in me is the strong connection I have with God. He guides and directs every detail of my life, and I trust Him implicitly."

PHILLIP B.
Occupation: Physician/Orthopedic Surgeon
Education: M.D.

"My life was going pretty well. I had been saved for four years. My practice was thriving. For all practical purposes, my life was good.

"I had been raised Catholic, but one day a friend invited me to a full gospel church. It did not take long for me to recognize that the people in this church had something that I didn't but I wasn't certain at first what it was. After attending church there for a while, I realized that it was the baptism in the Holy Spirit that these people had and I wanted it.

"At a Sunday night service I went to the altar and got on my knees before God. Two members of the church prayed with me. I made up my mind I was not leaving that service until God filled me with the Holy Spirit.

"Suddenly, I began to have the most incredible feeling I have ever experienced. I felt tremendous peace and joy that went on and on and even into the next day. I became more sensitive to the Holy Spirit's direction in my life. I have more insight into Scripture now. I have felt God's love more deeply because of this awesome gift. I often pray in tongues prior to performing surgery as I ask for guidance. I also pray in tongues when I'm fearful and I receive peace.

"Overall, I'd say that I have more power as a Christian. I am so grateful that God gave me this gift. It has made me a better husband, father, and physician. I am at a much deeper level in my Christian walk."

DAVID D.
Occupation: Minister
Education: Three years of college

"The baptism in the Holy Spirit helped me to go from believing in the Lord to walking and fully trusting in Him. I had been saved for twelve years, but I knew something was missing from my relationship with God. Some friends invited me to their apartment to pray. They prayed with me to receive the Holy Spirit. I began to have feelings of elation like I had just stepped into another realm. I also felt the love my friends had for me and how happy they were for me.

"Immediately, I had more intimacy with God. It gave me more staying and fighting power. Of course, I also became more sensitive to the voice of God. About two years later I responded to His call to the ministry.

"I personally feel such closeness to the Lord when I pray in the Spirit (tongues). Knowing that I'm talking directly to God gives me a sense of security and connection."

ROBERT F.
Occupation: Sales
Education: B.A. Degree

I was at a Saturday morning men's prayer meeting. I remember thinking that if the baptism in the Holy Spirit was from God, then it must be good and I wanted it. I had been saved several months and had been taught that it was the next step after salvation, so I wanted everything that God had to offer me.

"We were in a circle praying, and it was very natural and really no effort at all as I began praying in tongues. I remember being excited that I had received. I was fortunate to have a pastor who taught me that praying in tongues was a way to communicate directly with God and that it empowered us to do what He called us to do.

"After receiving the baptism, God began to permeate every part of my life. I believed that I could hear from Him and that He would speak to me and direct me. I seemed to be in constant communion with Him.

"I cannot imagine being a Christian without the baptism in the Holy Spirit. It has completely changed my life. I went from being a very negative, cynical person to being very positive and optimistic. I went from doubt to great faith and trust in Him. I realized that God is real and wants to be intimately involved in *my* life. I went from being a loner to having many personal relationships and close friendships with other Christians. I went from being a quitter to having the ability to persevere and press through to victory. He has given me power to overcome anything in life.

"When I pray in tongues, I know that God is not a distant God and that I can communicate with Him whenever I want. I can know His presence. I am comforted when I pray in the Spirit.

"I have been involved in youth ministry with boys in my church for several years now. I have seen many boys changed dramatically after receiving the baptism in the Spirit. Some were rather unruly troublemakers before receiving, but now are boys that their parents are proud of. The Holy Spirit changes lives at every age."

SUSAN A.

Occupation: Director of Activities, Therapeutic Boarding School
Education: M.S. Degree

"I was about seven years old when I received the baptism in the Holy Spirit. I think I had been saved only a few months. I was lying in my bed, and my dad and I were talking and praying before I went to sleep. I asked him about the baptism in the Holy Spirit because I had just heard about it at chapel meeting at the Episcopal school I attended. He asked me if it were something that I would want. Instantly, I said 'Yes,' and he said a simple prayer for me to receive the baptism. The first thing I remember is feeling really warm all throughout my body. It was a comforting feeling. My dad encouraged me to start praying, and as I did, new and different words started coming out of my mouth. They were words of a different language. My dad said, 'That's it! You got it.' I was still warm and I asked him, 'Is there fire on my head?' I remembered what happened on the day of Pentecost and thought the same was happening to me. My dad said, 'I don't know, maybe.' He encouraged me to pray in my prayer language every day.

"According to my parents, I was strong-willed, stubborn, and bossy as a young child. Over the years, the Holy Spirit has tempered my personality in these areas. I believe that because I have been filled with the Holy Spirit for the majority of my life, I have been able to stay away from temptations that I otherwise would have fallen into. It has been the glue that has held me to Jesus and even allowed me to draw closer to Him.

"I have used my personal prayer language (tongues) as a tool for intimacy with God that has ultimately helped me navigate the rough waters of life. During the toughest two years of my life, it kept me going. It was the one thing I clung to, and it ultimately helped to build me back up and fight the fight that was before me—and ultimately have victory!

"The infilling of the Holy Spirit was definitely the vehicle to greater intimacy with the Lord. I felt a greater personal connection to God. After being baptized in the Holy Spirit, whenever I heard people talk about God, whether in church or elsewhere, I felt as though they were talking about someone I knew personally rather than someone I knew about. I definitely spent more time in prayer. In fact, it was only after the baptism in the Holy Spirit that, I began to develop a prayer life.

"As an adult, the Holy Spirit has given me a greater insight and understanding of the Scriptures. He has opened several opportunities for me to teach the Bible to adults. I'm not exactly certain what this teaching ministry will lead to, but I am certain that He is leading me, and I'm totally committed to following Him."

ANNETTE P.
Occupation: Disabled
Education: B.A. and one year of graduate school

"I received the baptism in the Holy Spirit at the same time that I was baptized in water. As I came up out of the water, I was speaking in tongues. I did not know exactly what was happening or what to do with it. I closed my mouth but could still hear the words in my head.

It brought me closer to God. It sustains me. I have had low self-esteem, but praying in tongues raises my self-esteem. It gives me a direct line to God. When I pray, I feel my prayers get answered faster now. I feel that my heart is softer, and I am kinder to people now because the love of the Holy Spirit has been laid across my heart."

THOMAS F.
Occupation: Minister
Education: Ministry training and ministerial credentials

"Amazingly, my wife and I both received the baptism in the Holy spirit at the same time. We were at an evening church service and had been saved for two months. It was a 'by faith experience.' I knew something had happened to me, and I just spoke out loud in another language. The entire next week I would thank God, close my eyes (no distractions), and speak in another language. This went on for one to two weeks until I knew that it was something I truly had received from God.

"I began to use my prayer language to speak to the Lord about almost everything. I seemed to have an understanding that God understood *me*. I knew internally, in my spirit, that I was touching God and I was being strengthened. I could feel something inside rise up in faith as I prayed. My faith was solidly increased.

"I also studied Scripture to see how it affected others and began applying these principles to my life. I can truly say that it worked.

"Praying in tongues is an ongoing part of my prayer life. It is a constant builder of my spirit-man and a gateway to the operation of the other gifts of the Spirit in my life. I would not give up my prayer language and the baptism in the Holy Spirit for anything or anyone!"

PAUL C.
Occupation: Welder
Education: High School Degree and three years of vocational college

"When I got saved in 1985, I had a zeal for the Lord but I wanted more. Five years later some people at church prayed for me to receive the baptism in the Holy Spirit but nothing happened.

"The next Sunday morning I went jogging before church. As I was returning to my apartment, God deposited a word in my spirit. I was not able to understand it, but it just would not leave me. Every time I prayed in this new language, I felt a direct connection to God without any hindrance.

"The baptism in the Holy Spirit changed my whole life. It gave me a new identity in Christ. It revolutionized my understanding of God's Word. I saw it from a whole new perspective.

"It softened me, but at the same time, gave me a boldness and assurance of overcoming power that lies within me to be used whenever I need it for every situation in life. Whenever I react in a fleshly way, all I do is connect to the power that comes from the Holy Spirit and my whole focus or view changes."

CINDY S.
Occupation: Medical Office Manager
Education: High School Degree

"I received the baptism in the Holy Spirit while in prayer at work one morning. We had been discussing the subject for some time. I had been praying to receive it since learning about it. While in prayer that morning, a new language came out of my mouth. The initial feeling I first felt was a little overwhelming to me. I didn't know what to think about it.

"As I grew in faith, the language became a prayer language I seemed to automatically know. I learned that I could ask God for interpretation, and then I had a greater sense of what I was praying for when I prayed in my prayer language.

"My spiritual life was changed in a positive way. I now understood what I was reading when I read my Bible. It was no longer just words on a page. It became alive! I could visualize what the words were saying to me.

"The baptism changed my life personally. I began to look at the world, people and circumstances, in a different way. I saw what was of God and what was not. It gave me a better awareness of things. The most significant change is that it has made me more aware of how He wants me to be more like Him."

KIM B.
Occupation: Homemaker
Education: Bachelor of Arts

"I was about four months old in the Lord when I received the baptism, with evidence of speaking in tongues while I was in college. When I had been prayed for before for Spirit baptism, the only reaction I had was a glow on my face that my unsaved roommate noticed when I got back to my dorm room. But later at a Christian conference, the speaker gave an altar call for all who wanted to receive it.

"I remember the exhilaration I experienced when I began speaking in tongues. A friend spurred me on, and it felt as though I were a baby saying her first words. I felt that I was experiencing God in a tangible way. It was a joyful moment for me and for those who had been praying for me. It took a while—we had to press in—but it was definitely worth it.

"As I pray in tongues now, it opens up a clearer connection to God. A Scripture will often come to me that meets the current need as I pray, and I get a sense of deep peace. The immediate effect after receiving the baptism in the Holy Spirit was distaste for worldly things. I had no desire for that lifestyle anymore. I had a hunger for the things of God and wanted to get alone with Him and hear Him speak to me. I became like a sponge, to quote my cell group leader. I wanted to take in all of God's Word that I could. It's all I wanted to talk about.

"I began to grow spiritually and to lead others. I believe I can discern God's will better now. This helps me in knowing my identity in Him. I do not swallow the lies of the Devil as often. My self-image and confidence level have greatly improved.

"I enjoy praying for others much more now because the Holy Spirit leads instead of me trying to figure out or conjure up something. I also look to God more than to people for what I need relationally.

"The baptism in the Holy Spirit has given me the undeniable revelation that God is near and He is actively involved in my life!"

NORMAN D.
Occupation: Physician/Internist
Education: M.D.

"I was born-again at age twelve but did not receive the baptism in the Holy Spirit until I was forty eight. I received at church after the third attempt. I was filled with surprise, excitement, and joy. There was a radical change in me. I gave up sinful habits almost immediately. I had a holy boldness to tell others about the Lord Jesus Christ. I *sold out* for Christ.

"The Bible made more sense and came alive for me. My faith grew. I had challenges and problems, but I had more strength to overcome them.

"I became involved in various ministries such as Full Gospel Businessmen's International. I eventually began teaching the Bible and praying with others to receive the baptism in the Holy Spirit. I have seen many lives changed as a result of this wonderful gift from God."

BETH B.
Occupation: Teacher, Spanish and French
Education: Bachelor of Science and 94 hours of language education

"The infilling of the Holy Spirit happened soon after my salvation through the ministry of some American missionaries in San Jose, Costa Rica. As I received, I felt the peaceful presence of God and listened to myself speaking in tongues.

"I was in a troubled marriage in a foreign land with small children to raise. God became my only hope and comfort. The baptism gave me strength and hope to persevere in a difficult life situation."

DANA L.
Occupation: Homemaker
Education: Three years of college

"I had only been saved a short time and was not attending church. I came from a Catholic background, but we never attended church. I would pray on my bedroom floor. I had been seeking the baptism for about a week and would feel like I needed to *release* more but wasn't sure what to do.

"I finally agreed to attend church, and the sermon just happened to be on the baptism in the Holy Spirit. It was something I knew very little about at the time. At the altar call, I went to the front, threw my arms in the air, and prayed in tongues. No one had prayed for nor with me. I was *very* shy, so this was totally out of character for me.

"God answered me in such a *huge* way! It was something that, as a new believer, I looked at and knew God was real. God shook me, literally.

"I believe it has changed my life completely. I really had not had much of a spiritual life before. My prayer time became more intimate and deeper. When I pray in the Spirit, I pray from deep inside, deeper than my thoughts or emotions, but rather from my heart and spirit. The baptism in the Holy Spirit has brought me closer to God. It taught me to hear His voice,

Holy Spirit: Agent of Change

understand His Word, and build my faith to reach into the spirit realm.

"It gave me the courage to give up my old life and pursue training in ministry. I believe that, without the baptism in the Holy Spirit, I would have never even considered deeper spiritual things. I have gone through some rough and lonely times, but the Holy Spirit reassures me that God is real in my life."

GERRIE C.
Occupation: Homemaker
Education: High School Degree

"I received the Holy Spirit through the Kenneth Hagin ministry team after I had been saved for about nine months. I spoke three words in tongues. Satan spoke to me and told me that I was making the words up. But I kept saying them, and the Holy Spirit gave me the assurance that they were from Him.

"I began to notice more boldness and power to solve and overcome problems. The Holy Spirit, with the baptism, has totally changed my life. I have greater discernment now. I know people who don't have the baptism and I can tell a difference.

"When I pray in tongues, I have more focus and am better tuned into God and what He is doing around me. The Holy Spirit is my best friend."

JOE H.
Occupation: Physician, Family Practice
Education: M.D.

"I had been raised Methodist and lived across the street from that church. I functioned as Sunday school superintendent until age twenty when I left home for college. While in college, I studied about Catholicism and became a Catholic. After about twenty years as a Catholic, the charismatic movement came along. By that time, I realized that I needed much, much more help from God to survive in this world. I became very hungry for God.

"One Sunday I went to a charismatic meeting. I noticed that my office nurse, who was Pentecostal, was sitting close to me. She had been praying for me for years without my knowledge. I remember asking her if there would be a service at her church that evening. That evening in her church I had my encounter with the Holy Spirit and all things became brand new.

"I experienced peace, joy, and the opening of my understanding about His kingdom. I felt such gratitude for what He had done for me. So, I asked Him what I could do for Him. His reply: 'Look right where you are.' Only then did I realize why I was working as a physician. I was no longer working for just my needs, but now I was working for Him.

"Now I found purpose for my life. Suddenly, I found enthusiasm and hope replacing the despair with which I had been living for months. My work was no longer a heavy burden but a source of joy and peace.

"Immediately, I desired to share the good news of what my Lord had done for me. When I shared with my office staff, they, in turn, shared back with me what He had done for them, which I found very exciting and stimulating to my new faith in Him. We decided to continue this sharing on a weekly basis. We began to invite our needy patients to join us and to receive our prayers for them. Before long, various local pastors began joining us in these weekly prayer meetings. They brought their encouragement and spiritual teachings.

"These weekly gatherings were much anointed with His presence and His healing power. We witnessed all kinds of miracles. Spiritually, we found ourselves growing rapidly. I continued to function in the Catholic Church but also attended a full gospel church in which I eventually received ordination for the ministry.

"I made overseas missionary trips for both churches. This was something I had never even considered doing before I received the baptism in the Holy Spirit. It brought about some significant changes in my personality. Instead of being withdrawn and shy, I became outgoing and friendly. Instead of being sad, I became joyful. I learned the true meaning and manifestation of love.

"The call to ministry came promptly and has persisted. Initially, I was leading worship and teaching the Bible. I now write a popular Bible weekly newsletter and preach in various churches. I also continue to share the gospel with my patients, daily, in my office, hospital and nursing homes.

"Praying in tongues has been a blessing to me. It ushers me into His presence with all those associated benefits. The more time we spend with Him, the more we become changed into His image and likeness."

Summary

It is clear from the above testimonies Spirit baptism produces powerful and lasting change in individuals. Moreover, personal testimony is a valid stream of evidence in the area of spirituality just as it is in the fields of law, medicine, and business.

These testimonies are from people from widely different educational, socio-economic, cultural, and religious backgrounds but are representative of the millions of Spirit-baptized believers throughout the world today. They are all highly functional individuals who are successful, contributing members of their communities and churches. Although these Spirit-filled believers received the baptism in the Holy Spirit in different ways and in different places, these Christians are amazingly consistent in their report of the experience and the consequential changes in their lives.

As these testimonies illustrate, these Christians all experienced a deeper revelation of their new identity in Christ (origin-revelation). They immediately felt a greater intimacy with Him and a deeper understanding of spiritual things including His Word.

Jesus said that we would receive power when we receive the Holy Spirit. This is a common theme throughout these testimonies. These believers reported more power in their lives to overcome life's challenges. They felt more desire and boldness to share the gospel with others. Increased self-confidence, faith, peace, and joy were common among them.

Rapid spiritual growth and more involvement in ministry activities were frequently reported.

These individuals ranged in duration of salvation from a few months to a few years which gave them a standard of comparison between the two spiritual experiences. They all report striking differences between the two experiences (salvation and Spirit baptism) which is consistent with the two different revelations associated with each one respectively, which will be discussed later in this book.

All of these people spoke in tongues upon receiving the baptism in the Holy Spirit, which they continue to use daily in their prayer life. They consistently reported that praying in tongues gave them power, strength, peace, refreshing, clarity of mind, and confirmed that God is real and present in their lives.

When we consider the four streams of evidence: the scriptural, scientific, logical and experiential, we see a magnificent convergence leading to one unmistakable, irrefutable conclusion. The Holy Spirit is the Agent of Change!

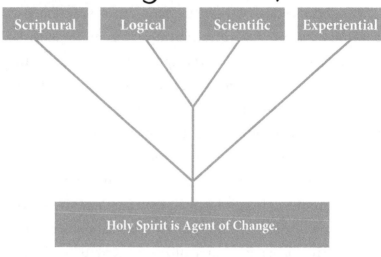

Figure 1. Holy Spirit Is Agent of Change, Convergent Analysis

CHAPTER 10

Common Questions Regarding Tongues

1. **When I receive the baptism in the Holy Spirit, do I have to speak in tongues?**

When you receive Spirit baptism, the Holy Spirit brings the fullness of Himself which consists of many things. He brings His love, peace, joy, kindness, patience, and all the rest of the fruit of the Spirit (Gal. 5:22). Which of those would you choose to reject? Tongues are just one of many wonderful things He gives us. The Holy Spirit is a gentleman; He will not force you to speak in tongues. He gives you the prayer language, and what you do with it is up to you. But you need to ask yourself, "Why wouldn't I want to experience all that the Holy Spirit has for me? Why wouldn't I want to step into the supernatural, spirit realm any time I choose?" If speaking in tongues is of God and is beneficial to you, as has clearly been shown, then why would you not want to experience it? Receiving the fullness of the Holy Spirit is not like going to a cafeteria where you are selective in what you choose. You must receive on His terms, not yours. Trust God and His word that tongues are a holy and awesome gift from God.

2. **When I receive the Holy Spirit, will I lose control and babble hysterically?**

You will not babble hysterically. Acts 2:2-4 tells us they spoke in other tongues. The Holy Spirit gave them their specific languages, but they had control over the expression of that language just as you have control over the expression of your native language. You can start and stop your spiritual

Holy Spirit: Agent of Change

language anytime you wish just as you can start and stop your native tongue. The Holy Spirit gives you the words, but you are in control of their expression. Since God is a God of order and control, doesn't it make sense that, in receiving the Holy Spirit, you will actually receive greater control, not less?

People often equate strong emotion with losing control. As you are praying in tongues and are being built up and strengthened in the spirit, it is true that it may trigger strong emotions such as intense love for God, joy, praise and adoration, boldness, and heightened faith. But are these bad emotions? Just because you may feel these intensely does not mean you are out of control.

There is a school of thought in Christian circles that we should divorce our belief system from all emotion. Our faith should not be based on feelings but on the word of God. While that reasoning may be true, I can assure you that a personal relationship with the living God through his Son Jesus will elicit strong emotions, which result from the realization that you have been redeemed from the pit of hell. Then, when you are filled with the Holy Spirit and speak in tongues, the reality of His existence and your intimacy with Him becomes so striking that it is impossible to not experience strong emotions, but that does not mean you are "out of control."

I have seen sports fans at sporting events do outlandish things. They may jump up and down, wave their hands and arms vigorously, scream and shout, cry, paint their faces and bodies, and even get into physical altercations. All of this is acceptable, but getting the least bit emotional over an encounter with God is frowned upon even by born-again Christians. Speaking in tongues is not a purely emotional event. It may occasionally trigger feelings, but those feelings are positive and healthy and expressing them does not necessarily equate with losing control.

I have seen many people receive the baptism in the Holy Spirit and begin to speak in tongues very softly and gently. I have seen others do it enthusiastically and loudly. The differences in the expression are more a function of their personalities rather than the experience itself. The Holy Spirit will work with and respect your personality and the specific ways you choose to express yourself. The experience is the same, but how it is expressed varies from individual to individual. The main thing for you to understand is that God will not make a fool out of you. You will speak in tongues, but you will be in control of it as the Holy Spirit gives you the utterance.

3. What are the benefits of praying in tongues?

The benefits are myriad, as we have already discussed. I view tongues as a therapeutic tool God has given us that we can use to generate the necessary power to address and overcome problems and challenges in life: "For God has not given us a spirit of fear but of power, and of love and of a sound mind" (II Timothy 1:7).

My view of praying in tongues is that it generates power much the same way that water running over a turbine engine in a dam generates electrical power. As we pray in tongues, we run our prayer language over our spirit, which somehow energizes us spiritually which, in turn, energizes everything else about us. I encourage Spirit-filled Christians to pray in tongues every day because we need this empowerment to face life's daily challenges.

Praying in tongues also benefits us by providing a daily reminder of the Holy Spirit's existence and presence in our lives. It is this awareness of His presence that affects the way we live. When we go through a crisis or challenge in life, we sometimes wonder if God has left us. The ability to pray in tongues serves as a constant reminder that "he dwelleth with you and shall be in you" (John 14:17).

This builds our faith and encourages us during difficult times: "But you, beloved, building yourselves up on your most holy faith; praying in the Holy Spirit..." (Jude 20). Praying in tongues allows us to keep our mind staid upon Him, which leads to perfect peace (Isaiah 26:3).

Tongues are also a bridge into the supernatural world. As we have already proven, tongues are a supernatural sign. Praying in the Holy Spirit often stimulates and empowers the operation of the other charisma. I often find that when I pray in tongues prior to seeing a patient for psychotherapy, the gift of wisdom will operate more quickly and more fully. The Holy Spirit will show me something very specific about a patient that would be impossible for me to know otherwise (gift of word of knowledge), which the patient then acknowledges in complete amazement. As the gifts of the Holy Spirit operate, they have often been the convincing catalyst that has brought many of my patients to a saving knowledge of Jesus Christ. I believe that praying in tongues daily releases the power that drives the other gifts of the Holy Spirit.

When we step into the supernatural by praying in tongues, it is often easier to hear from the Lord. Many Spirit-filled Christians report they often receive answers to prayer or questions they have asked the Lord during or just after they have prayed in tongues for a while. This makes perfect sense. If tongues transport us into the supernatural where God lives, we are more likely to hear what He has to say if we are in His presence vis-à-vis being in the natural world where it is much noisier.

4. In what way will praying in tongues change me?

As a therapeutic tool, tongues gives us the strength to make many positive changes, several of which we have already discussed. One of the most important ones, however, is the ability to control our tongue. A wagging tongue does more damage to an individual's life than any other member of the body does: "But no one can tame the tongue; it is a restless evil and full of deadly poison" (James 3:8). This verse tells us that our tongue has the potential of literally killing someone. Moreover, it is a loose cannon because no one can tame it. Many patients I have seen in my clinical psychology practice have been deeply wounded emotionally, even unto the point of death, because of what significant others have repeatedly said to them. People often minimize the impact of their words, but God says otherwise: "Hide me from the secret counsel of evildoers, From the tumult of those who do iniquity, Who have sharpened their tongue like a sword, They aimed bitter speech as their arrow, To shoot from concealment at the blameless ..." (Psalms 64:2-3). The psalmist is saying that the tongue apparently has the ability to cut us deeply like a sword and pierce our heart as an arrow. That is a deadly weapon and, yet, people, including Christians, wield it very nonchalantly with little concern for its devastating impact.

The Bible has much to say about gossips and slanderers. Many Christians who would not think of engaging in sexual immorality, drug addiction, alcoholism, pornography, or profanity, but immerse themselves in gossip and slander without a second thought. How serious does God take this? Romans says: "...being filled with all unrighteousness, wickedness, greed, evil; full of envy, murder, strife, deceit, malice; they are *gossips, slanderers*, haters of God, insolent, arrogant, boastful, inventors of evil, disobedient to parents, unloving, unmerciful..." (Romans 1:29-31, my emphasis). Notice that He equates gossips and slanderers with murderers and haters of God. He tells us we should not associate with such people (Proverbs 20:19).

Jesus spoke specifically to this problem: "Not what enters into the mouth defiles the man, but what proceeds out of the mouth, this defiles the man" (Matthew 15:11). It appears, then, that we all have the potential within us to defile, not only ourselves, but others as well because of the incontinency of our tongues. There is something within each of us that loves to hear a juicy tidbit of gossip about someone. Gossip columnists in Hollywood or New York make a lot of money bearing tales about famous people. Tabloid newspapers and magazines make millions of dollars writing sordid stories about famous people. They would not be in business if they did not appeal to our more prurient desires. Now, you may be saying, "That does not apply to me. I'm not a gossip." Then you are not paying attention because Scripture says that no one can tame the tongue (James 3:8).

So, what do we do about this dilemma? We let God tame our unruly tongue! When we pray in tongues, we yield our tongue to the control of the Holy Spirit. As we do this more and more, an amazing thing begins to happen. We gain more control over what comes out of our mouth in our native language! There appears to be a correlation between how much we pray in tongues and how much we speak positive, uplifting words to others. God gave us tongues to help us bring our native tongue under His subjection. What a powerful tool!

5. Do I have to speak in tongues to be saved?

Absolutely not! We have already clearly shown that salvation and Spirit baptism are separate spiritual experiences. Salvation through Jesus Christ redeems us from the wages of sin, eternal death, and assures us of eternal life (Romans 6:23). Spirit baptism gives us power to serve God and fulfill His plan on earth (Acts 1:8).

6. How does tongues make me a better Christian?

I want you to think of it in terms of your faith. God has given each of us a measure of faith (Romans 12:3). How important is faith? According to Hebrews: "And without faith it is impossible to please Him for he who comes to God must believe that He is, and that He is a rewarder of those who seek Him" (Hebrews 11:6).

It is with our faith that we gain God's approval (Hebrews 11:2). We are told that we should live by faith (Romans 1:17). It is our responsibility, however, to nurture and increase our faith. God's Word instructs us on exactly how we should do that: "But you, beloved, building yourselves up on your most holy faith; praying in the Holy Spirit" (Jude 20). Praying in the Holy Spirit (tongues) increases our faith in several ways. First, as previously said, it increases our conscious awareness of His presence in our lives. Second, Paul teaches us, "Faith comes by hearing, and hearing by the word of Christ" (Romans 10:17). When we pray in tongues, the Holy Spirit Himself gives us the words to speak. Therefore, when we hear ourselves pray in tongues we are hearing the word of God. Our mind may not understand what we are saying, but our spirit does. Moreover, when we hear ourselves do something for which we have no natural ability, our faith is built up because we know we are participating in the supernatural. How can your faith *not* be increased when you hear a miracle with your own ears? As your faith grows, so does your power in prayer: "And all things you ask in prayer, believing, you shall receive" (Matthew 21:22). Imagine the impact you can have if you operate in more prayer power. Your whole Christian life will be transformed. Tongues are a tool for accomplishing that goal.

7. Why do full gospel/charismatic Christians place so much importance on tongues?

Although tongues are certainly a miracle from God, I believe that Spirit-filled Christians often overemphasize the role of tongues to the detriment of the Holy Spirit. I cannot stress strongly enough that it is not solely tongues that you should seek but rather the Holy Spirit. Tongues are but one precious gift that He brings with Him when He takes up residence within you. It is not just an external sign that you should seek but rather intimacy with the third person of the triune God. Make sure your focus is on Him and Him alone rather than a sign or supernatural ability that He will give you. The rest will take care of itself.

8. Is it true that when I pray in tongues the Devil does not know what I am saying?

This is a popular belief in Spirit-filled circles. I doubt, however, that it is true. I can find no Scripture to support this belief. We know that on the day of Pentecost they prayed in tongues and were understood by many who were there. We also know that some who receive the baptism in the Holy Spirit receive a prayer language that is a known language on the earth today. If we, as humans, can recognize and understand someone's tongues, why would it be any different for Satan? I believe Satan is certainly multilingual because he speaks to people of the earth in their own language.

It may be a moot point, but I do not think it really matters that much one way or the other whether Satan understands a person's prayer language (tongues) because God understands what we are saying and He is the only one that counts. Satan can certainly understand what I pray for in my native tongue, and it does not stop God from answering my prayers. Why would it be any different if Satan did understand my devotional tongues? God is sovereign and, when He decides to answer us, no devil on earth can stop Him.

CHAPTER 11

Holy Transition: The Process of Change

As a clinical neuropsychologist, I am fascinated by the phenomenon of transformation. Our goal is to help people make meaningful changes, which is often a complicated process. Transformation can occur gradually or rather suddenly. In nature, for example, the amazing transformation of the caterpillar into a beautiful monarch butterfly is a gradual process. Transformation in physics often indicates a change from one form of energy into another and may occur suddenly. Whether the transformation is gradual or sudden, a series of steps occur that result in change. The Holy Spirit's goal is to change us into the likeness of Jesus Christ. As in nature or science, this process of holy transformation follows a specific sequence. It looks like this:

Spirit (origin revelation) → mind (values) → worldview → behavioral choices (holy living)

Profound and lasting change occurs in each of us as the Holy Spirit moves us through this sequence. He uses many things to facilitate this process, but He is the primary Agent of Change behind all of it. Let us look at each segment of this sequence.

Spirit (Origin Revelation)

When we are filled with the Holy Spirit, a spiritual revelation happens in our spirit, and we realize we are children of God (Romans 8:16). The Holy Spirit bears witness with our spirit that we are spiritual beings. Our spirit was created by God and was with God before we were in the flesh (Jeremiah 1:5; Zechariah 12:1). The infilling of the Holy Spirit revives or regenerates our spiritual memory of our spiritual origin, i.e., our spirit was created by God. This spiritual memory causes our regenerated spirit to yearn to be reconnected with God. Hence, the new vigor for the things of God. Our spirit is renewed at salvation, but the infilling of the Spirit infuses it with a supercharge of God's vitality and connection with Him (intimacy).

The spirit of a human constitutes his essence. There is no life without the spirit. Adam was mere dust until God breathed his spirit into him. It is at this core level that a human being is changed when Spirit baptism is received. The believer's spirit and the Holy Spirit are now irrevocably and immutably connected and intertwined with each other. Until this occurs, any changes in his soul (mind) after salvation may be only temporary and also may be very slow in coming. The human spirit is the foundation of man. All else is built upon it.

The spirit determines what happens in the soul (mind). If it has no revelation of its true origin, its belief system will be of the mind. That is, the spirit will be ruled by the soul rather than the reverse. Even a born-again Christian who has not received Spirit baptism will believe with his soul (mind) and thus be influenced and controlled by it. There can be renewal of the mind, but it will be limited in its power to change a person until there is *origin revelation* in the spirit. At Spirit baptism, this revelation explodes within the spirit and births new power, the power described by Jesus (Acts 1:8).

This *origin revelation* is at the essence of Spirit baptism. It is the certain knowledge and truth that we are first and foremost spiritual beings. We are eternally connected to God (Spirit) by our spirit because He created it. He knew us (and we knew Him) before we were put into a fleshly body. The spiritual memory of this preexistent relationship with Him is embedded in our spiritual DNA and is revived and enlivened again by the Holy Spirit when He takes up residence within us. It is this revelation that produces such dramatic change in us. The rate of change depends upon the amount of revelation initially, but the impetus for it is the revelation given by the Holy Spirit to our spirit.

The origin revelation is the deep understanding given to our spirit by the Holy Spirit that we are more than just body and soul (mind). It is the realization that we are truly made in God's image. God is Father, Son, and Holy Spirit. Similarly, God made us to be three elements, body, soul, and spirit, which should function as one even as the Trinity functions as one. Unfortunately, this design is not fully manifested in many people because they are only aware of the body and the soul (mind). If they are aware of the spirit at all, it is only minimally so and have no revelatory and experiential understanding of its origin.

The origin revelation carries with it an understanding of a nebulous concept—eternity that previously was ill-defined or nonexistent in the individual. Eternity is an abstract concept difficult to grasp. It refers to infinite time that has no beginning and no end. The human mind thinks in linear, finite terms. There is a beginning and an end. Time is measured in quantifiable units. Jesus referred to Himself as the Alpha and Omega, the beginning and the end (Revelations 1:8; 21:6;

22:13), finite terms, so that we could better comprehend His identity. At the same time, we are told that He is eternal. The human mind cannot grasp it, but the spirit is preprogrammed to understand eternity because it once lived there and will once again. However, first, it must receive origin revelation from the Holy Spirit, and it is this understanding of where we came from that increases our intimacy with God. We can only understand eternity on the spirit level.

The revelation must be experiential through the Holy Spirit rather than an intellectual assent of the existence of eternity. Otherwise, it is merely an abstract intellectual concept that has little, if any, power to change us. When we have the revelatory experience that our true essence and identity is an eternal spirit created by the eternal, living God, everything about us begins to change. The reality of our eternal existence with the eternal God becomes so striking that it begins to pervade and dominate everything about us. It is the origin revelation that unequivocally answers the existential question: "Is this all there is?" The answer is emphatically, "No!" In addition, it is this answer that gives meaning and significance to the finite temporal world in which we live. Without a revelatory and experiential glimpse of the eternal, life is meaningless and without hope, which is one reason the rate of suicide is at an all-time high. God created us in His image, that is, eternal, to exist with Him eternally. Once this fact is revealed to our spirit by the Holy Spirit, all things change.

Another aspect of the origin revelation is the sudden understanding of our spiritual genealogy. With the appearance of several genealogy websites on the internet, interest in family genealogy has exploded. The desire to trace our family ancestors as far back as we can appears to be inherent in each of us. Evidence of this is given in Genesis 5 where Moses traces the genealogy of Adam; Genesis 9 and 10, Noah's genealogy; Genesis 11, Abraham's family line. In the New Testament we are given in Matthew 1, the genealogy of Christ. These genealogies would not have been so painstakingly listed if family origin was unimportant to God. These genealogies document our physical, genetic origins.

Many adopted individuals desire to know who their biological parents were even though they love and respect their adoptive parents as their true parents. This longing to know from whom they came runs so deep that they may feel incomplete until they obtain this knowledge. Adoptees report a sense of closure, completion, and peace once they learn of their biological origin even though they may have no relationship with the biological parents.

This inherent need to connect with our origin is not just biological but also spiritual. This need for origin revelation is embedded so deeply within us, we are incomplete until the connection is made. Moreover, just how is this accomplished? Galatians informs us: "And because you are sons, God has sent forth the Spirit of His son into our hearts crying Abba! Father! Therefore, you are no longer a slave, but a son; and if a son, then an heir through God" (Galatians 4:6-7). At the moment we are baptized in the Holy Spirit, He is crying Abba Father into our spirit and mind (soul) thus imprinting our spiritual heritage deeply within us. It is a supernatural key unlocking the mystery of our true origin. Deep is calling to deep at that very moment (Psalms 42:7).

The imprinting process is said to occur during a critical period shortly after birth in some animals. Newly hatched chicks, for example, tend to follow the first moving object that captures their attention whether it is human, animal, or inanimate.[58] This phenomenon is poorly understood. Some believe it is instinctual while others believe it is a learned behavior. Nevertheless, it is profound and produces lasting effects on an organism. At the moment we are filled with the Holy Spirit, we are imprinted with the knowledge of our origin and with the knowledge of our true eternal parent. Just as a chick imprints on its mother and will follow only her, we are imprinted on the Father by the Holy Spirit and will now follow only Him (John 10:3-5).

A central feature of the origin revelation is intimacy. Isn't it interesting that the Holy Spirit cries into our spirit and soul Abba rather than Yahweh, Jehovah, Elohim, El Shaddai or one of the many other names of God? Why Abba? Abba comes from a Hebrew root word meaning "Papa" and implies a greater familiarity and intimacy with the paternal parent than the more formal addresses for father mentioned above.[59] The American equivalent would be "Dad" or "Daddy."

---

58 Gary R. VandenBos, ed., *APA Dictionary of Psychology*, (Washington, D.C.: American Psychological Association, 2007).

59 R. Laird Harris, Gleason L. Araher, and Bruce K. Waltke, *Theological Wordbook of the Old Testament*, (Chicago: Moody Bible Institute, 1980).

The imprinting of Abba into our spirit creates a profound dimension of intimacy with the Father and reveals a startling reality—that we are truly His adopted children for eternity. The intimacy engendered by this origin revelation creates a feeling of completion and wholeness in Him because we now know and understand that our true identity is not separate from God but rather is embedded in Him. This deeper level of intimacy with God produces the dramatic changes we observe in Christians who have received Spirit baptism. Greater intimacy always produces change.

Another aspect of this origin revelation is a sense of belongingness. The Holy Spirit reveals that we absolutely belong to God and that this relationship is permanent. This spiritual adoption as a child of God is quite different from an earthly adoption in its effect on the adoptee. Many adoptees report feelings of having been abandoned by their earthly mother. Many carry with them a fear of further abandonment for the rest of their lives.[60] There is no fear of abandonment with Spirit baptism. On the contrary, the Holy Spirit reveals to us the absolute certainty that we belong to God forever. The Lord confirmed this truth: "I will never desert you, nor will I ever forsake You" (Hebrews 13:5).

This Scripture becomes a living, breathing reality when the Holy Spirit releases the origin revelation within our spirit. All fear of abandonment rapidly begins to fade away. We begin to realize that, while humans may reject us, our heavenly Father

---

60 Nancy Verrier, "The Primal Wound: Effects of Separation from the Birthmother on Adopted Children," Terry Larimore, http://terry Larimore.com/PrimalWound.html.

will never reject us. Our internal security gradually increases which begins to manifest externally in the form of changed behavior patterns and changed emotional functioning. This permanency in belongingness creates an inner peace, a feeling of being absolutely safe, and an overwhelming certainty of being loved beyond measure. What earthly parents often fail to achieve even after years of parenting, God achieves in one fell swoop with Spirit baptism: "For my father and mother have forsaken me, but the Lord will take me up" (Psalms 27:10).

This need to belong is so fundamental within humans that it serves as a driving force and influences cultures and societies. When this need is frustrated and unsatisfied, it can lead to the development of abnormal subcultures. The proliferation of street gangs and organized crime throughout the world is a classic example. Young people are attracted to street gangs because they offer a sense of family membership, albeit a counterfeit, dysfunctional one. The need to belong is inherent to our identity, which is, at best, partly defined by to whom we belong. It is so strong that humans would rather have a negative identity than none at all. Therefore, individuals latch on to the first thing that fills this need to belong. The street gang offers a counterfeit form of the parental, family unit. It has a family hierarchy and structure with the more senior members serving as the authority figures (parents) who set the rules and dispense rewards for good behavior and punishments for bad behavior. The gang has its own family identity defined by traditions such as initiation rites, wardrobe (colors), insignia, hand signs, handshakes, and activities. Although the behavior patterns and activities of street gangs are dysfunctional, criminal, and sinful, their central reason for existence is to satisfy the inherent need to belong, which was not satisfied in each member's biological family of origin. If parents are unable to or simply fail to provide a godly, family environment that satisfied the child's deep need to belong, Satan will offer his perverted, false version, which ultimately leads to destruction.

This sense of belongingness is also conveyed in Galatians 4:6 by the specific phrase: "God has sent forth the Spirit of His Son into our hearts." It does not say the Spirit of the Father although that can be implied. It does not say the Holy Spirit although that is also implied. Rather, it says the Spirit of His Son because that specifically speaks to the parent-child relationship.[61] It is this connection with the parent that gives the child his sense of belongingness and ultimately his identity. The origin revelation given by the Holy Spirit meets this deep need and produces profound change at the deepest level.

Spirit baptism provides the impetus for and pathway to the origin revelation. It may come in fullness instantly upon the in filling of the Holy Spirit, or it may come in degrees and stages as a believer matures spiritually. The will of the Father is for all of His children to fully understand their eternal family of origin and have the spiritual experience of belonging to that family and, specifically, their eternal Father. The Holy Spirit facilitates this by continually bearing witness with our spirit that we are children of God.

---

61 Reverend Tommy Faulk, personal communication, May 9, 2009.

Mind (Values)

Receiving the origin revelation and understanding our true spiritual identity is the core root that leads to everything else that makes us who we ultimately become. For example, it directly influences our values. Author Hunter Lewis, in his book *A Question of Values*, defines the term *value* as: "...it should be synonymous with personal evaluations and related beliefs, especially personal evaluations and related beliefs about the 'good,' the 'just' and the 'beautiful,' personal evaluations and beliefs that propel to action, to a particular kind of behavior and life."[62]

Lewis contends humans choose their values by four, and only four, interior mental modes. These can be summarized as:

1. Sense experience—using the five senses to arrive at personal evaluations.
2. Deductive logic—utilizing reasoning.
3. Emotion—relying on feelings to arrive at conclusions.
4. Intuition—relying on the unconscious mind to arrive at truth.

Additionally, Lewis offers two major synthetic mental modes that may combine the four basic modes in myriad ways:

1. Authority—utilizing the four basic modes as authority is evaluated and then one's faith is placed in that authority.
2. Science—values are based on empirical observation. Lewis writes: "...Christianity has often been associated

---

62 Hunter Lewis, *A Question of Values: Six Ways We Make Personal Choices That Shape Our Lives.* (Crozet, VA: Axios Press, 2000), 7.

with authority, although it makes a direct emotional, intuitive, and logical appeal as well."[63]

This mental mode, says Lewis, can be applied to such beliefs as the resurrection of Jesus Christ by "relying on or not relying on the testimony of church or Bible."[64] This type of value system is based on faith in a higher moral authority. The challenge is in deciding who will be that moral authority.

Lewis perspicaciously observes that "… human beings cannot separate the way they arrive at values from the values themselves."[65] This is precisely the point, and it is why the Holy Spirit produces such dramatic, sudden change in a person's value system. Some argue, as does Lewis, that divine revelation is merely a combination of these mental modes of gaining moral knowledge. Perhaps that would be true if we eliminate the human spirit and its relation to the Holy Spirit from the values equation. That is equivalent to eliminating the earth's rotation from the explanation of day and night. It is simply insufficient.

While it is accurate that humans form their values through the mental modes mentioned above, it is a mental error to assume that these are the only ways in which we can gain moral knowledge. Humans are composed of more than just mind and body. They also have a spirit, which originated with God, which is Spirit. All of these mental modes are ways of *knowing* something and we all use them daily in myriad ways, but they

---

63 Ibid., 11.
64 Ibid., 10.
65 Ibid., 13.

depend primarily on the functioning of the mind. There is, however, another deeper, more profound way of knowing, i.e., spiritual. As we are made up of body, soul, (mind), and spirit, we can know something through all of these modes.

Some argue that the values themselves are more important than from where they originate or how we arrived at them. That approach quickly deteriorates into moral relativism, which maintains there are few, if any, moral absolutes in the universe. What is good, just, and true for you may not be for me.

For example, Nazi Germany espoused the value of Aryan Supremacy. This value ultimately led to the slaughter of over ten million human beings who were judged inferior based on that value system.

The Bushido code of feudal Japan stressed the values of courage, loyalty, and hara-kiri, and the latter emphasized a preference of suicide over dishonor. This value system continued to prevail during World War II leading to *kamikaze* attacks on allied troops resulting in thousands of deaths on both sides.

The Mayan civilization of the Yucatan was highly advanced in many facets of life, but they believed human blood sacrifices necessary to appease their gods.

Obviously, it is not merely the values that matter but rather their origin that determines their truth, validity, reliability, permanency, and impact on the human race. Faith in a higher moral authority is meaningless and potentially destructive if that authority is man or a human institution. This may, itself, be a value judgment but it is well-founded.

It is the intimate, absolute certainty of God's existence produced by the origin revelation through Spirit baptism that determines and shapes a Christian's value system. The Holy Spirit conveys God's values first to our spirit and then to our mind. We may then use the mental modes cited by Lewis to evaluate these values. However, it should be emphasized, the values themselves originate with God. They are not merely created by the human mind. Christians choose to adopt His values because, through the origin revelation, we understand that we are His adopted children. The Holy Spirit bears witness with our spirit to this absolute truth. That is what separates Christianity from human-made religions and human-made value systems. It is this deep knowing in the spirit that determines and shapes the knowing in the mind (Psalms 42:7). God's values are absolute and they are absolutely good.

The Holy Spirit has a central role in this process: "…because the love of God is shed abroad in our hearts through the Holy Spirit who was given to us (Romans 5:5)." God's primary value, love, is revealed to our spirit, and the Holy Spirit then begins to teach our mind: "And do not be conformed to this world; but be transformed by the renewing of your mind, that you may prove what the will of God is, that which is good and acceptable, and perfect" (Romans 12:2).

As this renewing process occurs, we progressively assimilate God's values. We may have already adopted some of His values after being born-again, but following Spirit baptism, they acquire a deeper significance and influence in one's life.

God's value system is revealed in His commandments (Exodus 20:23) and character (Galatians 5:22).

Most people agree that God's values such as love, truth, mercy, honesty, fidelity, justice, individual responsibility, honor, and life are acceptable and worthwhile. The problem is in how people choose to define these values and in the behavioral choices, they make in living them out.

Worldview

If we accept God's definitions of these values rather than our own, then our worldview begins to change. As the Holy Spirit renews (changes) our minds, we begin to view the world and everything in it through spiritual eyes, specifically, His eyes. People, events, and even nature itself are no longer seen as separate from the spirit world but in some way connected to it and God's divine purpose and plan. This is not to imply some type of pantheism that believes that God is literally in everything on earth, but rather that we begin to see the world through the eyes of the Holy Spirit. We begin to evaluate everything based upon God's value system, which determines what is acceptable and good.

Behavior Choices (Holy Living)

This new worldview begins to influence the kind of behavioral choices we make, which determines the type of life we lead. Many Christians give intellectual assent to God's value system, but it is not manifested in the choices we make. This is due largely to the absence of the origin revelation in our spirit person. We know in our mind what is good, acceptable and perfect, but we have neither the spiritual revelation nor the power to live it out. The infilling of the Holy Spirit, on the other hand, provides us with knowledge in the spirit, mind, and body and the desire and power to live according to God's perfect will and values. The Holy Spirit becomes our advisor and guide in the choices we make. He heightens our awareness of, not only the immediate consequences of our behavioral choices, but also the long-term and even eternal consequences of those choices. Many Christians think of God as being far away in heaven looking down on us but not really being involved in our lives or caring about specific decisions or choices that we must make.

If we can accept the basic premise that God has a purpose and plan for each of us, then why is it so hard to believe that He cares about the specific choices we make? Because His ways and thoughts are higher than ours are, it is easy to conclude that He knows which choices and decisions are best and will lead to the fulfillment of His perfect plan for us. Conversely, He also knows which choices will lead us away from or delay the realization of His will for us.

Poor choices may be made based on a worldview lacking any spiritual vision. This worldview is based on a distorted, dysfunctional value system not composed of any absolutes and, therefore, is not of God. Every choice we make in life has consequences—either positive or negative. The Holy Spirit leads and empowers us to make the right choices and avoid the wrong ones: "But now you also, put them all aside: anger, wrath, malice, slander, and abusive speech from your mouth. Do not lie to one another, since you laid aside the old self with its evil practices, and have put on the new self who is being renewed to a true knowledge according to the image of the One who created him..." (Colossians 3:8-10). Laying aside evil practices is a choice one makes. We desire to make that choice because the origin revelation reveals "a true knowledge according to the image of the One who created him." We identify with Him by internalizing His values, worldview, and behavioral choices.

If someone holds a value that death is more important than life, then his or her worldview will be such that everything occurring in the world is related to the value of death. That, then, will influence the choices he makes such as agreeing with practices such as suicide, euthanasia, abortion, or genocide.

Let us recap this process of holy transformation:
Spirit (origin revelation) → mind (values) → worldview → behavioral choices (holy living)

The Holy Spirit initiates, motivates, shapes, and directs the flow of this process in each of us. It is all dependent upon receiving that deep and profound revelation in our spirit that God exists and that we are truly his adopted heirs. All else flows out of that reality and truth. How quickly the transformation occurs is determined by the degree to which we are submitted to God and obey His leading in the process. Regardless, the sequence of the process is under His control and is immutable. The result is the same—a changed life.

Some Christians may argue there is no difference between being born-again and being Spirit baptized as it relates to these stages of transformation. The defining difference between the two experiences is in the nature of their respective revelations. The revelation in the born-again experience is one of redemption and salvation. The revelation in Spirit baptism is of our true origin and identity. Both revelations are from and of God but differ in their impact and depth of change each produces.

CHAPTER 12

Moment of Truth: Demonic, Demented, or Divine?

In proving the deity of Jesus Christ, Josh McDowell, noted author and apologist, logically clarified the possible alternative explanations for His identity. Jesus was either a liar, lunatic, or Lord. If He isn't Lord, as He asserted, then only two other alternative explanations remain. McDowell cogently ruled out these other two alternatives, liar and lunatic.[66] Similarly, we can apply a logic tree to the baptism in the Holy Spirit (Figure 2).

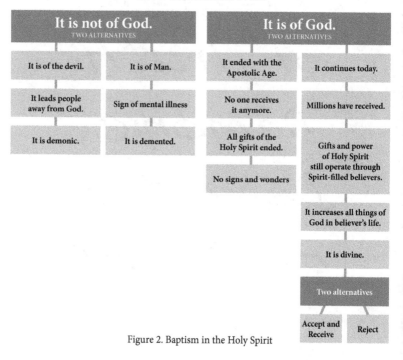

Figure 2. Baptism in the Holy Spirit

---

66 Josh McDowell, *Evidence That Demands a Verdict*, vol. 1, (Reprint, San Bernardino, CA: Here's Life Publishers, 1986).

Holy Spirit: Agent of Change

As we have done in previous chapters, let's examine the syllogistic reasoning of the opponents of Spirit baptism. It goes something like this:

Primary Premise:
The baptism in the Holy Spirit and the gifts of the Holy Spirit were of God but were only for the apostles and ended with the apostolic age.

Secondary Premise:
Those claiming today to receive the baptism in the Holy Spirit with evidence of speaking in tongues are either demon-possessed or severely mentally disturbed.

Conclusion:
Today's full gospel/charismatic movement is not of God.

If any of the premises can be shown to be false, as we have discussed earlier, then the conclusion is also false. The primary premise that Spirit baptism was exclusively for the apostles and ended with the apostolic age is either true or false. If it is true, then there are two and only two alternatives to explain what is happening among Christians in every denomination throughout the world today. If this premise is false, then Spirit baptism continues to exist today, and there are two and only two alternatives. Let's summarize the evidence for each of these.

1. Is the primary premise true?
We have shown scripturally and logically that Spirit baptism (the promise) was for subsequent generations and all who

believe in the Lord Jesus Christ (Acts 2:38-40; Mark 16:17). Signs, wonders, and miracles continued to operate right into the last chapter of Acts. They did not diminish in power and frequency. Paul taught extensively on the proper use of the gifts of the Spirit. More importantly, he taught church members, not apostles. Paul obviously believed that every born-again, Spirit-filled believer was given certain gifts of the Spirit and should operate correctly in them. I Corinthians 12 is not merely a history chapter. It is a pragmatic discourse on the gifts of the Holy Spirit, their purpose, and proper usage in the eternal Church.

We have shown in chapter six that the contention that Spirit baptism, signs, and wonders passed away when "the perfect is come" is casuistic reasoning. The "perfect" is clearly not the completed canon of Scripture. The perfect refers to the person of Jesus Christ. We anxiously await His return.

The gifts of the Holy Spirit, including tongues, were not restricted to the day of Pentecost. Numerous credible reports of the appearance and reappearance of the gifts emerged through the centuries in the Christian Church.[67] No expiration date is given anywhere in the Bible for any of gifts of the Holy Spirit.

If this primary premise is true, then it leads to two alternative explanations: Spirit baptism is of the Devil or it is of human origin.

2. Is Spirit baptism of the Devil?

If Spirit baptism with evidence of speaking in tongues is demonic, then those who receive it would pursue a life of sin

---

67 Phillip Schaff, *History of the Christian Church*, vol. 1, (Grand Rapids, MI: William B. Eerdmans Publishing, 1910).

and refute the deity of Jesus Christ: "By this you know the Spirit of God; every spirit that confesses that Jesus Christ has come in the flesh is from God, and every spirit that does not confess Jesus is not from God; and this is the spirit of the antichrist, of which you have heard that is coming, and now it is already in the world" (I John 4:2-3).

Spirit-filled Christians enthusiastically confess Jesus Christ as Lord and Savior and believe that He came in the flesh, was crucified, died for their sins, was resurrected, and lives today making intercession for them with the Father. According to the Scripture cited above, this would definitively rule out the prospect that they are possessed by a demon spirit: "Whosoever denieth the Son, the same hath not the Father: but he that acknowledgeth the Son hath the Father also" (I John 2:23).

Is there any other way to discern whether something is or is not of God? As we discussed earlier, we can judge by the fruit it produces: "The one who says, 'I have come to know Him,' and does not keep His commandments, is a liar, and the truth is not in him; but whoever keeps His word, in him the love of God has truly been perfected. By this we know that we are in Him: the one who says he abides in Him ought himself to walk in the same manner as He walked" (I John 2:3-6). In keeping His commandments we know that we are to love God and love our neighbor as ourselves. Do Spirit-filled Christians keep these commandments? Emphatically, yes!

A number of positive changes take place in a person after Spirit baptism. The word of God comes alive in a way never before experienced and becomes the central guide to a Spirit-filled believer. What previously was a rather confusing history book now becomes the living word of God that gives continual revelation on how to live in relationship with God and with others. The desire and actual time spent in prayer is dramatically increased. Spending time in church and with other Spirit-filled believers becomes a necessity for spiritual growth rather than an obligation. Sensitivity to sin and a willingness to repent are characteristic of the Spirit-filled life. A passion for evangelizing and missionary work is a prevalent characteristic. The Spirit-filled believer desperately wants to bring as many people as possible into the kingdom of God. They are also very willing to bring financial stewardship to those efforts.

Spirit-filled believers are ardent worshipers. Full gospel worship services are lively and characterized by the joyful outpouring of love and adoration of Jesus. Some may disagree with the style of worship, but none can dispute the intensity of love expressed and at whom it is directed.

These are all good fruit (increased Bible study, prayer, evangelization, and financial support). A bad tree cannot bear good fruit. Attributing Spirit baptism to the demonic without one shred of evidence to prove it is not only prejudicial but extremely harmful to the body of Christ. This erroneous and fallacious teaching is itself a work of the Devil because it has prevented millions of Christians from receiving their rightful inheritance in Christ and thus operating in the full power of the Holy Spirit. Now, I ask you, who do you think benefits most from that belief system? Satan knows that, as long as he can keep God's people impotent, he is in no real danger. He knows that when Christians receive the baptism in the Holy Spirit and their concomitant gifts, they become dangerous warriors with the power to do serious damage to his kingdom and to take territory that rightfully belongs to God.

Are Spirit-filled Christians perfect? Absolutely not. They are just as capable of sin as other believers, particularly if they do not submit fully to God's sanctification process. The Holy Spirit, however, does give additional power to resist and overcome sin.

Spirit baptism leads people into a deeper relationship with God. It does not lead people away from God. The belief it is of the Devil simply does not hold up under careful examination.

3. Is Spirit baptism of human origin?

Opponents contend that Spirit-filled believers who speak in tongues are mentally disturbed or ignorant, illiterate, impressionable people. While it is true that, in the early part of the twentieth century, many who received Spirit baptism, were relatively uneducated and from lower socioeconomic levels of society, this was also true on the day of Pentecost. The type of person receiving Spirit baptism in no way determines its validity and veracity any more than it would for the truth of salvation. It is for all who the Lord calls. Judging whether something is of God by who receives it is prejudicial. Attributing Spirit baptism to the effects of mental illness is unsubstantiated.

It has been shown through psychological research that Spirit-filled believers are no more prone to mental disturbance than other Christians and, in fact, many even exhibit better mental health. The cavalier assumption that Spirit-filled Christians who speak in tongues are either mentally disturbed or are merely speaking gibberish is not supported by any psychological or medical research.

To the contrary, research suggests that Spirit baptism may actually improve one's mental health. This would be consistent with Paul's contention that praying in tongues is edifying. That is, it builds up and strengthens a person. As has been shown in this book, many highly-educated, intelligent, prosperous, highly functional individuals have received the baptism in the Holy Spirit with evidence of speaking in tongues. These individuals lead fruitful lives and freely testify to the life-changing power of this spiritual experience. This spiritual reality can no longer be dismissed as something weird done by those ignorant holy-rollers. The Holy Spirit has invaded every Christian denomination: Catholic, Baptist, Methodist, Lutheran, Episcopal, and many others. He has filled people from every race, culture, and walk of life. Physicians, attorneys, psychologists, businessmen and women, teachers, counselors, skilled workers, and laborers have received. God is no respecter of persons. Even many traditional leaders admit that the full gospel/charismatic movement is the fastest growing Christian movement in the world today.

It has been shown that the primary and secondary premises are false, and, therefore, the conclusion must also be false. That leaves one, and only one, alternative. Spirit baptism is of God and it continues to exist today. Millions continue to receive this spiritual blessing and operate in the gifts of the Holy Spirit.

It greatly enhances one's spiritual life and empowers each individual to fulfill his or her specific call from God.

Receive or Reject

The alternative—that it is of God—leads to two, and only two, alternatives: Receive or reject. This is your moment of truth! You can choose to or not to seek the baptism in the Holy Spirit. It is a freewill choice. The Holy Spirit will not impose Himself on you. He is a gentleman. He never goes anywhere that He is not invited. However, you can no longer reject it on the grounds it is of the Devil or it is a sign of mental illness. Those conclusions have been shown to be invalid. Spirit baptism is either demonic, demented, or divine. You must decide.

The scriptural, logical, scientific, and experiential evidence clearly supports the conclusion that Spirit baptism occurring today is divine—of God! You may accept this evidence but still choose to not take this next step in your spiritual walk. You may see it as an option that Jesus gave to us to exercise or not as we see fit. Let me remind you here of a Scripture I cited earlier: "He that believeth on me, as the Scripture hath said, out of his belly shall flow rivers of living water. But this spake he of the Spirit, which they that believe on him should receive: for the Holy Spirit was not yet given: because that Jesus was not yet glorified" (John 7:38-39).

The key word here is *should*. This implies that Spirit baptism is a commandment from the Lord, and, therefore, it is our duty as born-again believers to be obedient and earnestly seek the infilling of the Holy Spirit. It is not optional as many Christians are taught. If you choose to not pursue this experience, please understand that this now becomes an issue between you and the Lord. It is no longer an issue between you and some false religious doctrine or tradition you have been taught. The error has been exposed. You must choose whether you will continue to live in error or step into the marvelous, radiating truth of the Holy Spirit. You must choose whether you want to stay stuck where you are or be transformed by the power of the Holy Spirit into the person God created you to be. If you are still not certain, I challenge you to pray and ask your heavenly Father if Spirit baptism is of Him and whether He wants you to seek and receive it. I am that confident of His answer to you. Open your heart and mind to His answer. Follow His truth wherever it leads you.

Moment of Change

If you have read this far, it is my hope that the Holy Spirit has begun to stir something within you. If you are already baptized in the Holy Spirit, I pray you have been encouraged by something in this book and that you can use this material to lead others into the fullness of the Holy Spirit.

If you have yet to receive Spirit baptism, now is the time to purpose it in your heart to seek this glorious experience. Let's talk about a few essentials to receiving.

First, only one prerequisite exists in order to receive the baptism in the Holy Spirit. You must be born-again. You must repent of your sins, confess Jesus as Lord with your mouth, and believe in your heart that God raised Him from the dead (Romans 10:9). If you have done so, you have taken on His righteousness and are cleansed of all sin. This is vital because the Holy Spirit will not occupy a sin-stained habitat. His first name is "Holy" and, therefore, will only inhabit a righteous vessel. Do not be confused here. You do not have to be perfect. You simply have to be made righteous by appropriating the shed blood of Jesus on your life. Simply acknowledge you are a sinner, repent of your sins, and invite Jesus into your heart.

Many struggle with receiving the infilling of the Spirit because they feel they are unworthy of such a holy experience. They believe they must somehow earn the right to receive the Holy Spirit. If that were true, then no one would receive salvation or Spirit baptism. None of us deserve either one. If we got what we deserved as sinners, we would not be here any longer. That is the beauty of God's mercy and grace. Mercy can be defined as not getting what we deserve. Grace is typically defined as unmerited favor from God. That is, we get something good that we do not deserve. It's interesting that, to be saved, people must have the revelation that they are sinners, they must repent, and they must believe Jesus is their personal savior. There is a revelation that salvation is a free gift that cannot be earned (Ephesians 2:8). And yet, when it comes to Spirit baptism, people believe that they must earn it and prove themselves worthy of it. Just as salvation was given freely to the entire world that glorious day at Golgotha, the Holy Spirit was poured out freely on the day of Pentecost for the whole world. Spirit baptism is a *gift* that has already been given, just as salvation is a free gift. All you need do is simply ask and receive (Matthew 7:7). You are made worthy of it through the shed blood of Jesus.

"But," you may ask, "what if I ask for the baptism in the Holy Spirit and He doesn't give it to me?" Jesus has an answer for you: "Now suppose one of you fathers is asked by his son for a fish; he will not give him a snake instead of a fish, will he? Or if he is asked for an egg, he will not give him a scorpion, will he? If you then, being evil, know how to give good gifts to your children, how much more shall your heavenly Father give the Holy Spirit to those who ask Him?" (Luke 11:11-13). God clearly wants all of us to "be filled with the Spirit" (Ephesians 5:18). He would not command us to do something without teaching us and empowering us to achieve it.

Second, you must initiate the first step. Remember that the Holy Spirit never goes anywhere without being invited: "Draw near to God and He will draw near to you" (James 4:8). Note that we must draw near to Him first before He responds. Some mistakenly believe that Spirit baptism occurs purely spontaneously at God's whim and we have nothing to do with it. God never imposes Himself on anyone. He waits upon us to purpose it in our hearts that we want to be closer to Him. Once you have asked Jesus to baptize you in the Holy Spirit, just focus all of your attention on Him. Clear your mind of everything else. Begin to praise Him and thank Him for all that He has done for you. This is how you draw near to Him. He inhabits the praises of His people (Psalms 22:3). The Holy Spirit's purpose is to glorify Jesus (John 16:14). The more we begin to praise and worship Jesus, the more the Spirit ushers us into His presence. Jesus is the baptizer. When Jesus sees that your main goal in life is to get closer to Him, He will accommodate you by filling you with His Spirit.

Third, you must be willing to yield all to Him. You must be willing to receive the Holy Spirit on His terms, not yours: "And we are witnesses of these things; and so is the Holy Spirit, who God has given to those who obey Him" (Acts 5:32). The key word here is *obey*. I call it *selling out to God*. Essentially, it is simply telling God, "I give my life to you. Do what you will with me. I am yours totally. I'll do whatever you want." Some may say, "Wow, that's really scary!" It would be if you were to say that to anyone but God. But God can be trusted absolutely. He always has our best interest at heart.

Obedience is not a popular concept in the post-Christian, humanistic era. It is often equated with oppressive control by others and is seen as contrary to individual freedom and pursuing one's own self-interest. Actually, the opposite is true. In being obedient to the Lord, unlimited freedom pervades every aspect of our life: "Now the Lord is the Spirit; and where the Spirit of the Lord is, there is liberty" (II Corinthians 3:17). So we see a linkage between obedience, the Spirit, and freedom. When there is disobedience to God and His laws and will, a dramatic reduction occurs in the degrees of freedom in an individual's life and in an entire society. The more that people reject God's will for their lives and their society, the greater the instability. This, in turn, requires governments to impose more and more laws, rules, and regulations in an attempt to control a population and prevent anarchy. Ultimately, history has proven, however, that humans have never been able to govern themselves. Without the Holy Spirit inspiring and motivating people to do the right thing, they inevitably fail miserably.

Obedience to God ushers in the Holy Spirit, which is the only safeguard against domination by others and ensures we live a life of true liberty.

Fourth, obedience to God requires that we repent of pride. He will baptize you in His Spirit but not on your terms. It must be on His and His alone: "Or do you think that the Scripture speaks to no purpose: He jealously desires the Spirit which He has made to dwell in us? But He gives a greater *grace*. Therefore it says, God is opposed to the proud, but gives grace to the humble" (James 4:5-6, my emphasis). James further tells us to "humble yourselves in the presence of the Lord and He will exalt you" (James 4:10).

Some people seek Spirit baptism, but they begin to dictate to God under what circumstances they will and will not receive. One Christian told me she was willing to receive the baptism in the Spirit but only if she could receive alone without anyone else around to see it happen. Another stated he would ask God for it but not if he had to speak in tongues. A gentleman who had been saved many years said that he would receive only if it was his pastor that would lay hands on him and pray for him. These attitudes reflect a certain amount of pride and a refusal to trust God and submit completely to Him. Humbling ourselves before Him and freely allowing Him to have His way with us *always* results in blessings.

One must understand that receiving the baptism in the Holy Spirit is not so much of you getting more of God as it is God getting more of you. That is what happens when you obey God and humble yourself before Him. This produces the proper condition of the heart necessary for Him to fill you with the Holy Spirit. It has nothing to do with your actions; it is all about your heart. Your main motivation for seeking the Holy Spirit is to have greater intimacy with the Lord.

When the Holy Spirit takes up residence within you He will bring all of His beautiful qualities with Him at an intensity that may be new to you. The love, peace, and joy you experience may trigger a number of emotions ranging from mild to strong. This is entirely normal. Do not worry about it. God will not make a fool out of you. If we can get excited at a sporting event or musical concert, we can certainly get elated by being filled with the Spirit of the living God. Just go with what you are feeling.

Next, expect God to give you your own prayer language. You may hear a word or sound in your mind, or you may feel something bubbling up from within. Trust God, open your mouth, and speak whatever is coming forth. Turn your analytical mind off. Every new language sounds strange to our ears, initially, but you will notice that the more you repeat it, the better you feel inside. This is what Paul meant when he said, "When I pray in tongues I am edified." It is important to speak the words out loud. It will build your faith and validate that something supernatural is occurring at that very moment. Some people receive only one word or even just a syllable, initially, while others may speak several words. It doesn't matter. What matters is that you are obedient and speak what the Holy Spirit is giving you.

To summarize the suggestions for receiving Spirit baptism:

1. Accept Christ as personal Lord and Savior.
2. Ask Jesus to baptize you in His Spirit.
3. Draw near to Him through praise and worship.
4. Yield to Him and be willing to obey Him in all things.
5. Set pride aside, humble yourself, and receive the Holy Spirit on His terms, when, where, and how He chooses to fill you.
6. Expect to speak in tongues.
7. Obey the leading of the Holy Spirit and speak forth whatever He gives you.

It is important to understand that Spirit baptism is not restricted to a church setting. Many people receive at church through the laying on of hands by other Spirit-filled believers. Scripture supports that practice. Others receive privately after praying and asking Jesus for it. There is no specific formula for receiving. One man, for whom I prayed to receive the Holy Spirit, received while driving His car, which contradicts the notion that people lose all control when receiving the baptism in the Spirit. Another was awakened out of a deep sleep in the middle of the night, filled by the Spirit, and began speaking in tongues. Others have been filled in restaurants, swimming pools, Bible study classes, and private homes. The Holy Spirit doesn't care where you are at the time. All He cares about is the condition of your heart.

What if you ask Jesus to baptize you and nothing happens at that moment? Don't worry about it. Keep seeking Him. He will never disappoint you: "And without faith it is impossible to please Him, for He who comes to God must believe that He is, and that He is a rewarder of those who seek Him" (Hebrews 11:6). The King James Version says He rewards those who *diligently* seek Him. Just make up your mind and heart that you are not going to stop asking until you receive. Too many people pray once or twice for something and, because they don't receive an answer immediately, they stop asking. God did not create us to be quitters. Note the parable of the woman and the judge. She persistently pleaded for legal protection from her opponent. The judge initially was unwilling but eventually granted her protection due to her unwavering persistence (Luke 18:1-5).

Another woman had suffered from a hemorrhage of blood for twelve years. After hearing about Jesus, she knew she would be healed if she could just touch His garments. She kept pressing through the crowd around Him until she was close enough to touch Him. She was immediately healed after touching His cloak (Mark 5:25-34). This woman was determined to receive her blessing.

These two women persevered in their quests until they received what they needed. They did not give up just because they didn't receive the first time. They persisted until they hit the "tipping point,"[68] that point at which God released what they were asking for and everything in their life changed.

A precious Christian lady gave me her testimony of how she received the baptism in the Holy Spirit. She had been seeking

---

68 Malcolm Gladwell, *The Tipping Point*, (New York: Little Brown, 2000).

it for a couple of years. She had gone to the altar at church and had been prayed for many times to receive it and nothing happened. She was discouraged and was tempted to just give up, but she kept reading the Scriptures and knew it was God's will that she should be filled with His Spirit. "Finally," she said, "one day I just took my Bible and went into my bathroom and locked the door. I told Jesus I was not coming out of the room until He baptized me in the Holy Spirit, no matter how long it took. I just opened my Bible and started reading out loud which then led into praise and worship. In a matter of a few minutes, I was speaking in tongues." What made the difference for this woman? I believe it was her determination to get what was rightfully hers from God no matter how long it took. God honored her persistence.

We are taught to pray without ceasing (I Thessalonians 5:17). This refers to, not only developing the habit of prayer, but also applies to the act of praying continually for specific things until one receives them. Some people receive Spirit baptism the first time they ask while others must persist for a while before receiving. We may never know all the reasons for these variations. It really doesn't matter. All that matters is that you seek until you receive.

What to Do After Receiving

1. At the moment a believer is filled with the Holy Spirit and begins to speak in tongues, I always encourage him or her to continue to repeat their prayer language out loud over and over again for several minutes. In doing so, the Holy

Spirit will give you assurance that you are experiencing a supernatural act of God. This is how He gives you the certainty that He is speaking through you. It is a way of building your faith.

2. Next, you must exercise your prayer language every day. Like everything else in life, the more you speak in tongues, the easier it becomes, and the more your language will grow. As you allow God to inhabit more and more of you, your spiritual vocabulary will grow. There is a direct relationship between the frequency of praying in tongues and spiritual maturity and power. The more you pray in tongues, the more real God becomes to you. It doesn't matter if, initially, you receive only one word. Keep repeating it daily and more will come.

3. Sometimes after receiving the infilling of the Holy Spirit, people will begin to have doubts about the experience. You must understand the source of these doubts: "And those beside the road are those who have heard, then the Devil comes and takes away the word from their heart, so that they may not believe and be saved" (Luke 8:12).

    Satan may begin to speak doubts to you: "Oh, you're not really filled. You just made up those words. You were just speaking gibberish. Who do you think you are that the Holy Spirit would fill you? You're nobody special!" Keep in mind that you never had any of these thoughts *before* you were filled with the Holy Spirit. These thoughts only came *after* you received. Why? Because it is Satan that is giving them to you. He couldn't prevent you from receiving, so now he tries to instill doubt in you to deceive you into believing that your experience was not the real thing. His goal is to prevent you from growing in the fullness of the Spirit because he knows that, if you do, you will become a dangerous powerhouse causing destruction and havoc to his kingdom. Jesus described Satan as the father of lies. There is no truth in him.

If those thoughts begin to pass through your mind, simply say, "I rebuke you Satan in the name of Jesus. Watch this!" And then immediately begin praying in tongues. As you do this, the Holy Spirit will bear witness with your spirit that what you are doing is of God. It will also give Satan and his demons the message that you reject everything he says and that you are certain you have received the infilling of the Spirit of the living God.

4. Get into the Word of God. Begin to read the Bible like never before. You will find that you now have a new hunger for God's Word and a deeper understanding of it. It will come alive to you in fresh ways because you now have the author living within you. Find a Bible study class or adult Sunday school class where you can go deeper into the Word of God.

5. Find a Spirit-filled church that believes in the baptism in the Holy Spirit. Fellowship with other Spirit-filled Christians. It is amazing how much you will learn and grow just by entering Spirit-filled circles. Find a mature, Spirit-filled Christian who is willing to mentor you in your spiritual walk.

6. Learn how to praise and worship God. One of the chief differences between a Spirit-filled believer and a non-Spirit-filled believer is in the nature and quality of their praise and worship. Before I received the baptism in the Holy Spirit, I attended a traditional church where the praise and worship part of the service consisted of singing two hymns and then listening to the choir sing a hymn. That was it. I never really felt engaged in worship. It was a fairly passive experience. God never intended for praise and worship to be only passive or quiet. He has a lot to say about this part of our relationship with him:

> Praise the Lord!
> Praise God in His sanctuary;
> Praise Him in His mighty expanse.
> Praise Him for His mighty deeds;
> Praise Him according to His excellent greatness.
> Praise Him with trumpet sound;
> Praise Him with harp and lyre.
> Praise Him with timbrel and dancing;
> Praise Him with stringed instruments and pipe.
> Praise Him with loud cymbals;
> Let everything that has breath praise the Lord.
> Praise the Lord! (Psalms 150:1-6)

This is a description of proactive praise that requires our total engagement. We are to let the high praises of God be in our mouth (Psalms 149:6). The traditional denominations often frown upon the lively praise and worship seen in Spirit-filled churches. They view it as irreverent and emotional. Jesus has another view: "And as He was now approaching, near the descent of the Mount of Olives, the whole multitude of disciples began to praise God joyfully with loud voice for all the miracles which they had seen, saying, *'Blessed is the king who comes in the name of the Lord; peace in heaven and glory in the highest!'* And some of the Pharisees in the multitude said to Him, 'Teacher, rebuke Your disciples.' And He answered and said, 'I tell you if these become silent, the stones will cry out!'" (Luke 19:37-40, my emphasis).

We were created to praise and worship God. One of the first changes you will notice when you receive the baptism in the Holy Spirit is your willingness to express your love for God through praise and worship. Prior to receiving Spirit baptism your praise and worship was determined and structured by external circumstances (e.g. church service), but after Spirit baptism, it is inspired and influenced by the Holy Spirit: "From Thee comes my praise in the great assembly; I shall pay my vows before those who fear Him" (Psalms 22:25).

Praise and worship is actually given to our spirit by the Holy Spirit. He begins to teach us how to freely praise and worship. His role is to lift up Jesus and exalt Him. He begins to reveal to us the unfathomable awesomeness of God the Father and God the Son in ways that our natural mind previously could not fully comprehend: "But a natural man does not accept the things of the Spirit of

God; for they are foolishness to him, and he cannot understand them, because they are spiritually appraised. But he who is spiritual appraises all things, yet he himself is appraised by no man" (I Corinthians 2:14-15).

When we are born-again, we will have a certain level of understanding of spiritual things, but when we receive the infilling of the Spirit, deeper truths are revealed to us: "But an hour is coming, and now is, when true worshipers shall worship the Father in spirit and truth; for such people the Father seeks to be His worshipers. God is spirit, and those who worship Him must worship in spirit and truth" (John 4:23-24).

One of the deeper truths that the Holy Spirit begins to reveal to us in fresh ways is the holiness of God. I never gave that a second thought until I received the baptism in the Holy Spirit. Who better to reveal the holiness of God than the Holy Spirit? As He continually reveals holiness to us, He develops within our spirit an intense love for God and a devotion to Him that comes bubbling forth in praise and worship. Worship is no longer a mechanical, stilted gesture performed by us because we are instructed to do so in church. You may find yourself praising and worshiping God in your car, the shower, at work, over coffee, or with a friend. It may spontaneously rise up within you whether you are in church or not. Praise and worship becomes a deep expression of your love for God rising from the innermost, deepest part of you (spirit). Moreover, it will become the most normal thing in the world to you. What is absolutely normal to you may appear extreme to non-Spirit-filled Christians because they do not yet have the deeper revelations of God.

They may consider you to be fanatic. Don't let that bother you. You are in good company. Peter, Paul, John, Stephen, James, Barnabas, and Timothy were all fanatics. What impact did they have? Oh, not much. They just changed the whole world, that's all! When people accuse me of being a fanatic in my love for God, I just redefine the term for them. "A fanatic," I say, "is just someone who loves God more than you. That's all." I would certainly rather be called a fanatic for God than a lot of the names I was called before I came to know the Lord.

Praise and worship is so inextricably wrapped up in the personality of the Holy Spirit that we automatically begin to identify with that trait when He takes up residence within us. Our expression of love takes on a whole new life of its own. You may feel a strong urging to raise your hands in praise of the living God. This may seem awkward to you at first but don't be embarrassed. This is simply the Holy Spirit inspiring and motivating you to openly and freely express your love for the Father and Jesus. Raising your hands or clapping them during praise and worship is entirely normative Christianity. If people raise their hands, clap, and shout to express their love and devotion at concerts or sporting events, then how much more normal should it be to do that for your heavenly Father with whom you plan to spend eternity? He is more worthy of our love and devotion than a rock star or an athlete. Performers may entertain you, but they cannot save your soul from the fires of hell. Praise and worship blesses God just as it would bless you if someone expressed their love for you.

As the Spirit teaches you how to abandon yourself to praise and worship, you will learn the various purposes it serves. Worship is powerful because it ministers to God. It can be used as a weapon of spiritual warfare because it breaks the spirit of oppression. It can also unveil the plans and strategies of Satan because it elevates us above his attacks.

The more you step out in faith and practice it, worship becomes easy and so much a part of you that it becomes analogous to a physical reflex like the knee jerk. When the Holy Spirit touches your spirit, you will automatically praise and worship the Lord and love doing it.

Another change the Holy Spirit works in us as we engage in regular praise and worship is humility. The more we focus on who God is through worship, the more humble we become as we compare ourselves to Him. The Holy Spirit's aim is to develop true Godly humility in each of us, so He can use us for His purposes. We cannot be trusted with the Holy Spirit's power without humility.

7. Make prayer a part of your daily routine. When I ask Christians if they pray, many answer, "Oh, yes, we say grace before every meal." After receiving Spirit baptism, prayer becomes more than some obligatory practice performed

before a meal or some ritual you run through at church. It now becomes the air you breathe. You will find yourself eagerly looking forward to getting alone with God and having sweet conversation with Him. Intimacy is developed through open, honest, and regular communication with Him. Most Christians find it agonizing to pray for as little as five minutes. After Spirit baptism, you have no real perception of time as you pray. You may spend two hours in prayer, and it seems like five minutes because in the Spirit realm there is no concept of time, only eternity.

As you spend time in regular prayer, the Holy Spirit may do a number of things to produce change in you. He may give you revelation, insight, and understanding about something you did not have before you prayed. He may do a healing in you while you are praying. He may soften your heart toward someone with whom you are angry. He may speak to you in ways that build your self-esteem. You may experience His love in a way that makes you feel valued, worthwhile, and significant. He may give you wisdom to solve a particular problem. He may even correct you about something. The end result of all of these is deep and lasting change in you for the better.

Spiritual, psychological, emotional, and characterological transformation is a direct function of how much time is spent in daily prayer. You cannot enter into God's presence, even briefly, without being impacted significantly. The more time spent in His presence, the more dramatically transformed you become. This is exemplified in Mo-

Holy Spirit: Agent of Change

ses: "And Moses entered the midst of the cloud as he went up to the mountain; and Moses was on the mountain forty days and forty nights" (Exodus 24:18).

It is apparent that, to accomplish great things for God, one must first spend much time with God. As a result of prayer, God transformed Moses from a stammering weakling into one of the most powerful men to ever walk the earth.

E.M. Bounds wrote prolifically on the subject of prayer. He stated, "Everything depends upon prayer, and yet we neglect it not only to our own spiritual hurt but also to the delay and injury of our Lord's cause upon the earth."[69] I believe, in referring to "spiritual hurt," Bounds meant not only that we will not receive from the Lord what we need, but also that we will stagnate in our spiritual and psychological growth. It is during prayer that the Holy Spirit can mold and shape us into a new creature fit for service to the Lord. Spirit baptism softens our hearts and makes us more pliable in His presence (prayer). So pray often and allow the time spent with God to change you.

8. You may find you can no longer separate your spiritual life from all other aspects of your life. That is as it should be. You will experience a new vibrancy and vigor in every aspect of your self. You will have a greater sensitivity to all things spiritual. You may begin to notice spiritual significance even in common, daily events. This new spiritual insight

---

69 E.M. Bounds, *On Prayer*, (New Kensington, PA: Whitaker House, 1973).

may be a bit overwhelming at first because it is so strikingly real. That is all right; don't panic. Share your experiences with a seasoned, mature, Spirit-filled believer who can explain them to you and keep you well-grounded. As you grow in the Spirit, these experiences will become second nature to you and you will welcome them.

I want to congratulate you for taking this next step in your walk with Jesus Christ. Spirit baptism is not to be viewed as the terminal, endpoint in your spiritual journey but rather the normal, next step that ushers in the deeper things of the Holy Spirit. Your Christian walk will no longer be boring. The Holy Spirit will take you on a thrilling, sensational adventure that will give your life true purpose and significance. So strap in and enjoy the ride.

NOTES

Chapter 3: The Transforming Power of the Holy Spirit and Apostle Paul

1 W.E. Vine, *An Expository Dictionary of Biblical Words*, (Nashville: Thomas Nelson Publishers, 1984).
2 Spiro Zodhiates, ed., *Hebrew Greek Key Study Bible*, (Chattanooga, TN: AMG Publishers, 1984).
3 Ibid.
4 Ibid.
5 Gary R. VandenBos, ed., *APA Dictionary of Psychology*, (Washington, D.C.: American Psychological Association, 2007).

Chapter 4: Who Is the Agent of Change and How Does He Work?

6 Gary R. VandenBos, ed., *APA Dictionary of Psychology*, (Washington, D.C.: American Psychological Association, 2007).
7 Ibid.
8 Paul Ai, personal communication, January 31, 2010.
9 Lynn W. Aurich and Mark D. Barrentine, The Isaiah Project: A Faith Based Crisis Response Ministry, (Lafayette, LA, 2005).
10 W.E. Vine, *An Expository Dictionary of Biblical Words*, (Nashville: Thomas Nelson Publishers, 1984).

Chapter 5: The Holy Spirit as Teacher

11 Gary R. VandenBos, ed., *APA Dictionary of Psychology*, (Washington, D.C.: American Psychological Association, 2007), 238.
12 Ibid.

Chapter 6: Vehicle for Change: The Baptism in the Holy Spirit

13 Spiro Zodhiates, ed., *Hebrew Greek Key Study Bible*, (Chattanooga, TN: AMG Publishers, 1984).
14 Gary R. VandenBos, ed., *APA Dictionary of Psychology*, (Washington, D.C.: American Psychological Association, 2007), 238.

Chapter 7: The Spirit Speaks

15 R.A. Torrey, *The Holy Spirit: Who He is and What He Does* (1927, Reprint, Shreveport, LA: Glimpses of Glory, 1997).
16 Ibid.
17 Ibid.
18 Josh McDowell, *Evidence That Demands a Verdict*, vol. 1, (San Bernardino, CA: Here's Life Publishers, 1986).
19 Gary R. VandenBos, ed., *APA Dictionary of Psychology*, (Washington, D.C.: American Psychological Association, 2007), 616.
20 Ibid., 616.
21 Torrey, *The Holy Spirit*, 98.
22 Howard M. Ervin, *Spirit Baptism: A Biblical Investigation*, (Peabody, Mass.: Hendrickson Publishers, 1987).
23 E.W. Bullinger, *Number in Scripture*, (Grand Rapids, MI.: Kregel Publications, 1984).
24 Ervin, *Spirit Baptism*, 176.
25 Spiro Zodhiates, ed., *Hebrew Greek Key Study Bible*, (Chattanooga, TN: AMG Publishers, 1984), 58.
26 Randy Hurst. "Christianity in China," *Today's Pentecostal Evangel*, April 5, 2009, 13.
27 Ibid. Hurst
28 Ibid. Hurst
29 John L. Sherrill, *They Speak with Other Tongues*, (Reading, UK: Spire Books, 1965).
30 Ibid.
31 Hagin, Kenneth E., *Tongues: Beyond the Upper Room*, (Tulsa, OK: Kenneth Hagin Ministries, 2007).
32 Ibid., 247.
33 Ibid., 248.
34 Mark Rutland, "Ordered Steps," in *Life in the Spirit: Devotions from the Pentecostal/Charismatic Revival*, ed. Robert White, (Minsk, Belarus: Spirit Life Books, 2000), 261.
35 Sherill, *They Speak*, 101.

Chapter 8: Psychology Speaks

36 Jesse Coulson and Ray W. Johnson, "Glossolalia and Internal-External Locus of Control, *Journal of Psychology and Theology*, no. 4, (1977): 312-317. These studies included: G.B. Cutten, *Speaking with tongues: Historically and psychologically considered.* (New Haven, CT: Yale University Press, 1927); J.B. Oman, "On Speaking in tongues: A Psychological Analysis," *Pastoral Psychology* (1964): 14, 48-51; F. Stagg, E.G. Hinson, and W.E. Oates, *Glossolalia: Tongue Speaking in Biblical, Historical,and Psychological Perspective,* (New York: Abingdon, 1967); W.W. Wood, *Culture and Personality Aspects of the Pentecostal Holiness Religion.* (Paris: Mouton, 1965).

37 I. Zeretsky, and M. Leone, eds., *Religious Movements in Contemporary America.* (Princeton, NJ: Princeton University Press, 1974).

38 V.H. Hine, "Pentecostal Glossolalia: Toward a Functional Interpretation," *Journal of Scientific Study of Religion*, no. 8 (1969), 211-226.

39 John Donald Castelein, "Glossolalia and the Psychology of the Self and Narcissism," *Journal of Religion and Health*, vol. 23(1984), 47-62.

40 Ibid.

41 Gary R. VandenBos, ed., *APA Dictionary of Psychology*, (Washington, D.C.: American Psychological Association, 2007).

42 H.M. Lefcourt, "Internal Versus External Control of Reinforcements: A review," *Psychological Bulletin,* vol. 65 (1966), 207.

43 N.T. Feather. "Some Personality Correlates of External Control, *Australian Journal of Psychology*, 1967, 19, 253-260.

44 P.D. Hersch and K.E. Scheibe, "On the Reliability and Validity of Internal-External Control as a Personality Dimension," *Journal of Consulting and Clinical Psychology,* vol. 31 (1967),609-614.

45 Ibid., 613.

46 V.C. Joe, "Review of the Internal-External Control Construct as a Personality Variable," *Psychological Reports*, vol. 28, (1971), 623.

47 Jesse Coulson and Ray W. Johnson, "Glossolalia," 314.

48 Lynn W. Aurich, "Risk Taking Behavior as a Function of Sex, Age and Locus of Control," (PhD diss., University of Southern Mississippi, 1975).

49 G. Javillonor, "Toward a Social Psychological Model of Sectarianism," (PhD diss., University of Nebraska, 1971), cited in Coulson and Johnson , "Glossalalia."

50 L.J. Francis and Mandy Robbins, "Personality and Glossolalia: A Study Among Male Evangelical clergy," *Pastoral Psychology*, vol. 51, (2003), 391-396. These studies included: L.J. Francis and S.H. Jones, "Personality and Charismatic Experience Among Adult Christians," *Pastoral Psychology,* vol. 45,(1997): 421-428; L.J. Francis and W.K. Kay, "The Personality Characteristics of Pentecostal Ministry Candidates," *Personality and Individual Differences*, vol. 18, (1995), 581-594; L.J. Francis and T.H. Thomas, "Are Charismatic Ministers Less Stable? A Study among Male Anglican Clergy. *Review of Religious Research*, vol. 39,(1997), 61-69; S.H. Louden and L.J. Francis, "Are Catholic Priests in England and Wales Attracted to the Charismatic Movement Emotionally Less Stable?" *British Journal of Theological Education*, vol. 11, (2001), 65-76; M. Robbins, J. Hair, and L.J. Francis, "Personality and Attraction to the Charismatic Movement: A Study among Anglican Clergy," *Journal of Beliefs and Values*, vol. 20, (1999), 239-246.

51 S.B.G. Eyesnck and H.J. Eyesnck and P. Barrett, "A Revised Version of the Psychotism Scale," *Personality and Individual Differences*, vol. 6, (1985), 21-29, cited in L.J. Francis and Mandy Robbins, "Personality and Glossolalia."

52 L.J. Francis and Mandy Robbins, "Personality and Glossolalia," 395.

53 Andrew B. Newberg and others, "The Measurement of Regional Cerebral Blood Flow During Glossolalia: A Preliminary SPECT Study," *Psychiatry Research:Neuroimaging*, vol. 148, (2006), 67-71.

54 J.T.L. Wilson and D. Wyper, "Neuroimaging and Neuropsychological Functioning Following Closed Head Injury: ET, MRI and SPECT, *Journal of Head Trauma Rehabilitation*, vol. 7, (1992), 29-39; Thomas James Callender, Lisa Morrow, and K. Subramania, "Evaluation of Chronic Neurological Sequalae after Acute Pesticide Exposure Using SPECT Brain Scans," *Journal of Toxicology and Environmental Health*, vol. 41, (1994), 275-284.

55 *Diagnostic and Statistical Manual of Mental Disorders*, 4th ed. (Washington, D.C.: American Psychiatric Association, 1984).

56 P. Bard, "Central Nervous Mechanisms for the Expression of Anger in Animals," in *The Second International Symposium on Feelings and Emotions*, M.L. Raymert, ed. (New York: McGraw-Hill, 1950); P. Bard and V.B. Mountcastle, "Some Forebrain Mechanisms Involved in Expression of Rage with Special Reference to Suppression of Angry Behavior." (Res. Publ., Ass. Res. nerv.ment.Dis.), vol. 27, (1948), 362-404, cited in S.P. Grossman, *A Textbook of Physiological Psychology*, (New York: John Wiley and Sons, 1967), 533.

57 Diana M. Goodwin, *A Dictionary of Neuropsychology*, (New York: Springer-Verlag, 1989), 48.

Chapter 11: Holy Transition: The Process of Change

58 Gary R. VandenBos, ed., *APA Dictionary of Psychology*, (Washington, D.C.: American Psychological Association, 2007).
59 R. Laird Harris, Gleason L. Araher, and Bruce K. Waltke, *Theological Wordbook of the Old Testament*, (Chicago: Moody Bible Institute, 1980).
60 Nancy Verrier, "The Primal Wound: Effects of Separation from the Birthmother on Adopted Children," Terry Larimore, http://terry Larimore.com/PrimalWound.html.
61 Reverend Tommy Faulk, personal communication, May 9, 2009.
62 Hunter Lewis, *A Question of Values: Six Ways We Make Personal Choices That Shape Our Lives.* (Crozet, VA: Axios Press, 2000), 7.
63 Ibid., 11.
64 Ibid., 10.
65 Ibid., 13.

Chapter 12: Moment of Truth: Demonic, Demented, or Divine?

66 Josh McDowell, *Evidence That Demands a Verdict*, vol. 1, (Reprint, San Bernardino, CA: Here's Life Publishers, 1986).
67 Phillip Schaff, *History of the Christian Church*, vol. 1, (Grand Rapids, MI: William B. Eerdmans Publishing, 1910).
68 Malcolm Gladwell, *The Tipping Point*, (New York: Little Brown, 2000).
69 E.M. Bounds, *On Prayer*, (New Kensington, PA: Whitaker House, 1973).

CPSIA information can be obtained
at www.ICGtesting.com
Printed in the USA
LVHW021225160121
676664LV00002B/3

9 780983 810568